Cartoons in Hard Times

Cartoons in Hard Times

The Animated Shorts of Disney and
Warner Brothers in Depression
and War 1932–1945

Tracey Louise Mollet

Bloomsbury Academic
An imprint of Bloomsbury Publishing Inc

B L O O M S B U R Y
NEW YORK · LONDON · OXFORD · NEW DELHI · SYDNEY

Bloomsbury Academic
An imprint of Bloomsbury Publishing Inc

1385 Broadway	50 Bedford Square
New York	London
NY 10018	WC1B 3DP
USA	UK

www.bloomsbury.com

BLOOMSBURY and the Diana logo are trademarks of Bloomsbury Publishing Plc

First published 2017

Library of Congress Cataloging-in-Publication Data
Names: Mollet, Tracey Louise, author.
Title: Cartoons in hard times: the animated shorts of Disney and Warner
Brothers in depression and war 1932-1945 / Tracey Louise Mollet.
Description: New York: Bloomsbury Academic, 2017. | Includes bibliographical
references and index. | Includes filmography.
Identifiers: LCCN 2017014775 (print) | LCCN 2017033276 (ebook) | ISBN
9781501328749 (ePDF) | ISBN 9781501328756 (ePUB) | ISBN 9781501328770
(hardcover : alk. paper)
Subjects: LCSH: Warner Bros. Cartoons. | Walt Disney Productions. | Looney
tunes. | Animated films–Social aspects–United States. |
Depressions–1929. | World War, 1939-1945–Motion pictures and the war.
Classification: LCC NC1766.U52 (ebook) | LCC NC1766.U52 W3735 2017 (print) |
DDC 791.43/75–dc23
LC record available at https://lccn.loc.gov/2017014775

ISBN: HB: 978-1-5013-2877-0
ePDF: 978-1-5013-2874-9
ePub: 978-1-5013-2875-6

Cover design: Louise Dugdale
Cover image © Eli K Hayasaka/Getty images

Typeset by Deanta Global Publishing Services, Chennai, India

To find out more about our authors and books, visit www.bloomsbury.com. Here you will find extracts, author interviews, details of forthcoming events and the option to sign up for our newsletters.

For Neil

Contents

List of Figures

Acknowledgements

There are so many people I would like to thank for helping me to accomplish this lifelong dream. First and foremost, I would like to thank the late Philip M. Taylor, without whom this project would not have existed. His belief and enthusiasm for the subject was what inspired me to realize that combining my two passions of History and Disney in academic research was possible. Secondly, I would like to thank all of my colleagues, past and present, at the School of Media and Communication at the University of Leeds. Thirdly, I would like to thank all the fantastic staff at the Margaret Herrick Library in Beverley Hills, the University of California Los Angeles Archives, the Warner Brothers Archives at the University of Southern California and the American Film Institute Archives. I would also like to thank all of my wonderful tutors, throughout my educational journey, but most especially Jonathan Davies, Steve Donlan, Jay Sexton and John Watts.

My biggest thanks, however, go to my family and friends, and my partner, Neil, to whom I would like to dedicate this book. I can never thank you enough for all of the support you have given me over the past three years.

List of Abbreviations

AAA	Agricultural Adjustment Administration
AFI	American Film Institute
CIAA	Centre for Inter-American Affairs
CWA	Civil Works Administration
FBI	Federal Bureau of Investigation
FDR	Franklin Delano Roosevelt
FERA	Federal Emergency Relief Administration
FHA	Federal Housing Association
FSA	Farm Security Administration
LT	Looney Tunes
MM	Merrie Melodies
NRA	National Recovery Administration
OIAA	Office of Inter-American Affairs
OSS	Office of Strategic Services
OWI	Office of War Information
PCA	Production Code Administration
SA	Sturmabteilung
SNAFU	Situation Normal All F**ked Up
UCLA	University of California Los Angeles
USC	University of Southern California
WPA	Works Progress Administration

Introduction: The Storyboard So Far

In the summer of 1941, Nelson Rockefeller and John Hay Whitney approached Walt Disney to make a series of animated shorts for the Office of Inter-American Affairs (OIAA). The OIAA was formed in 1940 and was primarily concerned with the financial problems of Latin American countries, but its role became limited to cultural relationships following the establishment of the Board of Economic Warfare (McCann 1973, 148). Rockefeller and Whitney wanted Disney to tour South America as a 'goodwill ambassador', believing that Disney's animation could be fundamentally important at curbing pro-Nazi feeling there. They offered to underwrite the cost of the trip and promised Disney $50,000 for making animated shorts fostering good relations between Latin America and the United States (Jackson 1993, 37). Disney set off with two dozen of his best animators in August 1941, leaving his studio in the aftermath of a disruptive strike, with the remaining artists fumbling through the animation for *Dumbo* (1941).[1] Disney had accepted his first state contract to produce propaganda through the medium of animation.

Nearly six months prior to the Japanese attack on Pearl Harbor, the Schlesinger Studios released *Meet John Doughboy* (1941). It was distributed by Warner Brothers, who were well known for the political undertones of their feature films.[2] Released the day after 4 July and just a short week following Germany's invasion of the Soviet Union, this animated production was unquestionably interventionist in its tone, calling for Americans to support the war and oppose anti-draft legislation. Despite the fact that the United States was not yet at war, these two studios quickly mobilized to present political messages through the medium of animation, recognizing its strength as an ideological platform.

---

[1] For further information on the Disney shorts produced for the OIAA, see Burton-Carvajal, Julianne (1994). 'Surprise Package: Looking Southward with Disney' and Cartwright, Lisa and Goldfarb, Brian, 'Cultural Contagion: On Disney's Health Education Films for Latin America'. In *Disney Discourse*, edited by Eric Smoodin, 132–9 and 174. New York: Routledge.

[2] See, for example, *Confessions of a Nazi Spy* (1939).

While the contribution of animation to the enormous body of literature on Hollywood's war propaganda has been recognized, the extent of this contribution has yet to be analysed in real depth. What is more, the current scholarship on animation falls short of any content analysis of animation before 1941,[3] with most works focusing on the ideological undertones of feature length animation in the late twentieth century, as well as animation's important role as propaganda during the Second World War. However, these contributions represent the culmination of animation's commentary on politics and society in this period. Cartoons produced by all the animation studios in America, but most especially the Schlesinger Studios and the Walt Disney Studios, provided their own interpretations of contemporary events, from Roosevelt's election, to the economic situation, to the pressures of total war.

This book will document this uncharted period of animation's history, from the presidential campaign of Franklin Delano Roosevelt in 1932 to the Japanese surrender in 1945, with the aim of finding an answer to the following fundamental question: How did the animation of the Walt Disney Studios and the Schlesinger Studios (distributed through Warner Brothers) provide a commentary on American politics and society?

In this period, the animated productions of these two studios underwent a significant transformation. They began as an experimental medium in the motion picture industry at the beginning of the 1930s, transmitting ideas through symbols and music. In the mid-1930s, as the medium progressed technologically, it changed from a vehicle for commentary on sociopolitical ideas into a powerful weapon of propaganda utilized by the American government in war.

The problem with animation

From the outset, it would seem that animation is something of a problematic medium for analysis by film historians. Leonard Maltin claims that there is a

---

[3] The current work in this area falls short of an in-depth analysis on the years 1933–45. These works touch upon the animation of this period, but do not consider its historical context and sociopolitical content. For example, Shull, Michael and Wilt, David. (1987). *Doing their Bit: Wartime American Animated Short Films*. Jefferson: McFarland; Schneider, Steve. *That's All Folks!: The Art of Warner Brothers Animation*. New York: H. Holt; Shale, Richard (1978). *Donald Duck Joins Up: The Disney Studio During World War Two*. Ann Arbor: UMI Research Press; Crafton, Donald (2012). *Shadow of a Mouse: Performance, Belief, and World-making in Animation*. Oakland: UC Press and Goldmark, Daniel and Kiel, Charles, eds (2011). *Funny Pictures: Animation and Comedy in Studio Era Hollywood*. Oakland: UC Press.

'snob barrier' between cartoon shorts and animated features which prevented any serious consideration of the former medium (Maltin 1980, viii). While Lewis Jacobs's contemporary study of film in 1938 highlighted Walt Disney's animated feature films as 'the highest expression of modern picture art in America', this seemed to elevate the animated feature, leaving its short counterpart cast aside into an area of Hollywood not worthy of critical attention (Jacobs 1939, 496). Despite being on the same bill as feature films, animation still remains an enormously understudied area of Hollywood filmmaking. As Joe Adamson has argued, it would appear that, 'When a man goes about writing an inclusive history of film, throwing out cartoons seems to be the first order of business, right after rolling up the sleeves and clearing the desk of rubber bands' (Adamson 1985, 11).

With the notable exception of the Disney Studios, many animation departments attached to the 'Big Five' during the 1930s were so far removed from the daily activities of the studios that many studio heads were unaware of their own cartoon production, or even unaware of their existence![4] Until fairly recently, this exclusion has been applied to all histories of animation. However, during the 1930s and 1940s, animated shorts were shown in theatres before the screening of feature films and became almost more popular than the features themselves. In an article in the *Saturday Evening Post*, one journalist commented that the essence of Americanism was 'spending millions of dollars to make spectacular movies' and 'sticking through them to see Mickey Mouse' (Jacobs 1939, 496). These cartoons received widespread circulation.

Over the last thirty years, the study of animation has started to flourish. Leonard Maltin focuses largely on the changing technology in animation, as well as the high turnover of staff between studios (1980). Similarly, Michael Barrier's extensive history on the American animation industry focuses largely on the differing techniques of the studios and the personalities and preferences of the animators involved, particularly the continued competition between Hugh Harman and Walt Disney for animated excellence (1999). There are also a significant number of general histories of animation, covering the medium's technological development

---

[4] See Jones, Charles (1989). *Chuck Amuck: The Life and Times of an Animated Cartoonist.* New York: Farrar Straus. Animator Charles Jones states in his autobiography that Friz Freleng maintains that Harry Warner believed that the Warner Brothers studio were responsible for the creation of the Walt Disney character, Mickey Mouse and when they discovered they did not, they shut the studio. See also Maltin, Leonard (1980). *Of Mice and Magic: A History of American Animated Cartoons.* New York: McGraw-Hill. Maltin has also commented that one spokesperson for a major studio denied the existence of an animation unit.

throughout the twentieth century.[5] Furthermore, the proliferation of work on animation theory and aesthetics, as well as dedicated scholarly journals on animation, has propelled its serious consideration within academic circles.[6] These works do not focus on particular studios, or on the content of the cartoon shorts produced during certain eras and on how they developed through time. Scholars such as Janet Wasko and Chris Pallant have done much to advance the study of Disney animation. While their works are comprehensive, they do not focus on the animated shorts of the 1930s and 1940s and their historical context.[7] Importantly, however, these works underline the premise of so-called 'classic' Disney and the essential characteristics of Disney's narratives.

Donald Crafton was one of the first scholars to recognize the importance of the messages within 'classic' cartoons. He has contended that 'failing to see beyond the childlike nature of animation simply perpetuates a fallacy of innocence' (Crafton 1993, 204b). Crafton's work speaks clearly to the adult themes running throughout animation, particularly his study of caricatures in Warner Brothers' animation. Crafton also stated that many of these cartoons have a 'hidden agenda' and contain certain 'social viewpoints' (ibid.). Indeed, veteran animator Charles Jones famously commented that 'these cartoons were never made for children. Nor were they made for adults. They were made for me' (Bogdanovich 1997, 699).

Sybil DelGaudio has also made the case for animation's incorporation of adult themes. Her work charts the use of animation for the purpose of education, documentary and propaganda. In the early teens, for example, she argues, Winsor McCay's *The Sinking of the Lusitania*, 'represented McCay's own outrage, as well as a depiction of the event' (DelGaudio 1997). DelGaudio's contribution is illuminating in its representation of animation as a medium for a sociopolitical agenda, asking the fundamental question, 'If truth be told, can "toons" tell it?' (ibid.) Can animation, a medium largely associated with light entertainment, be channelled for a more serious purpose? Subsequently, the

---

[5]   See, for example, Cavalier, Stephen (2011). *The World History of Animation*. London: Rotovision; Bendazzi, Giannalberto (1994). *Cartoons: One Hundred Years of Cinema Animation*. London: John Libbey; Beckerman, Howard (2001). *Animation: The Whole Story*. New York: Allworth Press; Soloman, Charles (1999). *Enchanted Drawings: The History of Animation*. New York: Alfred Knopf Doubleday and Grant, John (2001). *Masters of Animation*. New York: Watson Guptill.

[6]   For example, Furniss, Maureen (2007). *Art in Motion: Animation Aesthetics*. London: John Libbey; Beckman, Karen (2014). *Animating Film Theory*. Durham: Duke University Press and the foundation of *Animation: An Interdisciplinary Journal* in 2011 and *Animation Journal* in 1996.

[7]   See Pallant, Chris (2011). *Demystifying Disney: A History of Disney Feature Animation*. New York: Continuum International Publishing Group and Wasko, Janet (2001). *Understanding Disney: The Manufacture of Fantasy*. New York: Polity Press.

content of animation came to be considered by scholars for the first time as more than just an opportunity for comedic expression.

Michael Shull and David Wilt's work *Doing Their Bit: Wartime Animated Short Films* was groundbreaking in considering animation as a historical source. Shull argued that animation should not be cast aside as simply 'funny animals' in children's cartoons (1987, 4). Cartoon shorts were shown in the same theatres as feature films, with the same audience and therefore should be accredited the same substantial treatment by historians as valid empirical sources. They have a dual layer of interpretation. While it is true that they largely follow the antics of animals or children in fantastical settings, for adults, animation has significant sociocultural implications for historians of the 1930s and wartime America.

Animation and propaganda

When analysing animation in terms of its historical and political content, it would seem that many of the same concerns surrounding the relationship between motion pictures and propaganda should be raised. Jacques Ellul has argued that 'the movies and human contacts are the best media for sociological propaganda' (1965, 10). What is perhaps more important for animation in the current research is the significance placed on the use of images to reinforce a particular ideology (Jamieson 1985, 134). Given that animation is an overwhelmingly visual medium, the prominence given to what an audience could actually see or understand within a frame is paramount to any consideration of this field. In addition, Ellul claimed that propaganda and persuasion were more effective when they conformed to the needs of a society. In content and in tone, animation corresponded with the national feeling within America. First, cartoons, with their caricatures of modern society and politics, as well as many references to the world of the fairy tale, provided a welcome landscape of escape, entertainment and laughter for a depressed and war-torn population. Secondly, the characters within these cartoons, particularly the figure of Mickey Mouse, became embedded in the cultural fabric of society (Smoodin, 1993). Their hopes and dreams became akin to those of the ordinary people of America. Animation did not just conform to the needs of the American people, it reflected them.

Jowett and O'Donnell's contribution to the discourse on the power of propaganda is also of interest here. Their claim that propaganda is also formed through the creation of myth is seminal to the study of animation. They contest that 'a myth is not merely a fantasy or a lie but rather a model for social action ... a story in which meaning is embodied in recurrent symbols' (2006, 272). Through the use of animated characters, the Walt Disney Studios and the Schlesinger Studios created their own models for social action. Animation utilized the same symbols and motifs present in Hollywood films of the 1930s and 1940s to comment upon the ideology and policies of Roosevelt's government.

The movies and propaganda

The idea that movies, one of the primary beneficiaries of the free society, could be used to channel ideology and thus be used for the purposes of propaganda was deeply unsettling for Americans. The close relationship forged between propaganda and the totalitarian regimes between the two world wars led to an enforced awareness of 'propaganda' as a concept. Following the activities of the Creel Committee in the Great War, propaganda and the institutions 'producing' it were viewed with great distrust.[8] Propaganda was thus labelled as something distinctly 'un-American' and undemocratic in nature. Furthermore, isolationist groups enraged by the extent of US involvement in the conflict were quick to seize upon revelations regarding anti-US propaganda. The notion that America had been 'duped' into joining the war by Britain attracted a considerable following and Americans became increasingly aware of any medium that attempted to shape their values. Indeed, Anthony Rhodes has even gone as far as to argue that 'the greatest obstacle to Allied propaganda in World War Two was the propaganda that preceded American entry into World War One' (1976, 139).

Scholarship by the likes of Clayton Laurie, Philip M. Taylor and James Chapman has made the case for democracy's deep connection with propaganda.[9]

---

[8] See Ross, Stewart H. (1996). *Propaganda for War: How the United States was Conditioned to Fight the Great War of 1914–1918*. London: McFarland; Mock, James R. and Larson, Cedric (1939). *Words that Won the War: The Story of the Committee on Public Information 1917–1919*. Princeton: Princeton University Press; Peterson, Horace C. (1939). *Propaganda for War: The Campaign Against American Neutrality*. Norman: University of Oklahoma Press and Cull, Nicholas (1995). *Selling War: The British Propaganda Campaign against American 'Neutrality' in World War One*. New York: Oxford University Press.

[9] See, for example, Short, Kenneth, ed. (1983). *Film and Radio Propaganda during World War Two*. London: Croom Helm; Laurie, Clayton, (1996). *The Propaganda Warriors: America's Crusade Against Nazi Germany*. Lawrence: University Press of Kansas; Chapman, James (1998). *The British at War: Cinema, State and Propaganda 1939–1945*. London: I. B. Tauris and Balfour, Michael (1979). *Propaganda in War 1939–1945: Organisations, Policies and Public in Britain and Germany*. London: Routledge & Kegan Paul.

Due to the strategy of 'truth' promoted by such forms of government, propaganda in democracies could not look or sound like propaganda (Roeder 1993, 2). Indeed, both Roosevelt and Churchill rejected propaganda as a concept, failing to give much authority to those institutions responsible for its dissemination during the war.[10] This made movies the perfect medium through which to relay a particular political message to the general public.

Much of the stigma that has plagued the study of animation originally characterized the study of feature film. Following the foundation of the *Historical Journal for Film Radio and Television* in 1981 by Kenneth Short, the case was made for film to be utilized as an empirical source.[11] These scholars felt that any analysis of film should be based on the contextual as opposed to the textual. According to this discourse, films produced within the 1930s and 1940s should be viewed as texts heavily influenced by the culture that created them. They should be analysed for political or social content in the same way any historical text should be examined. Consideration of film by historians has moved steadily over the years from informational propaganda films such as newsreels and documentaries to feature films. This change has brought the paradigm surrounding film history into the realm of film theorists, keen to separate feature production from historical scrutiny. Such scholars have made the case for each production to be analysed internally, with the emphasis being on factors of composition rather than circumstance.[12]

These scholars reject historians' interest in finding contextual understanding from Hollywood productions. In an article for film journal *Screen*, Higson suggested that historical approaches place emphasis on 'representation, rather than points of view' (1983, 84). He implies that focus should be on the narrative and visual perspective of the director, and not of the audience understanding of the film text. However, it would seem that to dismiss a film's relative historicity is to dismiss not only its director's vision, but the nature of

---

[10] See Winkler, Allen (1978). *The Politics of Propaganda: The OWI 1942-1945*. New Haven: Yale University Press and Steele, Richard W. (1985). *Propaganda in an Open Society: The Roosevelt Administration and the Media, 1933-1941*. Westport: Greenwood Press.

[11] For works written in this tradition, see in particular, Pronay, Nicholas and Thorpe, Frances (1980). *British Official Films in the Second World War: A Descriptive Catalogue*. Oxford: Clio; Pronay, Nicholas and Springs, D. W., eds (1982). *Propaganda, Politics and Film 1918-1945*. Macmillan and London; Taylor; Philip, M., ed. (1988). *Britain and the Cinema in the Second World War*. London: Palgrave; and more recently Fox, Jo (2007). *Film and Propaganda in Britain and Nazi Germany*. Oxford: Berg.

[12] See Neale, Stephen, ed. (2002). *Genre & Contemporary Hollywood*. London: BFI; Higson, Andrew and Ashby, Justine, eds (2000). *British Cinema: Past and Present*. London: Routledge; Higson, Andrew and Maltby, Richard (1999). *Film Europe and Film America: Cinema, Commerce & Cultural Exchange 1920-1939*. Exeter: University of Exeter Press.

film itself. Film is not produced within an ideological vacuum, and while one cannot ignore the director's vision, it would be similarly complacent to ignore the historical context into which the film was released. Despite this tension, film scholars began to chart the intrinsic connection between history and film and the ways in which the latter could be used as a window into the attitudes and ideologies of the past.

As film and synchronized sound reached technological fruition at the beginning of the 1930s, so too did the medium of animation. When animation began to appear on the bill for feature films at the beginning of the 1930s, there were only a few studio names in the industry that began to attract significant attention. As such, any study of animation in this period must revolve largely around the activities of two particular studios: the Walt Disney Studios and the Schlesinger Studios, who distributed through Warner Brothers. These studios led the way in character animation in the 1930s, with characters such as Donald Duck and Porky Pig, and indeed, continue to hold popularity in the present day for their animated feature films and short subjects.

The Walt Disney Studios

The Walt Disney Studios has arguably produced some of the best animation in motion picture history, earning twenty-nine Oscars before Disney's death in 1966 for both feature films and cartoon shorts and considerably more since, most recently with *Frozen* (2013) and Disney–Pixar's *Inside Out* (2015).[13] The Walt Disney Company brand is nothing short of a global phenomenon, with theme parks, retail outlets, several motion picture production companies, cruise lines and holiday resorts. The company also merged with ABC Television Studios in 1996, acquired Pixar Studios in 2006, Marvel Entertainment in 2009 and Lucasfilm in 2012, further asserting its hold over global entertainment culture.[14]

Disney's unquestionable dominance in pop culture, both in the period under study and in the present day, has led to considerable problems with its scholarly treatment. Elizabeth Bell, Lynda Haas and Laura Sells highlighted the challenges

---

[13] *Frozen* won the Academy Award for Best Original Song with 'Let It Go' and Best Animated Feature. *Inside Out* also won the latter award in 2015.

[14] See 'Disney Completes Marvel Acquisition', available at http://corporate.disney.go.com/news/ corporate//2009/2009_0831_disney_and_marvel_entert ainment.html (accessed 21 January 2013) and 'Disney to Acquire Lucasfilm', available at https://thewaltdisneycompany.com/disney-news/ press-releases/2012/10/disney-acquire-lucasfilm-ltd (accessed 31 October 2015).

faced by those wishing to engage in a consideration of any Disney film. They have argued that 'legal institutions, film theorists, cultural critics and loyal audiences all guard the borders of Disney film as "off limits" to critical enterprise' (1995, 3). For a long time, Disney's elevated position within the paradigm of global culture led to an exclusion of any serious consideration of their animation. Steven Watts identified this tension as a conflict between popularity and critical reception. He has argued that 'Disney's enormous popularity has contributed to dismissal in critical circles. Commercial success has been viewed in inverse proportion to cultural significance' (1995, 84). The problem with Disney seemed to be the paradoxical underlying notion that populist sentiment cannot be viewed in unison with cultural importance. Furthermore, due to Disney's well-known association with the fairy tale, many scholars have viewed Disney's productions as artificially created productions, having little cultural value.

Among the first to criticize Disney animation was Francis Clark Sayers. Sayers accused Disney of creating nothing more than a 'soap opera' that was in no way related to everyday life. Jack Zipes has also laid many charges at the door of the Disney Company, particularly regarding its Americanization of the fairy tale. He contends that 'Disney 'cast a spell' over the classical fairy tale, infusing viewers with false hope, losing its original value system and replacing it with his own escapist world view' (1994, 74). Both of these scholars seem to adhere to the notion that Disney is worthy of special treatment due to its distance from the culture of its origins. To an extent, this is true. The animated world of Disney is as fantastical and escapist as its creator. Disney himself detracted from the underlying meanings of his own pictures, famously stating, 'We just make the pictures and then let the professors tell us what they mean' (Rollin 1996).

However, despite Disney's own ideological indifference towards his films, scholars have been unable to ignore the messages within Disney animation. Against the backdrop of an inherent critical awareness of media content, Richard Schickel's biography of Walt Disney, *The Disney Version: The Life, Times, Art and Commerce of Walt Disney* was one of the first to acknowledge the value system inherent in Disney films. He has argued that Disney transmitted ideology 'appealing to the worst aspects of middle class conservative values' (1968, 4). Similarly, Ariel Dorfman and Armand Mattelart characterize Disney animation as dangerous in its transmission of an aggressive American imperialism (1975). Marc Eliot's early damning biography of the studio head, *Walt Disney: Hollywood's Dark Prince*, uncovered Disney's apparent links to the FBI and his extensive work for the Committee on Un-American Activities to uncover communists within

Hollywood (1993). Henry Giroux's work received a hostile popular reception for arguing that Disney's cultural power was somewhat dangerous, given the company had built their reputation on 'wholesome entertainment, largely free of power, politics and ideology' (Giroux 1999). These works recognize that Disney's productions are far from innocent in their underlying messages and, furthermore, claim that the widespread popularity of Disney animation makes such media content effective at disseminating harmful ideologies.

Janet Wasko has made the case for a serious scholarly treatment of Disney. She claims, 'There is a general sense that its product is only entertainment. ... However, it is important to consider Disney seriously and to insist it is a legitimate focal point for cultural and social analysis.' However, the conclusions reached are similar to those laid out by critics such as Watts, Zipes and Schickel. 'Disney values', she maintains, 'are to be associated with "conservatism, homophobia, ethnocentricity, cultural insensitivity and superficiality"' (Wasko 2001, 3). While there is no denying the radical conservatism of many of the productions, much of the early literature on Disney focuses on little else. As such, these works are deductive in nature, analysing any Disney animated production in exclusive, not inclusive, terms.

However, the tide is beginning to turn in favour of the productions of Disney as a way to tap into a seminal part of American culture. There emerged a new constructive body of work on Disney that did not limit itself to the critical framework laid out by Schickel (1968) and Giroux (1999). Bryne and McQuillan's analysis of the neo-liberal era of Disney introduces a new notion for animation scholars to consider. The levels of interpretation of Disney texts are constantly evolving due to the rapidly changing ideological fabric of society. As such, they argue that the terms of critical engagement with these texts must change. They contend that scholars 'must not just ask questions about Disney', they 'must ask questions about the questions we ask about Disney' (1999, 7). Scholars must now consider the wider cultural, social and political frameworks of Disney productions and uncover what they reveal about concurrent periods of American history.

In this vein, Paul Wells underlined the problematic façade of innocence within Disney features, and recognized their power in exacerbating social tensions in a particular context. He argues, 'One only needs, however, to place a Disney cartoon in an explicit political context to see how this apparent innocence merely disguises a whole gamut of ideological possibilities' (1998, 207). Douglas Brode was one of the first Disney scholars to examine Disney animation in a somewhat positive light and to take these frameworks into real consideration. He argues that the evolution of ideology in Disney animation during the 1930s and 1940s was crucial to the formation of a radicalized value system that played a key part in the youth revolution of the 1960s (2004). The importance of Brode's scholarship lies in recognizing the underlying importance of the values transmitted through Disney animation and their far-reaching consequences. Brode underscores the social realities of the ideologies relayed within Disney's narrative frameworks. In previous literature, too much attention has been drawn to Disney's own political attitudes. The conclusions drawn from these have subsequently coloured scholars' judgements on the animation itself before any detailed analysis had been carried out. A similar conclusion is reached in Brode's edited volume *Debating Disney*. He contends that while the ideological undertones of many of the earlier productions are, indeed, problematic, it is necessary to look to audience reception and to context to truly understand the meaning and intentions of these productions (Brode, 2016). Similarly, Amy M. Davis's work on gender makes an astonishing case for the need to abolish traditional gender stereotypes in Disney productions, painting the features in a positive light distant from the original criticisms of Zipes and Sayers (2005a, 2013b). However, all of these works largely exclude the animated shorts of the 1930s and 1940s from analysis.

Some ideological analyses of Disney shorts have been carried out. For example, Russell Merritt has carried out an intense ideological examination of the Disney 'Silly Symphonies', but his analysis is based around the shorts' exploration of childhood (Merritt 2005). Eric Smoodin also taps into the cultural context of early Disney animation in the sound era. Smoodin's work accentuates Disney's intrinsic connection to Depression culture: 'Mickey Mouse became part of the Depression era narrative of afternoons at the movies and thus became a national monument of transnational capitalism' (1993a, 65). Smoodin's later editorial on Disney gives weight to the conclusion that Disney is now being seen as fundamental to the undercurrents of American society. He argues, 'As film studies came to the fore with the developing branch of cultural studies which linked it to the social sciences, Disney's sense of importance has increased once more in terms of the construction of national character' (1994b, 5). This highlights that the importance of Disney's productions lies not in the conservative nature of its narratives, but in its contribution to culture at a time of immense social and political upheaval. Kevin Shortsleeve's article 'The Wonderful World of Depression: Disney, despotism and the 1930s' is also of interest here. While Shortsleeve's analysis is fundamentally negative, his argument helps to underline a simple truth. Disney achieved his success in much the same way as Franklin Delano Roosevelt's (FDR) New Deal appealed to the American people. He achieved this status by 'associating his products with American iconography', situating them in and among images, myths and symbols of popular American heritage (Shortsleeve 2004, 18).

This contribution is not specific to the 1930s and 1940s. Nicholas Sammond's work on the connection of Disney to American childhood has done a great deal to call attention to Disney's contribution to the formation of national character. He has argued, 'Disney was represented as an interceding between an ideal past and an unrealized ideal future, distilling the best impulses of that past into a digestible form that would reappear as the present corrected in that future' (2005, 366). Indeed, Sammond draws links between Disney animation and its inherent ideology and hence draws conclusions about Disney's influence on society today. While there is no denying Disney's effect on culture in contemporary society, it seems pertinent to address where this influence came from, and how Disney came to be so inherently connected to American life. The answer to this question can only be answered by looking to Disney's first productions: the short subjects of the 1930s and 1940s.

The Schlesinger Studios

While the Walt Disney Studios dominated the field of animation during the 1930s, its biggest rival, the Schlesinger Studios (who distributed through Warner Brothers), increased in its output and importance to the medium, emerging from the classical period as the most prolific and successful studio in terms of animated short subjects. The Schlesinger productions have not attracted the same amount of criticism as the Disney Studios, nor has the studio generated as substantial a consideration by academics. While this may seem surprising, considering the extensive scholarship surrounding Jack and Harry Warner's contribution to the politicization of Hollywood, the two brothers paid little attention to their animation unit. The studio that gave birth to household names such as Bugs Bunny, Daffy Duck and Porky Pig was not actually under the direct control of the politically active Warner brothers, Harry and Jack, until Schlesinger sold his assets in 1944. Indeed, the only real explicit connection between Warner Brothers and Schlesinger's animation studio was their stipulation that each cartoon should include one full chorus of a song from a Warners' feature film (Maltin 1980, 220). Despite the fact that Warner Brothers' theatrical shorts won six Academy Awards and created more cartoon stars than any other studio, the literature surrounding their productions is far from adequate. Unlike Disney, Warners' animation and its characters have not come to dominate modern popular culture. The brand of Warner Brothers' animation does not carry the same weight of social expectations or ideological implications, nor have the productions attracted the attention of scholars.

Due to the long-standing neglect of the cultural importance of animation, for many years, there was no literature on Warner Brothers' animation. Steve Schneider's work, *That's All Folks: The Art of Warner Brothers Animation* serves as the only substantial history of Warner Brothers' animation. Schneider has argued that, 'The problem [with WB animation] was, no-one ever really paid much mind. In all the encyclopaedias of film history, in all the vivisections of pop culture, non-Disney animation was ignored, scorned or given the shortest of thrift' (1994, 17). Similar to the restrictions on Disney archival access, a major issue with research on Warner Brothers' animation is the elimination of many of the archival materials of this period, which makes research into the productions very problematic. Scholars must rely on interviews with animators working in the studio, and their biographies to uncover the contextual background in which the cartoons were made.

While Disney pushed for further realism in his cartoons through constant technical innovation, the animators at the Schlesinger Studios, during this period, were restricted both in time and in budget. The Warner Brothers studio acted as a hive for creativity and imagination, but with strict constraints in terms of product quality. The animators constantly 'battled for higher budgets with Leon Schlesinger, who resolutely refused to cut his profit margin by spending more on the product' (Maltin 1980, 224). In an interview with famous animator Charles Jones, the importance of the animation conducted in a studio fondly nicknamed 'Termite Terrace' is underlined: 'We had freewheeling sessions [there] with all of us together and that's where the experimental stuff came from; all the series themselves came from those sessions' (Bogdanovich 1997, 706). The core of the Warner Brothers' staff was physically separated from the rest of the unit by Schlesinger. Avery later told his biographer:

> I guess Schlesinger saw the light; he said, 'Well I'll take you boys away from the main plant. He put us up in our own little shack over on the Sunset lot, completely separated from the Schlesinger studio, in some old dressing room or

toilet or something, a little cottage sort of thing. We called it Termite Terrace. And he was smart, he didn't disturb us. We were all alone out there and he knew nothing of what went on'. (Maltin 1980, 226)

General histories of animation reveal that unlike Walt Disney, who exercised a heavily controlling influence on the work of his animators, the animators at the Schlesinger Studios were given substantially more freedom. As Tom Sito has argued, 'What made Leon Schlesinger ideal was that as an executive, he understood the separation needed between the creative and financial aspects of animation. He focused on budgets and schedules and otherwise, left the artists alone' (Sito 2006, 41).

Well-known animators such as Charles Jones, Tex Avery, Frank Tashlin and Robert Clampett took on the responsibility of directing the animation and as such had control over every element of the finished product. As Jones has confirmed, 'The director not only tries to explain to the animators what he wants in terms of bodily action, but he creates and gives them the key drawings. At least the directors did at Warner Brothers. At Disney, for instance, the directors did very little drawing but at Warners, we did a lot' (Bogdanovich 1997, 705).

Joe Adamson's biography of Tex Avery is illuminating in providing an insight into the way in which the animation unit operated at Warner Brothers. He confirms the autonomy of Warner Brothers animation, 'The action in an animated cartoon is so completely under the director's control that it becomes a medium in which the film maker's imagination not only can run absolutely riot, but genuinely has to' (Adamson 1985, 27). Adamson's analysis confirms that the animated shorts at Warner Brothers were the epitome of their creators' imaginations. This paints the animators as the channelling ideological force behind the cartoons themselves.

While the literature on Warner Brothers' animation is still scarce, some scholars have recognized the cultural significance of the productions. The works in which Warner Brothers' cartoons have been considered always draw a comparison with Disney, and as such, these studies become deductive in nature, examining the shorts in terms of what they are not, as opposed to what they are (Barrier 1999). Furthermore, research into the cultural significance of Warner Brothers' animation often transforms into a bitter discourse surrounding the Walt Disney Company. Kevin Sandler's work is one such charge (1998). However, it has also been argued that despite constant comparison with Disney,

Warner Brothers developed a socially conscious interpretation of the animated cartoon, displaying a certain self-awareness missing completely from their rivals' productions. Paul Wells has identified the difference as a contestation of what was considered conventional in the medium:

> In insisting upon subjecting the unities of the cartoon to interrogation and revision, the Warner Bros animators proved that parameters of the form could address aesthetic principles and socio-cultural conditions in a way that offered a fresh insight and pertinency, challenging any notion of a 'mainstream' orthodoxy. (2002, 51)

Mitchell Cohen's analysis is groundbreaking as for the first time, the tone and content of the animation is explored in real depth. He argues, 'They [The WB cartoons] were the more consciously contemporary cartoons, utilising up to date pop tunes, events and cultural references to make their satire particularly pointed' (Cohen 1985, 34). Cohen draws the link between the content of the animation and their cultural references, laying the foundations of Shull and Wilt's argument for using animation as a historical source. Cohen also points to the heavily adult themes inherent in Warners' animation, through their use as propaganda during the war; 'The LT (Looney Tunes)/MM (Merrie Melodies) conviction that the aggressor will eventually be destroyed was translated into patriotic propaganda during the first half of the Forties' (ibid., 36).

Michael Birdwell's article on the Private Snafu cartoons is certainly of note to historians of Warner Brothers' animation, as, again, the content of the animation is analysed. He charts the creation of the unit headed by Theodore Geisel, better known by the name Dr Seuss, which produced twenty-six instalments in the Private Snafu saga. These cartoons, he notes, 'gave Hollywood animators the opportunity to experiment with political and topical humour, allowing them to chart new territory and play a role in the eventual destruction of the production code' (Birdwell 2005, 206).

While it is natural to be more aware of the content of animation produced specifically for the military as propaganda, this awareness must first be applied to animation produced outside the confines of the government's propaganda guidelines. Animation was recognized by the government as having the power to be able to carry strong ideological messages; historians must now chart where this power came from and how it was wielded before and during the war.

Chapter outline

This book outlines the content and context of animated short subjects produced by the Walt Disney Studios and the Schlesinger Studios during the period from 1932 to 1945. These two animation studios not only produced the most animated productions in this period, but they each also provided a commentary on social and political life in America.

Chapter 2 concerns itself with the so-called 'honeymoon period' experienced within the United States during the presidential campaign of 1932 and after the inauguration of FDR in 1933. The argument is made that certain animation productions endorsed the new president's campaign and policies through their narrative and music. Chapter 3 is centred on animation's depiction of Depression America and its awareness of the New Deal from 1934 to 1937. Many historians argue that 1937 is the year in which the New Deal came to an end due to the cutbacks imposed upon the president by Congress in a need to balance the budget. Chapter 4 highlights how the productions of these studios put forward a message about America's position in the world, specifically in relation to the international stage. It focuses largely on animation's depiction of other nations and their regimes, through the use of caricature and narrative during the years 1936–41. 1936 was the year in which Hitler's invasion of the Rhineland against the Treaty of Versailles caused significant political upheaval within Europe. It also marks the beginning of the Spanish Civil War and the height of Mussolini's military action against Abyssinia in North Africa. America remained 'neutral' to a point during these years; however, the animated productions of these years provided commentary on the international arena without being subject to the amount of censorship imposed upon the feature films of Hollywood during this period. Chapter 5 focuses largely on the new sense of nationalism created in America through the policies of Roosevelt, specifically following the 'quarantine speech' in Chicago in 1937 (Dallek, 1979). This was achieved through the consistent use of national phrases, music, history and the animation of well-known American figures or landmarks.

Chapters 6 and 7 demonstrate the culmination of animation's involvement in forging ideological contexts through their narrative. Using unpublished internal documents from the Disney Studios, these chapters demonstrate the techniques at work during the production of 1930s animation and their formalization for use in propaganda at war. Chapter 6 focuses solely on shorts produced by the Disney and Schlesinger Studios sponsored by the US Treasury, and the productions sponsored by the Centre for Inter-American Affairs (CIAA). Chapter 7 deals with productions referencing the war and the international situation, but those that were not funded by the government, confirming that the productions of these studios provided a substantial commentary on politics during the war, much like Hollywood feature films of the same era.

Through the combination of unpublished internal documents from within the Disney Studios during the war, contextual analysis and an original content analysis of the animation from 1932 to 1945, it is argued that the techniques used in the 1930s to convey ideological and political meaning were formalized and documented for use within war propaganda. The animation produced by the Disney and Schlesinger Studios since 1932 interprets the Depression, the international situation and the war for its audiences, leaving a heavy ideological imprint for historians to excavate.

2

The Roosevelt Honeymoon 1932–4

The way in which the majority of Americans rallied to the support of FDR in the 1932 election campaign is well documented. The president elect managed to secure an absolute majority, which had not happened since the election of Franklin Pierce in 1852 (Edsforth 2000). Nearly twenty-three million voters chose FDR in the greatest vote ever cast for a presidential candidate (Brogan 1950). What is less well documented is the extent to which FDR and his new administration received an astonishing backing from the film industry in Hollywood.

Giulana Muscio's work *Hollywood's New Deal* remains one of the only pieces of scholarship to chart this support in some detail, characterizing the intrinsic connection between Hollywood and politics during the 1930s, and drawing attention to the 1932 election. Muscio states, 'Both the New Deal and cinema had a stabilising effect on society that was strengthened and sustained by a reinterpretation of the idea of Americanism, such that the thirties have been identified with the desire for a "new national vision of popular culture and the country"' (Muscio 1996, 2). The movies in the 1930s had an intrinsic connection with political culture that cannot be underestimated. This even escalated to the level that many of the studios actively promoted the administration of FDR. During Roosevelt's presidential campaign of 1932, Jack Warner staged a Motion Picture Electrical Parade and Sports Pageant at the Los Angeles Olympic Stadium on 4 September 1932. Universal, too, actively promoted the president's policies.[1] While Roosevelt's Press Secretary, Stephen Early, was keen to underline that the White House would not actively endorse any 'promotional' movie made on the subject of Roosevelt and his policies, Hollywood rose to the challenge regardless. Their campaigning reached a political climax with the 'Hollywood for Roosevelt'

---

[1] Universal asked McIntyre for permission to use a photo of Roosevelt in *Moonlight and Pretzels* (1933).

campaign (Rosten 1941). In 1940, it was estimated that more than 85 per cent of the industry supported Roosevelt (Brownstein 1990, 79).

Due to the inherent connection between politics and film in this decade, many historians have scrutinized the content of movies of the 1930s, analysing their underlying political messages. Allen Woll has made much of the role of musicals in the era at promoting community spirit and unity within society, particularly within the first few years of the decade (1983). Indeed, musicals emphasized the importance of synchronicity and togetherness within a populace. *Gold Diggers of '33* (1933), *42nd Street* (1933) and *Footlight Parade* (1933), all Warner Brothers features, spoke to the resilience and optimism of the American people in a time of Depression and how these traits can lead to material success. James Cagney as the lead in *Footlight Parade* is an avid 'New Dealer' and even states the phrase, 'We're giving you a new deal,' in the film's dialogue.

Andrew Bergman's scholarship *We're in the Money: Depression America and Its Films* makes a strong case for the ways in which movies championed the work of the federal government in 'cleaning up' the town. He argues that films such as *I Am a Fugitive from a Chain Gang* (1932) and *Wild Boys of the Road* (1933) reflect Jack Warner's 'unwavering faith in the work and policies of FDR' (Bergman 1971, 93). *Wild Boys of the Road* even features a judge that resembles FDR who sends the film's youths back to the safety of their homes while standing beneath the NRA eagle. Warner Brothers defined the social consciousness film in the 1930s and continued to make films surrounding the ethos of the 'common American man', and painted FDR in the role of an unsung hero, working to better the lives of the working class.

Such films, released in the earliest years of Roosevelt's presidency, emphasized the importance of the policy of the New Deal to rejuvenate America, the importance of Roosevelt's personality, injecting confidence into a depressed populace, and the importance of togetherness and working hard to get America out of Depression.[2] Thus, despite the fact that the inter-war period has clearly been recognized for its intrinsic importance to the history of cinema, in terms of both its style and for the formation of Hollywood as an influential political institution, an in-depth analysis of the animation of this era remains absent. The animated

---

[2] While outside of the confines of this study, the irony of the author's argument becomes clear if one analyses the Universal short subject, *Confidence* (1933). In this animated short, the original Disney character, Oswald the Lucky Rabbit, seeks help from the president for his depressed hen farm. The hens are 'depressed' and are eventually helped through an injection of 'Confidence' obtained from FDR himself.

shorts of Walt Disney and of other animation studios were shown on the same film bill as the live action features that have received so much attention from film historians of this decade. Most scholars mention only the Disney Silly Symphony *The Three Little Pigs* (1933) as having a cultural significance to the national mood due to the tone of its title song, 'Who's Afraid of the Big Bad Wolf'; however, this remains the only animated short subject to have received such attention.

Using examples from the popular trade press, the *Motion Picture Herald* and the *Motion Picture Daily*, this chapter charts the way that Walt Disney's animated characters found an outlet through which to support FDR and his policies, which filtered through from the politicized forum of the industry periodicals into the narratives of many of its productions in the first two years of the new president's term.

The Hollywood trade press and the new president

Following the results of the 1932 election in FDR's favour, the Hollywood press were quick to congratulate the new president on his victory. As Dennis Brogan has argued, 'The Roosevelt name was magic' (1950, 20) and the industry was quick to capitalize on its appeal. The first edition of *Motion Picture Herald* in 1933 welcomes its readers optimistically into the New Year: 'Happy 1933! Sure it's the same as 1929 because good times are here again thanks to the Laughing Lion!' (*Motion Picture Herald*, 18 February 1933).

Hollywood movies even used the New Deal to advertise their pictures. The advertising line for *42nd Street* was cited as 'The Inauguration of a New Deal in Entertainment' (*Motion Picture Herald*, 25 February 1933). The film even had a special showing in Washington on the inauguration weekend, advertising itself alongside FDR's ascendancy to the presidency (*Motion Picture Herald*, 4 March 1933). MGM's Globe Trotter Travelling Studio 'proudly' took its place in the Inaugural Parade in March of 1933 (ibid.). In July, when Roosevelt appealed to American industry to adopt a uniform policy of higher wages under the National Industrial Recovery Act, he received an instant telegram from Will Hays of the Production Code Administration, pledging support of the agreement by all major producers, effective from the end of July 1933 (*Motion Picture Herald*, 19 July 1933). Hollywood, in these years, was proud to be associated with the new administration and used the president's new policies to promote its new films and programmes.

However, fuelling passion for the New Deal into advertising was not simply confined to the live action feature films and the big studios. Disney animation also used the New Deal and the appeal of Roosevelt to promote itself within the industry. Disney's early distributor, Columbia, used the rhetoric of Roosevelt's new presidency in its advertisements. An advertisement in the 25 March 1933 edition of the *Motion Picture Herald*, featuring Mickey Mouse, advertised the slogan 'Keep 'Em Happy with Columbia Short Subjects!' The advertisement also included a speech bubble from the character of Mickey Mouse, stating 'Banks are open, market's shooting up – beer will soon flow freely. USA will balance the budget. Farm and unemployment relief are on their way – a grand new deal all around!'

The animated world considered itself a part of the promise of the New Deal and, through advertising, endorsed the policies of the new administration. Mickey Mouse was even invited to be a special guest star at the New England Prosperity Festival in May 1933 and had a specially constructed street, 'Mickey Mouse Mall' named after him. *Motion Picture Herald* overtly recognized the connection the animated star had with the new thread of hope pulsating throughout society: 'School children, merchants, police and unemployed rallied about a mythical pencil line which somehow has become vitally symbolical the country over for children, young and old' (20 May 1933).

What is perhaps most striking is that the character of Mickey Mouse was even allowed his own editorial slot in the popular film periodical *Motion Picture Daily* in this period. The author, stated as 'Icklemay "Ousemay"', is accompanied by a large print of the cartoon character and written in the unmistakeable intonations of Mickey Mouse, containing references to Minnie Mouse, Walt Disney and his fellow cartoon colleagues, Horace Horsecollar and Clarabel Cow. The editorial contains endorsements of the new administration put forward by the 'character' himself, drawing a direct link between Disney animation, its characters and support for the New Deal.

In the editorial, 'Mickey' calls attention to the widespread support his studio had received from the presidential family. He states that 'the biggest thrill of my life' was when he 'read all the lovely things Mrs. Roosevelt said about my pictures' (*Motion Picture Daily*, 10 June 1933). 'Mickey' is likely referring to the well-known comment made by the First Lady who stated that her husband 'loved Mickey Mouse and he always had to have that cartoon in the White House' (Gabler 2007, 195). 'Mickey' establishes a relationship between himself, the Disney Studios and the New Deal by reaching out to the presidential household.

While 'Mickey' is flattered by the attention he has received from the household, he seems humble and even harbours his own political ambitions. Later in the editorial, he states that as 'eight thousand managers lobby for a mouse', that ought to get him somewhere in Washington and contemplates whether there will be a place for him in the 'Mouse of Representatives' (ibid.). Mickey further underlines his support for the president by stating that someday, 'I want to meet Mr. Roosevelt and shake his hand and tell him that he is our mouse beloved president' (ibid.).

Even outside of the realms of the cinema screen, animation was actively engaging with the political atmosphere in the trade press within the years 1932 to 1934. Donald Crafton has argued that there is little overtly political content in Hollywood cartoons (2011, 71). However, when the animated world was actively involving itself within the political culture of Hollywood in these years and playing its own role within the so-called Roosevelt honeymoon through editorials, parades and advertising, perhaps it is worth taking another look at the content of the cartoons in this period. While it has been argued that the early Disney cartoons are deeply committed to the 'old American tradition of individual initiative and enterprise' (Sklar, 'The Making of Cultural Myths – Walt Disney', 1980, 63), through the analysis of the characters, personalities and music from within the cartoons released by Disney and Warner Brothers, it is clear that the force of the animated world was behind the administration of Roosevelt.

Mickey's Nightmare (1932)

Mickey's Nightmare was released in August 1932. While this cartoon was in production, the nation had seen the collapse of four hundred private charities in New York and an estimated sixty million out of a total population of one hundred and twenty-six million people living 'hand to mouth' (Edsforth 2000, 77). Moreover, unemployment was estimated to be upwards of thirteen million (Leuchtenberg 1963, 2). Financial pressures were increasingly taking their toll on the average American family, with thousands of men leaving their wives and children in an attempt to find work. Many families had to turn to private charities in order to make ends meet. The central institution of the family became a burden unto itself. This cartoon, released before the promise of the New Deal and at a time when America's economy was at its lowest ebb, encapsulates the spirit of these times directly, simply through the troubling nature of Mickey's dream. It stands in stark contrast to a later cartoon which centralizes the same social issues, but portrays an inherently different ideology.

Mickey's Nightmare opens with Mickey dutifully saying his prayers before bed time. His bedroom is modest but comfortable. Mickey then begins to dream. His vision opens as the embodiment of the typical American Dream. He proposes to Minnie and they quickly get married and settle down together. They have their own home and garden in the suburbs and are living in the throes of the idyllic 1920s, where America's economy is booming and home ownership was increasing by the day (Masnick 2004). A stork soon delivers a baby to the house and Mickey is congratulated by Pluto on becoming a father.

However, one manageable child soon turns into fifty children. Mickey's idyllic life is transformed into the epitome of the Depression burden – a house full of mouths to feed. The children gradually destroy every element of Mickey and Minnie's American Dream. The car is ruined, as are the various commodities owned by the newlyweds. Mickey's carefree life is suddenly filled with a responsibility not associated with 1920s America. Furthermore, the absence of Minnie within this cartoon places the emphasis even further on the father figure as the sole breadwinner of the household during the Depression. The dream ends with Mickey literally trapped by his responsibilities with no sign of rescue. His children have tied him up and surround him, so he is unable to escape. Mickey wakes up, smashes the Cupid statue next to the picture of Minnie by his bedside and cheers the reality of his life.

Mickey's experience within this cartoon channels the burden of family associated with a pre-New Deal America. It emphasizes the responsibility of a wife and children to the average male, here portrayed as Mickey. The fact that this short was released in 1932, at the height of America's struggle with the Depression, situates this animated short directly within the forum of economic and political debate. Mickey and Minnie are home owners and sport many commodities in their comfortable house. These are gradually destroyed throughout the animation, signifying the destruction of the materialistic culture of the 1920s. Far from being the 'American Dream' experienced by a middle-class figure of Mickey's background, due to the current economic climate within this 1932 cartoon, Mickey's wife, house and children are a 'nightmare' he is only too happy to escape from. The world created by Disney's animation engages itself with real social issues central to the everyday struggles cutting through the fabric of a previously prosperous society.

The Three Little Pigs (1933)

Few cartoons of this era have attracted as much attention from historians as *The Three Little Pigs*. Widely regarded as one of Walt Disney's most successful cartoons of the *Silly Symphony* series, the animated tale of the pigs' battle with the Big Bad Wolf has been highlighted as culturally and socially significant. Richard Schickel has drawn attention to the cartoon as being 'more Hoover than Roosevelt ... stressing self-reliance, conservative building and keeping one's house in order' (1968, 154). However, Robert Sklar has linked the animated short with the euphoria inherent in society after the election of Roosevelt. He argues that 'the film's popularity likely stemmed from its expression of New Deal spirit' (1978, 204). Michael Shull and David Wilt have also linked the wolf in *The Three Little Pigs* with 'the Depression and ... fascism' (1987, 23). Both the popular press and the trade press expressed the importance and popularity of this cartoon and its underlying ideology. A *Motion Picture Herald* review of the picture from October 1933 cites the animation as being 'the best colored short in many a day. Have had patrons come back to see it a second time and numerous phone calls' (21 October 1933). The Pigs were even associated with New Deal philanthropy as they were used to distribute prizes in a contest awarded by W. C. Ricord Junior in December 1934 (*Motion Picture Herald*, 1 December 1934). Contemporary observer on the movies, Lewis Jacobs, made the case that *The Three Little Pigs* 'has a message of striving together which was emphatic after the election of Roosevelt's famous appeal to the Americans. The film became a heartening call to the people of the troubled country' (1939, 505).

The narrative and characters of the animated short, *The Three Little Pigs* embrace the values of the new administration. Our attention within this cartoon is drawn first to the characters of the pigs themselves. *The Three Little Pigs* set the benchmark in what animation historian, Leonard Maltin, has characterized as 'personality animation' (1980, 41). We are introduced to the three pigs, two of which have similar carefree personalities. They put little effort into the construction of their houses, find the time to play their musical instruments and sing in celebration of their lot. These two pigs represent the epitome of the ideology inherent within 1920s America. They are living the American Dream, embracing their lives filled with wealth and fortune. Both are dressed in smart uniforms. The pictures on the walls of their houses reinforce this carefree attitude. The pig in the straw house is shown dancing in a Hawaiian grass skirt;

the second indulges himself with the sport of boxing. Each of these photographs shows leisurely pursuits, indicative of an egotistical ideology and suggests that these pigs care little for the joy of family or community. These pigs are put into direct contrast with the third 'practical' pig. The 'practical pig' is dressed in worker's overalls, indicative of the fact that he does not take much pride in his appearance. He does not adhere to the carefree attitude of his peers, and works long and hard constructing his house with 'wolf proof paint' (Figure 2.1).

The 'practical pig' is resourceful. He does not accept his fortune, he works to maintain and strengthen his personal defence against the world. On the walls of his brick house, the 'practical pig' celebrates family, with a picture of 'Mother' placed on the wall. Simply through the personality of these three characters, this animated short presents a clash of alternative ideologies: one consistent with a pre-Roosevelt America, and the other consistent with the philosophies inherent in the New Deal.

One must pay attention to the music within this animated short. The ideology of the cartoon is relayed through Frank Churchill's lyrics. The practical pig sings, 'I'll be safe and you'll be sorry when the wolf comes through your door.' The pig infers that through his hard work and graft, he will be immune to any outside threat, while the other two pigs simply laugh off the danger posed by

Figure 2.1 *The Three Little Pigs* (1933). Walt Disney Treasures.

the wolf and continue to dance and sing. When the carefree pigs have their houses destroyed by the wolf, the error in their ideology is highlighted by the lyrics of the practical pig. He sings, 'Only bricks and stones are wolf proof.' Furthermore, as many historians have signified, it makes sense to embrace the idea of the wolf representing the Depression, we can uncover further meaning behind the refrain 'Who's Afraid of the Big Bad Wolf?' Throughout the narrative, the carefree pigs laugh off the Depression and its clutches. However, instead of fighting the menace of the wolf when he arrives, they run away and do little to change their current situation. The practical pig, however, is motivated and takes direct action to combat the danger. He hits the wolf over the head with a brush and eventually burns the wolf's rear end with boiling turpentine. Again, the personality of the practical pig demonstrates the direct consequence of Roosevelt's plea to the American people to take action and work to combat the Depression.

The Wise Little Hen (1934)

The Wise Little Hen was released on 9 June 1934 into a somewhat different historical and economic background than *Mickey's Nightmare*. FDR had alleviated the banking crisis, set the American currency to the gold standard and launched the New Deal officially with the establishment of the National Recovery Administration. Most importantly for the context of this animated short, the new president had set to work on stabilizing the agricultural sector with the establishment of the Agricultural Adjustment Administration (AAA). Accompanying the NRA bill through Congress, the AAA was aimed at tackling the desperation of the situation in the countryside by providing government subsidies for farmers (Kennedy 1999, 702). FDR also passed the Farm Mortgage Act, which enabled the government to readjust farmers' mortgages (Kennedy 1999). The mentality that accompanied this agricultural policy was, as Albert Romasco has argued, not far removed from the German economic concept of autarky (1983, 241).

The idea of economic self-sufficiency in the countryside is well demonstrated by the personality of *The Wise Little Hen*. This animated short has largely been made famous due to the debut of the famous Disney character, Donald Duck. Such attention has left the short under-researched in terms of its sociopolitical content. This analysis suggests that not only does the animation adhere to the early New Deal policy of self-sufficiency in farming, but it also constitutes a further rejection of the 1920s ideology found within the two carefree pigs in *The Three Little Pigs*. This is accomplished through criticism of the personalities of Donald Duck and Peter Pig and veneration of the work ethic of the hen.

The short opens onto the farming lands inhabited by the hen and her chicks. The hen seeks help to plant her corn to provide food for her family. She has multiple dependents; however, unlike the nightmare world experienced by Mickey in 1932, these chicks only enhance her work ethic. She calls upon Peter Pig, a single 'man', with no dependents, to help her plant her corn. Much like the carefree pigs, Peter is unproductive in his day-to-day life and is shown simply dancing around in his back yard. When asked to help, the pig states that he has belly ache and groans, shirking off any responsibility thus demonstrating his rejection of the community work ethic found within the New Deal. When the hen approaches Donald, he also complains of a belly ache, leaving him unable to help the hen. The hen, undeterred, simply works with her chicks and they plant the corn together. Once her corn seeds have grown, the hen once again seeks help from Donald and Peter for the harvest. The pair have now formed an 'Idle Hours Club' and again complain that they have belly ache and cannot help her (see Figure 2.2). The hen harvests the corn with her chicks and cooks plenty of food for herself and her children. When the time comes to reap the true benefits of all her hard work by eating the corn, Donald and Peter are only too happy to help but are given Castor Oil for their supposed belly ache, leaving the hen and her chicks to eat the corn.

Again, through personality animation, the cartoon is able to relay its underlying ideology. The hen is from a humble background and throughout the story only wears a shawl to cover her shoulders and head. Her chicks have no clothes, emphasizing their vulnerability. She provides a stark contrast to both Donald and Peter who are fully clothed. They are reminiscent of the carefree pigs and the 1920s spirit of material culture as they both take pride in their appearance by wearing smart clothes. The hen is not afraid to ask for assistance from her neighbours and, more importantly, is undeterred when Donald and Peter refuse her request for help. The hen thus becomes completely self-sufficient, making enough food for herself and her children.

This perfectly exemplifies Roosevelt's early intentions for the agricultural sector. Donald and Peter, however, represent the antithesis of what Roosevelt wished to inject into society – apathy. Midway through the cartoon, Donald and Peter have established an Idle Hours Club. Much like the second carefree pig, they associate themselves with leisure pursuits. We can see a boxing poster

Figure 2.2 *The Wise Little Hen* (1934). Walt Disney Treasures.

pinned up on the side of Peter's house and there is also a tennis racket lying nearby. Both ignore the honest living demonstrated by the hen. Much like the practical pig, she values family and hard work above all else, evidenced by the family pictures hung on the walls in her house. As the hen reaps the rewards of her hard work, Donald and Peter's laziness is punished as they are left hungry.

The Wise Little Hen also uses music to enhance this ideology. At the opening of the animated short, the lyrics of the narrative speak to the hen's need to plant her corn, so she is 'not left short when winter comes again'. The winter of 1933 leading into 1934 in the United States has been described by many historians as 'the worst in its history' (Louchheim 1983, 188). The harsh weather had antagonized the crises in the rural sector and spurred Roosevelt to call for the formation of the CWA (Civil Works Administration). While historians can only debate over the inference in this cartoon, it is possible that the hen is working so hard to prevent a devastating repetition of the previous winter. At the close of the cartoon, the chorus sings that 'although her friends [Donald and Peter] have seen the light, they've nothing but a plight as with all her might, she'll eat the corn herself'. The lyrics highlight the wise self-sufficiency of the hen as the 'light' in the story; however, no solution is offered to Donald or Peter, showing that they will not receive any reward unless they are willing to work hard.

While the Disney cartoons maintained a level of subtlety in their references to Roosevelt and the New Deal, the same cannot be said of other animation produced during this period. The most remarkable feature of Warner Brothers' animation is the use of caricature and explicit references to Roosevelt's policies. These are analysed below by way of a comparison with the Disney productions and also as a note on techniques that Disney employs later in the decade.

Bosko in Person (1933)

Bosko in Person was released on 11 February 1933. While this was before the official inauguration of President Roosevelt, emergency meetings with Congress had already been held in order to address the various banking crises (Edsforth 2000, 99). During the election campaign, culminating in November 1932, FDR 'radiated confidence' in public. While he was well aware of the deteriorating economy and the gravity of the task entrusted to him, while in public, he always avoided the appearance of alarm or worry. His charismatic personality at public events resulted in the construction of a striking caricature of Roosevelt in some of the animated productions of 1933. The first of these was in the Looney Tunes cartoon *Bosko in Person*.

The tone of *Bosko in Person* is noticeably different from other Looney Tunes animation of the time. Far from being set in the comfort of the farmyard or on the agricultural plains prevalent within Disney animation, Bosko separates himself from his audience, performing a show that the audience of the cartoon must watch. At the beginning of the cartoon, Bosko and his girlfriend Honey dance in sync together with optimism reminiscent of Warner Brothers' musicals such as *Golddiggers of '33* and *Footlight Parade* (Bergman 1971). For the first time, the action is on the stage, instead of set within the confines of everyday life. This adds a sense of urgency and importance to what the audience are made to witness and emphasizes that Bosko and Honey are building up to the main attraction of the show.

Furthermore, there are no problems in the short that could be identified with the complexities of everyday life. Within the production, Bosko sings, 'Everything's okay, you see.' The emphasis in the music drawn to these words seems to suggest the presence of a previous crisis that has now been resolved. *Bosko in Person* also aligns itself with the support of Hollywood, as Bosko and

Honey impersonate stars such as Jimmy Durante and Maurice Chevalier, avid supporters of the new administration.

However, the most interesting premise of this cartoon is undoubtedly at its end. Bosko starts to beat on a drum that features a lively caricature of the president elect (Figure 2.3).

This, in itself, is striking. Rules were instituted prohibiting the use of images or of the voice of the president in any audio visual message for commercial or promotional use (Muscio 1996, 56). Bosko asks, 'Is everybody happy now?' while the audience cheers for their new president. FDR comes to life from within the drum and toasts his future and his audience with a beer in hand while Bosko and Honey dance off stage.

There are several things that can be deduced from this cartoon's active endorsement of the new administration. Roosevelt was seen as a man of the public and was sensitive to the way he was presented to the American people. As Muscio has argued, 'He maintained close contact with public opinion by travelling widely and reading mail sent to the White House' (1996, 56). In this sketch, FDR drinks a beer and dances with Bosko. Honey follows them off stage, waving an American flag, while the national anthem plays majestically in the

Figure 2.3 *Bosko in Person* (1933). Looney Tunes Golden Collection.

background. In this sketch, Roosevelt is not only linked to the audience through his toast, but also linked to American nationalism and American greatness. The optimism with which Honey waves her flag, the happy tones of the music and Bosko's dancing draw the audience into a new era, signifying the union of the animated world and the politics of the 'real' world. The use of the flag and the national anthem, in particular, were to become signifiers of American greatness and nationalism in animated productions of the late 1930s, as America drew closer to war.

Furthermore, it must also be noted that animated productions did not appear to be subjected to the same scrutiny as live action feature films, in terms of their censored content. Despite the pervasive reach of the Motion Picture Production Code, and the prohibition on images of the president, *Bosko in Person* clearly shows the president elect, toasting the future with animated characters.

Bosko the Musketeer (1933)

Bosko the Musketeer was released in September 1933. The Hundred Days has passed, the NRA was in operation and the New Deal was in full swing. In this short, Bosko is walking through a meadow, picking a daisy to the romantic refrain 'She loves me, she loves me not.' He goes to see Honey, who quickly points out that she is impressed by strong soldiers. Bosko dreams of impressing Honey, and so, in a daydream, he walks into a retelling of the Three Musketeers and does battle.

Determined to become the musketeer Honey wants, Bosko arrives at a bar and becomes the fourth Musketeer. He is determined to find something that will make the Musketeers unbeatable as they come up against some local thugs. He soon finds the cure. In the middle of battle, Bosko uncorks and glugs down a bottle of 'New Deal "3.2."'[3] With its magical curing powers, he and his musketeer friends are able to defeat their foes, he is able to impress Honey and they live happily ever after.

This cartoon puts across a direct political ideology. First, Bosko's problems are solvable through only one cure. He cannot gain the confidence to defeat his

---

[3]   As the quality of this short is poor, it is unclear as to whether the beer Bosko drinks is labelled 'New Deal 32' or 'New Deal 3.2', which could be referring to the strength of the alcohol permitted when Roosevelt repealed the Prohibition Act in 1933. However, either way, the author's argument still holds, as reference to the New Deal as the cure to society's ills still seems clear.

foes without the bottle of 'New Deal 3.2'. Bosko drinks the policies of the New Deal as a physical liquid. This would suggest that the animation is identifying the New Deal as the cure to the 'sick' American society. Or perhaps the fact that Bosko's ability as a musketeer is increased significantly by the ingestion of 'New Deal 3.2' would infer that the enemy is a lack of confidence or lack of belief in one's own abilities or Roosevelt's 'fear of fear itself'.

While the true identity of the enemy in this short is unknown, the use of metaphor within this cartoon allows historians to identify another technique utilized in animation in this period in order to put across political ideology. Animated productions often gave physical form to complex concepts. While the audience cannot see the finer details of 'New Deal "3.2"', they can see its positive effects on the common American man, Bosko. This short therefore endorses Roosevelt's central policy of the New Deal. There are no overtly political references within the narrative of this cartoon. On the contrary, *Bosko the Musketeer* is a daydream in which Bosko dreams of impressing Honey through his fighting prowess. However, through use of metaphor, a political inference is made in an otherwise simplistic animated short.

Conclusion

From its infancy, animation actively involved itself within the political discourse of Hollywood and of society. Both on and off screen, the characters within animation contributed towards the widespread endorsement of the new administration, engaging its characters with the concept of the 'Roosevelt honeymoon' that took hold in the United States from Roosevelt's election until 1934. From 1933, the Disney Studios was channelling ideology through its narratives and characters, embracing the communitarian ideology of the New Deal through the practical pig and the wise little hen. The actions of these characters are juxtaposed against other characters in the stories, who hold self-serving and complacent attitudes towards their life and work.

The personality animation that proved able to transmit such ideologies in Disney cartoons had not yet developed within the Warner Brothers' animated shorts. As stated by famous Warner Brothers' animator, Charles 'Chuck' Jones, 'The biggest thing Disney contributed was that he established the idea of individual personality. ... The breakthrough really was Three Little Pigs – that's where personality was developed. All of us who followed were obviously keyed off by that – and it's just bad history to ignore it' (Bogdanovich 1997, 711). Jones admits that the Warner Brothers animation team were not yet at the stage where they were able to create individual personalities for their characters. Thus, their animated productions were held back in their ideological progression through their lack of technological development.

However, Warner Brothers used different means in order to put across its message and connect itself with political discussion. Instead, their animators used symbols and caricature. In the production *Bosko in Person*, the animators combined the two to infuse a new liberal ideology within its cartoons. Roosevelt holds a beer and toasts the future of his new administration and the American people, situated within the audience of this cartoon. The beer, holding connotations of the intended repeal of prohibition, was heavily symbolic of a new era for the country. The use of symbolism is also pertinent in their later production *Bosko the Musketeer*. Instead of attempting to relay the ideology within the New Deal through a personality trait of a character, or even through narrative, Warner Brothers' animation simplifies the complicated nature of the New Deal through evoking a transformation of its state. It is converted from an abstract concept into a physical liquid. When Bosko drinks the liquid, he is able to defeat his enemy. Thus, without directly engaging into a political debate over the validity of New Deal policy, the animators simply showed that the liquid is successful by allowing Bosko to succeed in his endeavours after drinking it.

What these animated productions do have in common is their use of music. At this stage, the medium of animation had only just mastered the art of synchronized sound, with Disney leading the way through the production of *Steamboat Willie* in 1928. With this breakthrough, the Walt Disney Studios continued to be more advanced in their utilization of sound within animation to impart a particular effect. Frank Churchill's song 'Who's Afraid of the Big Bad Wolf' is a particular charge. As many have argued, regardless of the fact that the effect of *The Three Little Pigs* was unintentional, it did, however, have a rallying effect on society (Zipes 1995, 35). The lyrical narrative within *The Wise Little Hen* has a similar effect, by asking a rhetorical question of the audience, 'Who will help her plant her corn?' This urges the audience to take responsibility and to disapprove when Donald and Peter refuse to come to her aid. It also references the reason why the hen must work so hard, providing the motivation behind her ideology. In *Bosko in Person*, Warners' also utilize music to put across their ideology. Bosko sings, 'Everything's okay, you see.' reassuring the audience of the positive change in society.

There are no explicitly political exchanges within the productions at this stage, nor do the narratives charge themselves with political agenda. However, the techniques these studios use throughout these early years of the 'Roosevelt honeymoon' are used in more advanced forms during the Second World War.

3

Animating Depression America 1934–7

Following the 'Roosevelt honeymoon' of the early 1930s, the narratives of these animated productions moved from veracious political endorsement towards a thoughtful social commentary on American life. In line with many of the Hollywood films of this particular decade, Walt Disney and Warner Brothers' cartoons embraced their ability to interpret the struggles of everyday Americans during the Depression.

In the 1930s, Arthur Schlesinger commented that 'movies in the 1930s were near to the operative centre of the nation's consciousness'. They provided a mirage into the complex layers of American society. As such, the content of movies in this decade has been the subject of intense scrutiny by film historians, hoping to tap into the political and social landscape of Depression America. The 1930s represented something of a breakthrough for Hollywood and are viewed by historians and film theorists alike as the 'golden age'. Despite the aggressive hold of the Depression over most Americans, cinema flourished and audience attendance remained high. It is in this decade that it seems almost impossible to separate film from its history and indeed, to exclude any political or cultural significance in the content of movies in this era.

Richard Steele has made the case for the separation of the movies from ideological messages. He argues that 'until the late 1930s, Hollywood's producers had been largely indifferent to political issues' (1985, 152). On the surface, it would appear that Hollywood's movies during the 1930s were nothing more than escapist fantasy with the primary role of entertainment, having little to do with the complexities of everyday life. However, as Andrew Bergman has argued, 'People do not escape into something they cannot identify with. Movies were meaningful because they depicted something lost or desired' (1971, xiii). In this vein, the realm of fantasy has also been recognized within current film scholarship as having a pivotal part to play in America's struggle with Depression. The idea that escapist and fantastical entertainment is of cultural importance for historians is particularly prominent for a study of animation, where narrative is based wholly in an imagined, hyperbolic and fanciful universe.

Having proved itself in the ability to reflect upon a change in society's mood with the inauguration of the new president, the animated shorts of this era began to provide a commentary on the economic and social changes in the United States, much like the live action feature films. How did people regard their new society, changed beyond recognition by Roosevelt's New Deal? How did these changes affect their aspirations, hopes and dreams of success? Through the vivacious personification of ideals and the unification of its poignant lyrics with narrative, Disney and Warner Brothers' animated productions came to portray the upheaval of traditional American values and the ways in which these values were overturned and replaced. The fairy tale world of Mickey Mouse, Porky Pig and their animal friends masks a sensitive realist portrayal of Depression America. Interestingly, these cartoons continue to embrace New Deal liberalism until the time FDR began to lose his hold on popularity in 1937. This lends further attrition to the argument that it is to the context of these shorts' production that emphasis should fall.

Within these years of the 1930s, animation embraced four key ideological concepts that historians have traditionally associated with the Depression, the New Deal and 1930s society. The first was a Jeffersonian rural idealism echoed in many Hollywood films of the era. This precept acknowledges the opportunity offered by the cityscape but fears the technological advancement that accompanies such urbanization. The second sought to underscore the changes taking place within the national mindset. Steadily, with the replacement of 1920s individualism by 1930s communitarianism, traditional values were overhauled. Their proponents were found within the personalities of Disney and Warner Brothers' characters. The third centred entirely on the social drama associated with a land of poverty. These shorts were able to portray the day-to-day angst of those wanting relief from their present situation, mostly through an obsession with becoming rich, hence alleviating the stresses of everyday hardship. The fourth is indicative of a growing political trend within society, and is most reflective of this transitional stage within animation. Though merely only an extension of its careful commentary on everyday life, the two animated productions within this category are able to transcend to a new level of ideological awareness, the foundations for which are built upon during the late 1930s and in the Second World War.

Rural idealism

The first of these concepts can be characterized as a Jeffersonian rural idealism and fear of technological advancement.[1] Historians have long documented Roosevelt's underlying belief that the cure for the nation's ills was a return to a simplistic life on the land. His biographer, Frank Freidel has stated that 'country life to Roosevelt was a way out of the Depression and a guarantee of permanent comfort' (1973, 79). Throughout the campaign trail in 1932, he had accused the Republicans of misunderstanding the real problems of farmers and spoke of 'national planning for farmers' and a 'reordering of economic life' based upon the idea of balance (Katz 1983). Romasco has also highlighted the resonance of the agrarian myth within society during the Great Depression (Romasco 1983, 186). Pivotal to this re-imagining of American economic thinking was a new policy for agriculture in the shape of the AAA.

Passed into law in May 1933, the AAA included such measures as production control, self-financing through processing taxes, participation encouraged by benefits payments and the purchase of surplus crops by the government to control the price of wheat. Most importantly, however, the Farm Credit Act was put into place, allowing for struggling farmers to avoid foreclosures by taking out short- and long-term loans (Kirkendall 1983). While the success of the AAA does not concern us here, it is the ideological foundations upon which the AAA and its preceding organization, the Farm Security Administration (FSA) were built that filtered through into the animated world of Walt Disney's and Schlesinger's cartoons. As Kevin Shortsleeve has argued, many animated productions 'reject the cityscape', preferring to embed themselves within the agricultural sector (2004, 93). This embrace was coupled with a fear of technological advancement.

Many historians have attested to the immense investment in machinery to jump start agricultural growth. Paul Bonnifield has made claims for a 'revolution' in the farming sector during the Depression years. He contends, 'The revolution in farming, resulting from tractors, combines, trucks and one way plows and other technological improvements, meant that many hired men were no longer needed' (1979, 106). In an increasingly competitive employment marketplace such as that existed in the 1930s, this created genuine fears for the future of

---

[1]   See Bergman, Andrew, (1971). *We're in the Money: Depression America and Its Films.* New York: New York University Press; Hearn, Charles (1977). *The American Dream in the Great Depression.* Westport: Greenwood Press and Kennedy, David M. (1999). *Freedom from Fear: The American People in Depression and War.* New York: Oxford University Press.

skilled work in the countryside and worries over the prospects for society in a world where men were being rapidly replaced by machinery. These fears are depicted within the animated world.

The Country Cousin (1936)

This short handles the elevation of country life principles when pitted against the wild throes of the urban landscape. The opening shot of the cartoon features the tiny shadow of Abner Country Mouse against the towering urban landscape of the big city, emphasizing the daunting and frightening challenges the city poses to the traditional ways of life. We learn that Monty City Mouse has sent a telegram to Abner Country Mouse, demanding that he 'stop being a hick and come to the city and live in splendour'.

However, when Abner arrives in the city, full of hope and optimism for his new life with his cousin, he is soon out of place with the high standards of city life. Abner is frowned upon when he gives in to his hunger pangs and begins to eat the feast laid before him. When he eats some tangy mustard, he accidentally drinks a glass of champagne to take away the spice and ends up drunk and rowdy, much to the horror of his wealthy cousin Monty City Mouse. Abner causes mayhem and after being chased out of the house by a cat, nearly gets killed by the flurry of cars and crowds of people, before running as fast as he can out of the city. Through the personification of the two conflicting ideologies of ruralism and urbanism, the animators of this short were able to signify its ideological direction.

Abner Country Mouse is a common American farmer, visiting the city with optimism and fervour. Much like many of the farmers of the 'dust bowl' during the 1930s, he was forced to the city for work. Monty, however, represents the promise of this new cityscape. He is a wealthy man, dressed in a smart suit and top hat, and enjoys the luxuries of food and imported alcohol. However, when these two are placed together, through the clash of their personalities, the animation is able to state that these two ideologies are ultimately conflicted. Abner is portrayed as the fun-loving and innocent mouse, who wants to live life to the full; however, Monty is portrayed as strict and selfish, constantly putting restrictions on Abner's time in the city and at the close of the animation, he deserts Abner when he is placed in danger through his encounter with a cat. Monty is self-serving and rejects the communitarian ideal to be found within the countryside.

Furthermore, once Abner is chased out of Monty's house by a vicious cat, Abner is nearly killed by several cars, trampled by the crowds of people walking the street and is sent dizzy by the endless noise and bustle of the urban landscape. The city is portrayed as a dangerous place and Abner's visit to Monty ultimately ends in him rushing towards the city limits back home to the countryside. Through the personification of the urban city in the character of Monty City Mouse, this short is able to elevate the ideals of the simple life in the countryside over the luxuries of life in the city. Abner faces death in the city as it fails to live up to the promises of Monty's telegram. He is able to indulge in luxury, but is ultimately rejected and put into danger because of this indulgence. Abner's eventual retreat home to the countryside to life 'as a hick' seems to suggest a preference for the simple life as opposed to the apparent dangers of life in the city.

Modern Inventions (1937)

Modern Inventions presents a complete rejection of the conveniences of the 'modern age'. The issue of the complete replacement of human labour by machinery was already a fear among many in society, particularly in the farming profession. Donald Duck enters the 'Museum of Modern Marvels' full of excitement for the discoveries he will make; however, he is soon disturbed and frightened by the changes offered by the uncompromising technology. After terrifying encounters with a robot butler, who continues to take Donald's hat, a bundle wrapper, a robot nurse maid and a robot groomer, Donald is angry with the inventions he sought out and rejects their work.

There are several components of interest within this cartoon. First, we must make note of the character of Donald. Donald is, at first, excited by his trip to the museum. We hear him marvelling over the technology during the first half of the short. He seems to be open to the idea of new inventions, although notably, he does not like the idea of having to pay for them. This could suggest reluctance for the tax payer to bear the cost of technological advancement in society. During the New Deal, Roosevelt invested heavily in new farming machinery for the agricultural sector, the cost of which was heavily resented by the American public, and eventually rejected by Congress as unconstitutional. However, by the end of the cartoon, Donald completely rejects the technology after his negative experiences, seemingly dismissing the need for new inventions within society.

We must also pay attention to the inventions themselves. Each is given a 'character' which Donald interacts with. This gives disturbing light to the idea of human replacement inherent in the fear of technology within 1930s society. Each of the inventions Donald comes across is a 'person' of sorts and their inefficiency is highlighted by their inability to act 'human'. The robot butler continues to take off Donald's hat, when he clearly wants to keep it on, showing the lack of sensitivity to individual wishes shown by machinery. The robot nurse maid, while able to rock 'baby' Donald to sleep, ends up squirting milk in his eye and restrains him with an iron bar, showing the dangers inherent in any machinery or inventions dealing with children. Lastly, Donald's encounter with the robot groomer is disastrous (Figure 3.1).

While inspecting the machinery, he is strapped into the chair the wrong way round. The groomer, unable to recognize this fact, continues to groom Donald's bottom as though it were his hair. It polishes his face with black shoe polish, a mistake that clearly, a human would not have made. By giving life and character to each of the machines and showing Donald's inability to interact with them as 'human', this short highlights the inability of these machines to replace human

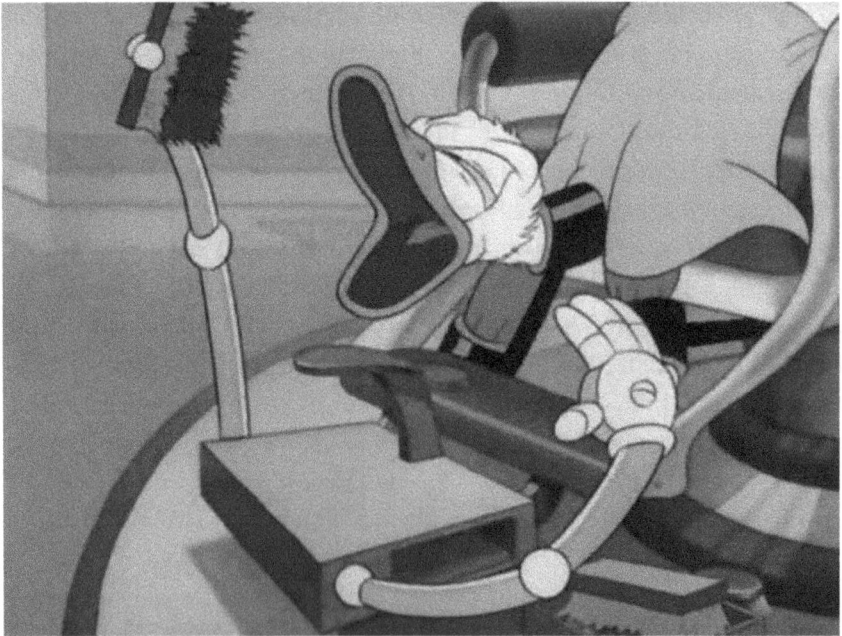

Figure 3.1 *Modern Inventions* (1937). Walt Disney Treasures.

labour. Donald is increasingly frustrated with each of the inventions and their lack of understanding of his human needs, solidifying the message of this cartoon as a complete rejection of technological advancement in the interests of replacing human labour.

Porky's Building (1937)

Porky's Building is a Warner Brothers' production. From the outset, the Warner Brothers animators demonstrated frankness in the ways in which they satirized everyday life. A title card at the beginning of the picture states, 'Any similarity of characters or happenings in this picture to actual people or events is definitely intended. … If you think we're going to sit around for days thinking up new ideas, you're pixilated!' This message demonstrates, in a rather tongue in cheek fashion, that the animators took their inspiration from their historical context to formulate characters and stories, placing the content of the cartoon directly within the sphere of relevance for historical study.

Porky's Building is set within a nameless city within America, although due to the impressive skyline and the reference to 'actual events', it is likely the urban landscape is Los Angeles. Porky and a rival contractor are put into a bidding war to build City Hall for the government. The fact that these two contractors are put into employment to construct a civil works building is indicative of the New Deal at work, showing the promise and opportunity lent by the urbanization of America (Blumberg 1979, 126–8). Both parties come up with the same price for the job and are pitted against each other to build the building, with the fastest builder winning the contract. Despite being within the realms of the city, Porky's building site uses 'rural' tools, getting the animals to help in mixing cement for his construction. Rejecting community enterprise and the simplicity of agricultural labour principles used in the city, Porky's rival states that he does not need labourers for his site anymore and emerges onto the screen with a 'brick laying machine'. While the obvious concern for labour replacement here is not quite as animated as Donald's encounter with the robots, the message is still clear.

While endorsing the fact that the urban landscape could hold opportunity, the short holds concern for the idea that man may soon be replaced by machine. While his rival Dirty Diggs steams into the lead with his new machine, Porky takes on the help of an enthusiastic rabbit sporting the title 'Super Colossal Brick Layer'. Porky is sceptical, but the rabbit soon proves the value of labour over machinery. Dirty Diggs's machine malfunctions and gets stuck in reverse, resulting in an explosion and a 'reversal' of all the work the machine had done. Porky rejoices in having won the contract through hard graft and through using labour, hence providing employment at the service of the City Commissioner.

Conflicting mindsets – the challenge of community living

Historians have long commented on the sense of cultural dislocation experienced by Americans following the Wall Street Crash. Ideals of individualism, materialism and wealth in forming the basis for success and upward mobility had crumbled with the onset of Depression, leading to the displacement of the American Dream.[2] What had once seemed certain became nothing but a myth. However, the New Deal, through its public work programmes and by making the state the basic arbiter of people's lives, a sense of community developed within American society. In the motion picture industry, this was forged through the implementation of the National Recovery Administration. Many key figures within the industry had to take a 50 per cent pay cut for eight weeks. This recognition and support of the government also took the physical form of the National Recovery Administration (NRA) Blue Eagle. Animation recognized this change, both politically and culturally. In the 1934 Walt Disney short *The Dognapper* (United States, dir. David Hand), the NRA eagle is even visible on the front page of the newspaper featured at the beginning of the story. Culturally, the ideology of community underlays the narrative of much of the animation of these years. Prosperity was possible, but only through society working together in pursuit of a common goal (Hearn 1977, 4). As Andrew Bergman has argued, 'Success, law, social unity and federal benevolence and social "concern" – these would be the ingredients of the fantasy America depicted for the rest of the decade' (1971, 61).

Such were the ideological foundations for what would become the new American society. As Ekirch has argued, the question was when the Great Society would transform into 'The Great Community' (1969, 22). Such ideas

---

[2] See, for example, Parish, Michael (1992). *Anxious Decades: America in Prosperity & Depression 1920–1941*. New York: W. W. Norton; Hearn, *The American Dream in the Great Depression*, and Ekirch, Arthur Ekirch (1971), *Ideologies and Utopias*. Chicago: Quadrangle Books.

were undoubtedly present within Hollywood in films such as *Our Daily Bread* (1934) and, as such, were translated into an animated interpretation of this new America. Not only was community at the heart of the push for upward mobility but emphasis was also put upon character to be the fundamental factor that would ensure success. The bestselling nonfiction book of the 1930s, *How to Win Friends and Influence People* by Dale Carnegie, highlighted the significance of values, behaviour and lifestyles within the culture of the 1930s. No longer was importance placed on material goods and wealth; success had to come from the inside out.

The following cartoons embrace this communitarian interpretation of the American Dream. Success was only forthcoming to those who are willing to work with others to achieve their life goals.

The Grasshopper and the Ants (1934)

The Grasshopper and the Ants was released in cinemas nearly a year after FDR was inaugurated as president of the United States. One of Aesop's Fables, the animated short was a treatise to the importance of the community work ethic. Much like *The Three Little Pigs*, the Disney Studios used personality animation to show the ideologies at work within this animated narrative. The Grasshopper seems reminiscent of 1920s individualism. He is a carefree spirit, who plays his fiddle, singing that 'the world owes us a living' and will provide for everyone. He laughs at the ant colonies around him, who are working together to save food for the winter. The Grasshopper sneers that winter is far away so he does not need to prepare for it just yet. However, winter soon arrives. The Grasshopper is left out in the cold and hungry. He is eventually taken in by the ants and is let into the colony. He quickly rejects his previous ideology and endorses the community spirit of the New Deal and of the ants, changing his song to, 'I owe the world a living.'

Personification is at work in this cartoon in order to channel communitarian ideology. The Grasshopper rejects the work ethic of the ants, preferring instead to indulge his musical hobby. He is even dressed in business attire, linking him to the bankers partly responsible for the Wall Street Crash. However, as he is exposed to the elements and left cold and hungry, he is forced to repent his ideology in order to survive the winter. In opposition to the Grasshopper, we have the direction of the Queen Ant, who takes responsibility for the other ants. They show her a great respect and are unwilling to be seen shirking their responsibility to the rest of the colony by relinquishing their work duties. This can be shown through the example of the ant, who, once spotted by the Queen Ant to be chatting to the Grasshopper instead of working, goes straight back to his duties.

Music also acts as an ideological unifier within this cartoon, as it does in the Silly Symphony *The Three Little Pigs* and the lyrical narration of *The Wise Little Hen*. Common across the ant colony, the Grasshopper tries to convert one of the ants to his way of thinking through his music, singing, 'The world owes us a living.' He believes that he does not have to contribute to society in order to get what he feels is owed to him. This is directly reminiscent of the 1920s interpretation of the American Dream. Due to the expanding nature of the economy, it became commonplace for Americans to expect a minimum standard of living. He tries to persuade the ant to 'play and sing and dance'. This is akin to the behaviour exhibited by Percy Pig and Donald in *The Wise Little Hen* who choose entertainment over work.

At first, the music isolates the Grasshopper from the ants around him. However, when the Grasshopper is finally accepted by the ants, it serves to unify him to their community. The Queen Ant invites him to play his music and the ants dance with him to his changed tune. He sings, 'I owe the world a living. I've been a fool the whole year long and now I'm singing a different song.' This seems to dispel any initial fears society may have had regarding the change in government in the United States, as Roosevelt managed to get many through the winter.

There is one further point of interest in *The Grasshopper and the Ants* and this concerns the symbolism utilized by the animators. The ant colony is hard working and motivated, and led by their Queen Ant. When the queen appears in shot with her chariot, however, she is led by a purple flag sporting a spade and a pickaxe. While the flag is not an exact replica of the Communist symbol, its inclusion is certainly suggestive (Figure 3.2). This short associates the New Deal with a positive re-imagining of Communist ideology. The Queen Ant, while shown to be kind and accommodating in her behaviour towards the Grasshopper, is nonetheless, a strict and respected leader, giving an impression that while the ideal of communism here is sound, due to the productive nature of the ants, good leadership is essential to success in this endeavour. It could also be argued that it makes reference to the success of the Soviet Union in achieving economic growth during the time of Depression.

Figure 3.2 *The Grasshopper and the Ants* (1934). Walt Disney Treasures.

Mickey's Pal Pluto (1934)

Pluto, in this early short, shows some glimmers of a self-serving attitude the Disney cartoons would later bestow upon Donald Duck. In this animated short, Mickey, Minnie and Pluto are wandering by a nearby stream and come across a bundle, floating on the river. They retrieve the bundle and discover it is full of abandoned kittens. However, once Mickey and Minnie take the kittens home and start to care for them, they begin to neglect Pluto. Pluto is thus faced with an ideological conflict, which is given life in the form of two apparitions: a Devil Pluto and an Angel Pluto. The Angel embraces the New Deal communitarian ideology, telling Pluto to share his food and drink with the kittens, whereas the Devil tells him to chase the kittens out of the house. This conflict repeats itself later in the cartoon when the kittens fall down a well in the garden and the Devil tells Pluto to leave the kittens down there, whereas the Angel tells him to save them.

There is a very clear ideological message within this cartoon and it is simply displayed through the actions of the character of Pluto himself. At first, embracing his selfish side, Pluto is unwilling to share his lot with the needy and homeless. It is made clear that Mickey and Minnie have little problem with sharing their home with those less fortunate, as they display no hesitation in taking in the kittens. This, again, provides a stark contrast to *Mickey's Nightmare* in which any additions to the family were thought of as a burden. Pluto, however, is resentful of the kittens when they try to drink out of his bowl. When he follows the Devil's advice of running the kittens out of the house so he does not have to share his food, he is sent outside by Mickey and has to do without. However, when Pluto follows the advice of the Angel later in the cartoon and saves the kittens, embracing the community spirit of the New Deal, he is rewarded with a juicy turkey by Mickey.

This animated short uses personification to address an ideological conflict (Figure 3.3). The opposing ideals of community and individualism are given physical form. These characters are able to state their purpose and their consequences for Pluto's life to the audience. In this instance, Pluto's embrace of the 'every man for himself' mantra leaves him out in the cold, without family or food. However, once he embraces the idea of a shared experience by rescuing the kittens, he is rewarded with a home, returned to his family and, most importantly, has more than enough subsistence for himself and for others.

Figure 3.3 *Mickey's Pal Pluto* (1934). Walt Disney Treasures.

The Golden Touch (1935)

The Golden Touch is a retelling of the story of King Midas. Midas wishes for everything he touches to turn to gold, however, soon finds he is not able to eat, drink or have social contact with anyone, leaving him saddened and alone. Symbolism is used throughout this cartoon in order to put an ideological message across. In a pun on the dollar bill phrase 'In God We Trust', Midas has an 'In Gold I Trust' sign on the wall. Instead of placing himself as part of a community, and putting his faith in faith, Midas chooses gold. He isolates himself from a community of believers, instead trusting only himself and his material wealth. Midas embodies the culmination of 1920s values. Consumed by his status, Midas is only concerned with his wealth of possessions and wants more of them. Goldie, the leprechaun who grants Midas his wish and who ultimately teaches him a lesson, is reminiscent of rural Middle America. He dresses as a commoner and rejects the importance Midas places on material wealth. What is interesting about this animated short is the way in which money is interchanged with food and drink. Many were both starving and homeless during the 1930s. A basic diet was seen as far more important than the status of wealth. Ultimately, this is the point of view eventually endorsed by Midas as he asks for a simple hamburger and onions in exchange for his curse to be taken from him.

Donald's Better Self (1938)

The narrative within this Donald Duck animated short echoes the conflict experienced by Pluto in *Mickey's Pal Pluto*. Both a Devilish and Angelic Donald fight for his attention and endorsement. He is distracted from a day of school by the Devil, who suggests that he go fishing and smoke a cigar. The Angel, however, tells him to get up and go to school.

Much as is the case in *Mickey's Pal Pluto*, personification of ideals is the technique used within this animated short to give life and direction to the conflicting 1930s ideologies. Donald usually follows the Devil's instructions; however, we can see his ideological progression within this short. After discovering the negative consequences of the Devil's advice, he allows himself to be guided to school by the Angel. By the end of the short, the Angel even becomes a part of him, showing his complete transformation in ideological grounding to the communitarian interpretation of the American Dream.

The Devil character, while linked to individualism, is also linked to the life of truancy and crime chosen by many in the 1930s. Donald skips school and is forced into smoking a cigar by the Devil. Donald is easily led astray and his foray into the 'dark side' of society is ultimately proven foolish by the Angel. Donald confides how awful the cigar tasted and eventually feels ill as a result of his truancy. This conveys the message that choosing this path will have a negative impact on your life, morals and health. However, this illness completely disappears once Donald chooses the 'right' path indicated by the Angel and goes to school to work hard.

Not in the money – the struggles of economic hardship

The current historiography of the social and economic impact of the Great Depression across America consists of endless social studies. For example, Blumberg's investigation of the impact of the Works Progress Administration (WPA) on the millions of unemployed in New York City (1979) and Starr's study of the way in which the Depression hit California (1996). Others consist of general works on the impact of the economic crisis on America as a whole.[3]

What historians can deduce is that the Great Depression hit all American families, whether as a direct impact through a loss of earnings or employment, as was the case in one in four families in 1934 (Bernstein 1987, 4), or through the heavy taxation of those with income, in order to fund Roosevelt's extensive alphabet agencies. What little money people had was spent on the daily bread, not on luxury goods, as was the case in the 1920s. This feeling of scarcity was an integral feature of 1930s culture. As Frederick Allen has argued, the Depression actually liberated most people from the shame of feeling poor: 'They felt no shame now in being short of money. Everybody seemed to be. They were all in the same boat' (1940, 109). Desperation became a natural part of everyday life as people struggled to afford rent and subsistence.

The idea of making money quickly in order to alleviate those in a state of poverty was an integral part of 1930s animation. Many Disney cartoons and to a larger extent, the Warner Brothers cartoons, concern themselves with a desire for a life of affluence. The Walt Disney Studios was no stranger to handling poverty. Far from the charge that Disney cartoons concerned themselves with a life of a fantasy and happiness, *Mickey's Good Deed* (1932) shows Mickey Mouse as being homeless. The number of homeless people between 1930 and 1934 in

---

[3]   See, for example, Kennedy, *Freedom from Fear* and Edsforth, Ronald (2000). *The New Deal: America's Response to the Great Depression.* Oxford: Blackwell.

New York State more than doubled (Crouse 1986, 58). Disney animation did not shy away from these difficult issues; it embraced them as part of its narratives.

Moving Day (1936)

Moving Day was released months before Roosevelt was re-elected as president of the United States. It seems to represent a further transition towards political commentary as it directly handles the significant money worries experienced by many within society and could be read as recognition that even though many structural changes had taken place within society to deal with the widespread poverty and unemployment, many still remained unable to pay rent and faced homelessness.

The short begins with a close up of a calendar, on which we discover that Mickey and Donald are one month overdue with their rent payments. Mickey and Donald pace the house, trying to think of a solution to their financial plight and suddenly receive a visit from the sheriff, Pegleg Pete. Pete serves them with a notice to dispossess their home and demands that he will sell their furniture in order to pay off their debt (Figure 3.4).

Figure 3.4 *Moving Day* (1936). Walt Disney Treasures.

Mickey and Donald quickly pack up their belongings and Goofy moves their grand piano. However, moving their things proves rather difficult, and through numerous troublesome encounters with animated objects, much of Mickey and Donald's furniture is destroyed. Pete returns, angry at the damage being done to 'his' property, but upsets a gas leak and the house itself explodes. Mickey, Donald and Goofy manage to escape with their things, leaving Pete alone with the empty shell of the house. Throughout the short, Donald and Mickey are terrified by the threat of the 'knock at the door' and the worries it will bring for their ailing financial situation. When Pete appears at the door, they plead that they will get the money he needs, although it is clear that they do not have the means to pay their rent.

This shows a direct engagement with a genuine social problem of the 1930s. The characters of Mickey and Donald are empathizing with the financial worries of many members of the audience. The short also highlights the futility of many luxuries purchased in the 1920s. Mickey and Donald have many household appliances which prove useless in their current situation; they serve only as fuel to enable Pete to get the money he is owed. These possessions also slow them down considerably in their endeavour to leave the house as quickly as possible before Pete returns. Goofy struggles with the grand piano, Mickey finds he has too many clothes that will not fit into his suitcase and Donald gets stuck inside a fish bowl.

The release of this cartoon *before* the re-election of President Roosevelt and *after* what many consider to be Roosevelt's most successful years in the presidency is also of note. This animated short takes into account the changes in society but also notes that however much things have changed, they perhaps have not gone far enough. The financial status of the majority has not been substantially altered. Steven Watts has commented that Disney cartoons in this era do not directly address the Depression; however, *Moving Day* is certainly an example to the contrary (Watts 1997, 63). The Disney studio animators weave this potent social issue directly into the narrative of this short, showing that Mickey and Donald are far from immune to the harsh realities of Depression America.

Milk and Money (1936)

Much like *Moving Day*, *Milk and Money* deals with financial troubles for homeowners during the Depression but relates this trouble to the agricultural sector more closely than the Disney short. Despite the Farm Credit Act and the AAA, the agricultural sector remained badly affected by the Depression, leading to the establishment of the FSA in February 1937 (Edsforth 2000, 219). This short highlights the main threat to farm owners within this period – mortgage foreclosure. Thirty-nine farm mortgages out of every thousand in 1933 entered foreclosure (Alston 1983).

The short opens with Porky's Father working on the farm. He introduces his son to the audience, ensuring that those watching are identifying with his situation. The pair are shown to be hard at work during the opening scenes of the short. However, they are soon visited by a debt collector introduced through credits as 'Mr. Viper', the snake. The man holds a mortgage notice to Porky and his Father and announces that if they do not have the money he needs by the following day, he will take the farm.

Noticeably, Mr. Viper interacts with the audience throughout the short, vowing, 'He'll never make it,' encouraging those watching to support Porky and his Father. Class and ideological undertones are further conveyed through the characterization of Porky and his Father in comparison to Viper, the former dressed in farming overalls, the latter in a smart coat and hat. Porky and his Father are shown to be humble and likeable; Viper is rich, cold and superficial. His villainous nature is further enhanced by the way he slithers away back to his horse and cart after speaking with Porky and his Father.

Worried for the future, Porky goes to the city and finds work as a milk delivery man. While he is browsing the advertisements, we are also given a further insight into the financial worries of the animated world. In the Personals section of Porky's paper, an advert states, 'Not responsible for any debts other than my own. R Wolfe.' This shows an awareness of debt throughout society in both the country and the urban landscape. While Porky is unsuccessful in his job as he accidentally smashes some of the milk bottles, he manages to win a horse race and a ten thousand dollar cash prize.

At home, Viper is waiting on the doorstep of the farm, while Porky's Father paces, worried for their financial future. However, Porky arrives quickly and pays off his Father's debt with his winnings. Porky and his Father are in a very desperate situation and yet Porky is resilient and never gives up hope and is financially rewarded by the end of the cartoon. Again, this seems to be in line with the ideology of the Great Depression. Many simply hoped to 'wait it out' and be rewarded with better times in the future (Ekirch 1969, 7).

There is one further element of note within this cartoon. At the short's end, after receiving his money, Viper is physically ejected from the animated world and lands in the credits screen, separate from Porky and his Father. This seems to suggest that there is no place in the animated world, indicative of society, for debt collectors such as Viper. He is quite apart in values and temperament from the rest of the American public and thus should be kept out of everyday life.

Milk and Money hence sits quite comfortably as an animated production providing a subtle commentary on the financial status of rural homes, the dangers open to this area of the economy and the spirit of hope within this sector for a return to prosperity. While the ending to this cartoon is undoubtedly idealist, the problems experienced by Porky and his Father were unquestionably real to many watching this production.

Porky's Poppa (1938)

In many ways, *Porky's Poppa* provides a commentary on economic crisis as well as providing a positive outlook on rural life. Again, as in the case in *Milk and Money*, the audience is introduced to Porky's farm through the children's nursery rhyme, 'Old Macdonald Had a Farm'; however, the lyrics are changed to include the line, 'And on that farm, he had a mortgage.' Like many of the Disney cartoons of this era, music plays a role here. The children's song is transformed to have an adult meaning, discarding the childlike values many attach to the animation of this period. The narrator also references popular culture of the time by stating, 'And today, as it must to all men, debt came to Porky's Poppa.' This is a direct reference to the popular radio show, *The March of Time*, which often headlined the death of a famous person with the exact same phrasing, with the simple substitution of 'debt' for 'death'.

In this short, the mortgage is personified as it is given arms and feet, allowing it to be a physical presence within the cartoon (Figure 3.5). Indeed, the mortgage is shown to be a heavy weight on Porky's Father's back, conveying its status as a burden on his life. This is a technique used considerably by the Disney Studios during the war, demonstrating with some certainty that Disney did find inspiration within many of the Warners' cartoons for its propaganda. This suggests that animation was reaching a highly developed stage in its ideological development as it proves able to take the abstract concept of mortgage debt and give it a physical effect on the characters within the animation's narrative.

Porky's Father is having financial problems largely because one of his cows has been quarantined due to hoof and mouth trouble. Porky decides to buy a 'creamlined' mechanical cow from a mail order service to improve production on the farm. Porky's Father is most impressed with the mechanical cow, which is able to make cheese and ice cream. However, Porky nurses their real cow, Bessie, back

Figure 3.5 *Porky's Poppa* (1938). Looney Tunes Golden Collection.

to health and the two go into competition. After a fierce battle, the mechanical cow is rejected by Porky and his Father as it is magically transformed into a vacuum and ends up sucking up all the hay on the farm. They declare Bessie the cow as the winner of the competition and are able to make money from her victory. Similar to *Modern Inventions* and *Porky's Building*, this animated production rejects the replacement of physical labour over any new inventions. While the achievements of the 'creamlined' cow are impressive, the technology involved is not reliable, as proven by the fact that the cow manages to produce useless invisible cream and transforms into a vacuum, which sucks up more than it produces for the farm.

Political tantrums

Historians are generally in agreement that the New Deal reached the end of its active and effective stage by the end of 1937.[4] Riding high on his victories of

---

[4] See Brinkley, Allan (1995). *The End of Reform: New Deal Liberalism in Recession and War*. New York: Alfred A. Knopf; Badger, Anthony (1989). *The New Deal: The Depression Years, 1933–1940*. Basingstoke: Macmillan and Eldridge, David (2008), *American Culture in the 1930s*. Edinburgh: Edinburgh University Press.

1936, the president took on the Supreme Court in an attempt to secure more power through which to implement further social security measures. However, cracks were beginning to appear in the well-crafted New Deal construction project and the court proceeded to 'knock out one after another of the key New Deal statutes' (Katz 1983, 127).

There was also some real concern within the Treasury over how much these social security measures were costing. As Romasco argued, 'By 1936, they [officials of the Federal Reserve and the Treasury Department] had become increasingly concerned with the danger of uncontrolled inflation' (1983, 224). This concern was justified. The American economy went into a further recession between September 1937 and June 1938, reversing many of the gains made since 1933 (ibid.). The level of industrial production fell farther and faster between 1937 and 1938 than it had since the years 1929 to 1930 (Bernstein 1987). Roosevelt also faced serious unrest in the labour sector, with a series of large-scale sit-down strikes in 1937 (2000, 268). This feeling of unrest, distrust and impatience with the government found its way into some of the animated shorts of the late 1930s.

Interestingly, despite the heavy criticisms of propaganda in the movies in this period, no rejections or adjustments to these animated productions were requested by the Hays Office.[5] By contrast, in the sphere of the live action feature film, the major studios were taken to court over the propagandistic content of their movies. This further emphasizes the importance of historians' need to look to the narrative of animation to uncover ways in which Hollywood contributed towards the formation of propaganda within society.

Porky's Road Race (1937)

Released in 1937, amid a politic scarred by labour conflict and recession, *Porky's Road Race* revolves around a car race, in which Porky races for a two million dollar prize; however, to win, he must beat a plethora of Hollywood actors and actresses.

While nothing of note is said by the animated characters themselves, political grievances are directly referenced. First, the prize of two million dollars on offer to the winner of Porky's Road Race is heavily taxed. On the

---

[5] Production Code Certificates Box 00179, Warner Brothers Archives, University of Southern California. The box contains all the Production Code certificated granted to the animated productions by the Hays Office. There are no requests for amendments to any of the cartoons released from 1933 to 1945.

sign addressing the reward for the winner of the Road Race, it states that 'first prize is $2 million (less $1,999,998.37 in taxes)'. This directly addresses the common grievance within society that the New Deal was costing the American public too much money. Throughout the 1930s, FDR was constantly asking Congress for further budget approvals to fund his many public works schemes, which he deemed essential to the American economy's recovery. However, these demands were met with constant opposition. This criticism is further highlighted during the race itself. While racing, the audience is given a glimpse of a WPA work site.

The site is abandoned, is not serving any particular economic purpose and is simply portrayed as a wasteful eye sore on the landscape of the race itself (Figure 3.6). Combined with the amount of taxes the American people were paying to support the New Deal, this animated short is suggesting that FDR's economic policy has, in part, failed to do what it set out to do. By portraying the WPA as a pointless, fruitless exercise, the cartoon is providing a direct commentary on the policies of the administration. Disney, however, found another way to comment on the frustrations of society with the current politic and they used their popular cartoon star, Donald Duck, to vent this frustration for them.

Figure 3.6 *Porky's Road Race* (1937). Looney Tunes Golden Collection.

Self Control (1938)

Released towards the end of what many historians would term the 'active' phase of the New Deal, *Self Control* seems to call into question the very premise on which the New Deal is based. During the period in which this animated short was produced, the United States had fallen back into recession. There were over four thousand labour strikes throughout the country and farm prices and industrial prices had fallen rapidly. It seemed as though the New Deal was failing. While FDR remained optimistic about the prospects of his government, stating in a fireside chat in October 1937 that Americans do not 'ask their Government to stop governing simply because prosperity has come back a long way', the New Deal was falling into disrepute. This challenge is adequately addressed within this short.

Donald Duck is relaxing in a garden and listening to his wireless. The radio announcer states that someone is going to be talking to the listeners about self-control. The self-control programme begins and the broadcaster opens with 'Hello my friends.' Donald preaches that he has never lost control, and vows that he will never lose control. However, as Donald tries to nap, he is continually bothered by animals and obstacles that disrupt his peace and quiet. While the wireless constantly coaches him to 'Laugh his troubles away', and to 'ignore petty crime', Donald eventually ends up ignoring the advice of the wireless, gets his gun and attempts to shoot the animals that are pestering him. While he is unsuccessful in his endeavour, he ends up not attacking the animals, but the wireless itself (Figure 3.7).

This animated short directly engages with the political forum of the late 1930s. The presence of the wireless providing advice for a member of the American public draws instant comparison with Roosevelt's fireside chats. Not only was the wireless the mainstay of the general public's connection with politics, but also the announcer providing advice to Donald even uses FDR's common opening line, addressing his listeners as 'my friends'. The voice on the wireless tries to guide Donald through his crisis, preaching self-control and patience. However, much like the American public's views of Roosevelt's politics during this year, Donald, who was never really an advocate of Roosevelt's community spirit, has lost his patience and self-control.

Interestingly, he does not attack the problems within his society – in his case, the animals that are disrupting him; the main force of his attack is reserved for his ideological guide over the wireless. This appears a striking rejection of

Figure 3.7 *Self Control* (1938). Walt Disney Treasures.

the administration by Donald, in keeping with the political tide of the time. While this is eventually overtaken by an overriding nationalism, at this stage, the politics and ideology of FDR are rejected.

Conclusion

The Disney and Warner Brothers' animated shorts of the 1930s wholeheartedly endorsed the concept of 'the simple life'. While these cartoons recognized that the changes wrought by urbanization could be positive, overall, the animated landscape fears technology and the way it encroaches upon the human contact inherent in everyday life.

In shorts such as *Porky's Building*, and to a certain extent, *The Country Cousin*, the opportunity of the urban landscape is acknowledged. It provides opportunity, luxury and certainly an experience of a different side to life. However, ultimately, each experience in the city ends in crisis. Donald is traumatized by his encounter with the robots in *Modern Inventions*, Abner Country Mouse flees the city in fear of the life he would be forced to lead there and Porky is conned by the manager of the construction project he is working on. Here, we begin to see the importance of personification to transmitting ideology through animation. In this transitional stage, Disney and Warner Brothers' animation began to seamlessly incorporate its favoured ideologies through the narrative of its productions.

However, both the communitarian ideology and its clash with old 1920s values firmly take their hold within the personalities of Mickey Mouse and Donald Duck respectively. Donald embodies a frustrated spirit of Depression America through his actions within these animated productions. Donald always strives to do the right thing, however, is easily distracted by his own selfishness. His moral conflict in *Self Control* and *Donald's Better Self* epitomizes the frustration with the limitations of this new ideology. The ideological emphasis is no longer just on the individual to gain social advancement; it relies upon the work of the whole community. Donald finds this limiting. We have already associated Donald with the ideology of the 1920s through the early 1930s cartoon *The Wise Little Hen* and his association with this rugged individualism grows. Donald does not see why he must be a part of the community and go to school, or 'keep calm' as instructed by his 'Rooseveltian' psychologist over the wireless in *Self Control* when he can handle things in his own way.

Mickey, however, never works alone. He is the epitome of the communitarian realization of the American Dream. The leader of most of the Disney cartoons, he always advocates the other characters working together in order to achieve an end goal of success in his endeavour. Hence we can deduce by the end of this phase in animation's ideological tuning, that the personalities of the characters within the animation itself are coming to the fore as important ideological imprints, Donald as the reluctant receiver of change, Mickey as its arbiter. Donald's 1920s values are inherent in his actions; however, they are always proved wrong by Donald's constant failure and unhappiness in opposition to Mickey's constant success. Donald thus became a symbol for American resistance to the changes imposed upon American society by the New Deal. His frustrations with government in the late 1930s animated shorts and his consistent struggles with the ideology it imposed on society transform him into a metaphor for a new 1930s individualism.

4

International Relations in Animation 1936–41

In a meeting that took place in early December 1942 between Allen Rivkin of the Motion Picture Division and Joe Grant and Richard Huemer, two of Disney's leading animators, the following minute was taken: 'We must wind up with some plus value, now that we have ridiculed the Hitlerian theory into complete destruction.'[1] A later correspondence between the three remarks, 'I gather you will have some good comic sequences in which the notable Nazi is fooled.'[2] Lampooning the Nazi state and ridiculing those that followed its teachings was second nature to the Disney Studios during the Second World War. However, animation's commentary on US fascist enemies in Europe did not begin with the bombing of Pearl Harbor or with the formal declaration of war on 11 December 1941.

Hollywood's own connections with the worrying international situation in the 1930s are well documented. Despite the isolationist attitude of much of the American public, Hollywood was quick to comment on the rise of fascism in Europe (Offner 1969, 12). From Walter Wanger's production of *Gabriel Over the White House* as early as 1933, to the thuggish attitudes of the youths in Cecil B. DeMille's *This Day and Age* (United States, 1933), fascism and the fear of the violence of Nazism made its way into the movies (Dick 1985). Following the release of Warner Brothers' *Confessions of a Nazi Spy* (United States, 1939, dir. Anatole Litvak) the Hays Office had imposed a ban on the production of anti-Nazi films. The ban was lifted in January 1940; however, by the summer of 1941, Hollywood's violation of US neutrality warranted an investigation (Schindler 1996). On 1 August 1941, Gerald P. Nye introduced a resolution calling for an investigation of propaganda disseminated by the motion picture industry. Films such as *The Great Dictator* (United States, 1940, dir. Charlie Chaplin)

[1] Memo from Allen Rivkin, 7 December 1942, f. 22, JKW520, Motion Picture Society for the Americas Records, Margaret Herrick Library, Beverly Hills.
[2] Letter from Allen Rivkin, 19 January 1943, f. 22, JKW520, Motion Picture Society for the Americas Records, Margaret Herrick Library, Beverly Hills.

The Mortal Storm (United States, 1940, dir. Frank Borzage), *Foreign Correspondent* (United States, 1940, dir. Alfred Hitchcock) and *A Yank in the RAF* (United States, 1941, dir. Henry King) all caught the attention of the Nye Committee for their commentary on the situation in Europe. Animation was left untouched by the authorities, even though its commentary on the international situation was arguably, just as explicit as the feature films of the period.

Following the breakdown of the disarmament conferences of the early 1930s, much like the feature films of the same period, animation began to target Nazism. Warner Brothers' *I Like Mountain Music* (1933) features Edward Robinson giving the fascist salute. *Bosko's Picture Show* (United States, 1933, dir. Hugh Harman) features a wealth of international awareness with its 'Out of Tone' newsreel reporting on world events. The cartoon features a caricature of the peace conference, in which many world leaders are brawling in open forum with each other (Figure 4.1).

The reel also charts events in the fictional town of 'Pretzel' in Germany, showing American personality Jimmy Durante being chased down the street by Adolf Hitler wielding an axe.

Figure 4.1 *Bosko's Picture Show* (1933). Looney Tunes Golden Collection.

When Mussolini sent extra forces into Ethiopia in February 1935, animation's campaign against the fascist threat went into overdrive alongside the feature film, with commentary on both fascist Germany and Italy (*Motion Picture Herald*, 19 October 1933). As Charles Aaronson stated in an editorial of July 1935, 'timeliness of subject matter' was partly responsible for the proliferation of the animated short subject during this period (*Motion Picture Herald*, 13 July 1935). The *Hollywood Spectator* also recognized that the content of animation in these years seems to 'bear a remote resemblance to … international figures' (10 October 1936).

While the rest of Hollywood was warned off the production of films demonstrating awareness of the international situation, the Disney and Schlesinger animation studios released productions with dramatic international undertones without being subject to the same scrutiny as the live action feature (*Motion Picture Herald*, 1 April 1936). Throughout 1936 and 1937, pleas in trade press were circulated to the Hollywood movie-making community, to maintain the purity of cinema and ensure that 'films must be kept free from propaganda' (*Motion Picture Herald*, 11 September 1937). Disney, however, used the personalities of characters already embedded within the American national mindset to form a commentary on the events in Europe, while Warner Brothers showed no reluctance in caricaturing major international figures and events within the fantastical boundaries of the animated world.

Mickey Mouse and Hitler never saw eye to eye. A 1944 edition of *Daily Variety* reports that in Coblenz, a novelty company started flooding the German market with Mickey Mouse lapel buttons. By an official decree, Hitler banned the sale of Mickey Mouse merchandise in Germany (*Daily Variety*, 12 June 1944). Disney was disappointed that his creation did not have international appeal. In an interview in 1934, he stated, 'Mr. A Hitler, the Nazi old thing. Imagine that! Well, Mickey is going to save Mr. A Hitler from drowning or something someday. Just wait and see if he doesn't. Then won't Mr. A Hitler be ashamed!' (Schickel 1968, 159). Walt Disney also contributed towards the war effort in England in 1940, allowing proceeds of the premiere of Fantasia at the Broadway Theatre in London to be put towards soup kitchens for the homeless in bombed areas of England (*New York Times*, 23 October 1940, 20).

Disney's own anti-Semitic leanings are well documented. Marc Eliot's biography of 1993 paints a picture of Mickey Mouse's creator as holding fascist views throughout his life and uses evidence of deleted scenes from the successful short *The Three Little Pigs* and Disney's activities during the Communist sweep of Hollywood in the 1940s and 1950s as evidence for his claims. Disney's critics also use the Nazi filmmaker Leni Riefenstahl's visit to the studio in 1938 as evidence for Disney's pro-Nazi leanings. While Disney undoubtedly knew who Riefenstahl was, he did not wish to get involved with any political controversy (Gabler 2007). Furthermore, Riefenstahl later reported that Walt expressed hesitancy over her visit, later claiming he had no idea who she was and had feared that he may be boycotted as a result of her visit (Riefenstahl 1993, 286).

Other biographers of Disney have readily disputed claims for Walt's supposed fascist connections. Disney's most recent biographer, Neal Gabler, highlights Disney's apathy towards politics, arguing that his Republicanism was perhaps a rebellion against his father, more than any real political fervour. Rather, Gabler states, 'His politics were marked by confusion or neutrality' (2007, 448). From the evidence collected in Chapter 3, it seems that Disney animation followed the populist political tide in the 1930s, supporting Roosevelt when he was popular but becoming more critical when the president was losing his influence within Congress and the Senate.

Richard Huemer, one of Disney's leading animators, stated that Disney was very particular about his politics and the politics of his employees. He claimed that Walt was 'definitely to the right. He couldn't stand those guys who were tinged with a little pink.'[3] While this does provide solid evidence for the case that Walt Disney had strong right-wing political leanings, it seems that Eliot's claims for discrimination against his employees based on these claims are easily reputed. Huemer goes on to argue: 'One thing about Walt though. Regardless of political opinions or religious convictions or whatever, his first consideration was what a person could contribute to the studio and the product. He was always willing to give the benefit of the doubt and was very liberal with those whom he employed. I think he would have used the Devil himself if he were a great animator' (ibid.).

Animation and the rise of Hitler

Three Little Wolves (1936)

Released amid two fascist crises, the theming of *Three Little Wolves* could not have been more on point. Following Germany's reintroduction of conscription and subsequent announcement of an air force contrary to the terms of the Treaty

---

[3] 'From This You Are Making a Living?' An Oral History of Richard Huemer. Interview with Joe Adamson, 1968. American Film Institute Archives. p. 134.

of Versailles, the world had one eye on Mussolini's activities in Africa and the other on Hitler's repudiation of the post-war European settlement.

The short opens with focus on the Big Bad Wolf and his three little wolves. The wolves are sat watching the Big Bad Wolf who is instructing them on the different cuts of meat that can be attained from the Pig. Strikingly, from the outset, the Wolf not only speaks in German, but also, throughout the short, speaks in a German accent. He asks the three little wolves, 'Ist das nicht ein Sausage meat?' While this is obviously not a direct translation, the fact that the Wolf is identified with Germany from the beginning of the short suggests that the main threat to the Pigs' safety is also German.

In no other interpretation of *The Three Little Pigs* tales, is the Wolf so directly associated with a nationality. On the contrary, the Wolf dons many guises throughout these animated shorts. However, the power and popularity of the characters in this series of shorts allows historians to guess at the proposed impact of this modification. The Disney animators allowed the villain of his story to be interpreted as German as early as 1936, before even any of Hitler's conquests in Austria, Czechoslovakia and Poland.

As in the previous tale, two of the Pigs are carelessly dancing through the woods, while the so-called Practical Pig is building a wolf pacifier. This construction is worthy of note. From the beginning, the Big Bad Wolf was the external threat to the safe living of the Three Little Pigs. In *The Three Little Pigs*, the Practical Pig builds his own house to keep the Wolf at bay. However, in the *Three Little Wolves*, a wolf pacifier is the construction worked upon by the Practical Pig. This suggests that the Pigs, our substitute for the American people, viewed pacifying Germany as the only way to tame the Wolf's destructive urges and appetite and keep America out of conflict.

While the Practical Pig works hard to construct his pacifier, he demonstrates that he is unafraid to go into battle if provoked. The two foolish Pigs sound the wolf alarm and the Practical Pig comes running into the forest with a gun immediately, prepared for battle. The Wolf tricks the foolish Pigs into coming into his house with his little wolves, dressing as Bo Peep with her sheep. The Pigs are cornered and attacked by the wolves and seasoned for the wolf family to eat. However, the Pigs trick the wolves into blowing the wolf alarm loud enough for the Practical Pig to hear. The Practical Pig hears the alarm and drags his wolf pacifier through the forest.

Peace is shown as the solution to the German threat. However, when the Wolf is thrown into the pacifier, the process is anything but peaceful. The Wolf is restrained, beaten and intimidated by the device. This suggests that perhaps the solution to the German threat was viewed as a show of strength through the guise of peace. After the Wolf goes through the pacifier, both he and the little wolves are catapulted away from the forest and away from the Pigs. After their victory, the Pigs come out of the Wolf's house, flying the white flag of peace. Noticeably, they are all three dressed in the American colours: red, white and blue. (Figure 4.2)

In this short subject, several different techniques are used in order for the narrative to convey a message. First, once again, personality animation is used to great effect. In an interview for the *New York Times* following the success of *Snow White and the Seven Dwarfs* in 1937, Walt Disney stated that one of the most important things about his animated characters was his need for them to have personalities. He stated, 'We don't want them to just be shadows, for merely as moving figures, they would provoke no emotional response from the public' (*New York Times*, 6 March 1938, 117).

From the outset, it appears that Disney felt it necessary to imbue his characters' personalities with traits the public would recognize. In this short, the strongest personality, that of the Practical Pig, takes the guise of the wary, vigilant American. We can see from his construction of the 'Wolf Pacifier' that he is sensible, alert and prepared for danger. From the impact of

Figure 4.2 *Three Little Wolves* (1936). Walt Disney Treasures.

The Three Little Pigs, the Practical Pig is already framed as the 'American' who is most economically secure and the one who holds the most important and traditional of American values. In this short, we see this character protecting his way of life from an external German threat. While he is not actively seeking the Wolf, he is prepared to face him, if provoked. This is demonstrated by the way in which the Practical Pig rushes readily into the forest when the wolf alarm is sounded and by the action taken when the Wolf kidnaps his kin. While it could be argued that the Pig is taking an interventionist stance, advocating action against the German threat, what is important to note is that the Pig is provoked. Ultimately, however, the Pig preaches peace, for at the end of the cartoon, he waves a white flag, demonstrating that though the threat is neutralized, the Pig never desired to go to war with the Wolf.

On the contrary, the German Wolf is aggressive and provocative throughout, in keeping with Hitler's actions in Europe when the cartoon was in production. Not only does the German Wolf actively plan to destroy the Pigs, but he is also teaching his young cubs to do the same, suggesting the indoctrination of the young German youth with destructive ideas. The short also uses sophisticated narrative devices in order to suggest the nature of the German threat. For example, the Wolf dresses as Little Bo Peep and claims that he has lost his sheep, with his young cubs literally donning the guise of wolves in sheep's clothing. This could suggest that the German threat should not be underestimated. While many had sympathy with the German public following the settlement at Versailles, the treatment of Jews in Germany under the new Nazi regime sparked a reactionary German boycott in New York as early as April 1933 (Offner 1969, 60). While the German threat may appear harmless, as Hitler publicly claimed he was taking back what was owed to the German homeland, the sinister trickery of the Wolf reveals its true intentions and its danger. While the Wolf does flee the scene after being tackled by the Pigs' pacifier, the very fact that the Big Bad Wolf has taught his philosophy to his little wolves suggests that a new generation of danger could be about to reveal itself to the world.

This short also uses music to instil this anti-German ideology into its audience. Previously, the title song for *The Three Little Pigs* sequence, 'Who's Afraid of the Big Bad Wolf' was identified as the American people's battle with Depression. Since the American economy was recovering at this stage, a new threat is now identified. The Wolf, speaking German, identifies Germany as the principal threat to the American people. The Wolf's cubs mock and cheer at the Pigs' song to the Big Bad Wolf.

Given the cultural importance of this song to the American public, the fact that the German cubs mock its significance would also have had a substantial impact (*New York Times*, 3 September 1933, x2). Once the Pigs have triumphed over the Wolf, the song is played again. This time, the Pigs emerge victorious, flying the white flag of peace. However, for the first time, the undertone of the song is militaristic, indicating that the Pigs are willing to go into battle against an external foe. One of the Pigs plays a drum and the three heroes march towards the audience victoriously, as though returning home from war. The Pigs are transformed into national heroes, willing to fight for their country's safety.

The economic and social importance of this song is hence transformed into a patriotic anthem for the American people, symbolizing their triumph over the German threat. The Pigs' vendetta against the Wolf develops further in the 1939 short *The Practical Pig* when the Practical Pig develops a 'lie detector' for his German foe. The production period for this short was in the midst of the Sudetenland crisis and it was released shortly before Hitler broke the Munich Agreement and entered the rest of the Czechoslovakia (*New York Times*, 7 April 1938, 19).

The foundations for government-sponsored propaganda were laid down with these cartoons and by the time war broke out in Europe, the characters had already assumed their roles. When Disney was called upon by the Canadian government to make a series of shorts supporting the purchase of war bonds, the result was a remake of *The Three Little Pigs* with minor modifications. These modifications were easy for the American public to accept, due to the characterizations that took place in the mid-1930s.

The Thrifty Pig (1941)

Disney was approached to make a series of shorts for the Canadian government in 1941, following a successful screening of sections of *Fantasia* and *The Reluctant Dragon* in 1939 for the National Film Board of Canada. Seeing the effectiveness to which animation could be utilized for educational purposes, Disney was thus contracted for twenty thousand dollars to make four shorts. These shorts were to be used to promote the sale of war bonds within Canada. The first of these was produced in April 1941 and released on 19 November 1941, just before the Japanese attack on Pearl Harbor (Shale 1978, 17).

Reusing footage from *The Three Little Pigs*, *The Thrifty Pig* follows the Practical Pig and his foolish kin as the now Canadian Pigs clash with the

Nazi Wolf. The Practical Pig builds his house with Canadian war bonds for protection from the Wolf. What was once simply an American safe haven for the Pigs turns British in tone, as Disney animators place a union jack flag in the Practical Pig's yard. The Pig's previous association with the common American man is now replaced by an affiliation with the ordinary Canadian as the War Savings Certificates with which the Pig builds his home hold the address 'All Over Canada.' Furthermore, this also indirectly associates a supposedly neutral America with the Allied forces, who were, at the time of the short's release, at war with Nazi Germany.

The Big Bad Wolf, as in *Three Little Wolves*, is portrayed as a foreign enemy to the Pigs. However, this short takes the insinuation further. Not only is the Wolf German, but also he is affiliated with the Nazi party, wearing a swastika armband. He also wears a hat and carries a bag emblazoned with the famous Nazi branding (Figure 4.3).

The Disney Studios built upon the propagandistic foundations of its 1930s creations to produce government-sponsored propaganda, implicating the Nazi menace, before America was even at war.

Figure 4.3 *The Thrifty Pig* (1941). Walt Disney Treasures.

She Was an Acrobat's Daughter (1937)

Despite comfortably painting the ultimate 1930s Disney villain, the Big Bad Wolf, as an established Nazi in 1941, the Disney Studios did not physically produce a caricature of the man, Hitler, until the following year with their Canadian production, *Stop That Tank* (1942). However, the Warner Brothers' studio produced many caricatures of the fuehrer throughout the 1930s. While their effort in *Bosko's Picture Show* was comedic, at such a time, there was not significant worry surrounding the rising strength of the Nazi state.

Considering the political fervour surrounding the release of the Warner Brothers feature *Confessions of a Nazi Spy*, taken from a series of newspaper articles in the same year, it is interesting that *She Was an Acrobat's Daughter* attracted no attention from the Hays Office, despite the obvious references to the international situation the animation includes (Roddick 1983, 162).[4]

The film has a similar structure to that of the earlier Bosko productions in that it makes several gags surrounding the content of the film bill in the 1930s, which naturally includes references to the newsreels. The awareness present within this cartoon proves not only animation's responsiveness to the international situation in the 1930s but also its willingness to provide a commentary on the world's events.

The first news story worthy of note is the reference to the US military expansion programme. Through his public works programmes such as the Public Works Administration (up until Congress forbade its use in 1935), Roosevelt had sanctioned the spending of eight hundred and twenty-four million dollars on building aircraft carriers, naval ships, aviation research facilities and bombers (Sherry 1990, 20). Following Germany's announcement of an air force and Japan's naval expansion, Great Britain and the United States began to build up their military forces in response. Using what little funding Congress would allow, Roosevelt used limited construction funds to build carriers, battleships, cruisers and large destroyers (Buel 1984, 208). This short acknowledged this construction in this newsreel with its reference to the ship building race. While animation parodies this naval race by referring to the length of the ship, it also makes a connection between Britain and the

---

[4] For further information on the uproar surrounding Warner Brothers release of *Confessions*, see 'Council Bans Use of Alien Uniforms', *New York Times*, 26 April 1939, p. 25 and 'Espionage in Hollywood', *New York Times*, 5 February 1939, p. x5.

United States, by including each in the story, indicating where a future military alliance could be forged.

Alongside this commentary, there is also a reference to the Nazi state. There is no textual commentary, nor is there any indication of what international situation the news is referring to. However, there is a brief appearance of Hitler on the screen (Figure 4.4).

This acknowledges that Hitler was 'news', even in the animated world. It is interesting that the newsreel also fails to provide a full view of Hitler, as the short provides only a side shot of his stature. This could be due to the restrictions in place surrounding the movie industry's commentary on international events. An extensive appearance of Hitler may have provoked controversy. However, what is also of interest is that one of the animated characters in the audience appears terrified of Hitler's figure. Nonetheless, the reluctance to provide a full caricature of Hitler shows that the animators knew that they were dealing with a sensitive subject. All of the other news stories presented on the newsreel were presented in full view.

Figure 4.4 *She Was an Acrobat's Daughter* (1937). Looney Tunes Golden Collection.

Donald's Better Self (1938)

In a further meeting between Allen Rivkin, Joe Grant and Richard Huemer during 1942, the ways in which the Good and Evil of the conflict during the Second World War could be portrayed in an animated production were discussed. The minutes state:

> A prologue would establish the birth and growth of man, his desire to better himself, his family and his social surroundings. During this progression, two types of man would evolve; Good Man and Evil Man. Evil would watch Good hungrily, seeing what personal privilege he would garner from Good's discoveries and developments, then evil would drop into the background as Good went about his business of making a better world to live in.[5]

As part of the Second World War propaganda effort, Disney animators Richard Huemer and Joe Grant sought out a personification of the conflict between Good and Evil and a visualization of their impact on the world around them, demonstrating for the audience the various potential outcomes of the struggle for world domination. However, this personification of concepts is already used throughout the 1930s and to particular effect in the 1938 Donald Duck cartoon, *Donald's Better Self*.

The sociological implications of this cartoon have been discussed in Chapter 3; however, this cartoon also has *political* implications that require further examination. When Donald is led astray by the Devil side of himself, or perhaps one could argue, the 'Evil Man', the Angel comes looking for him and confronts the Devil. 'Have no fear,' says the Angel, 'I do not intend to fight.' The Angel, or perhaps one could argue, the 'Good Man' initially adopts a pacifist stance with the Devil. However, the Devil is provocative and hits the Angel, bundling him up and throwing him into a nearby lake. The Angel, angered by the attack, announces that his action was 'the last straw'. Provoked, the Angel takes to the skies, taking the shape of a bomber aircraft (see Figure 4.5). The Angel propels into the Devil, who is subsequently buried into the ground.

This cartoon was released in March 1938 and consequently would have been in production during 1937, in the middle of the Spanish Civil War and amid Roosevelt's renewals of the Neutrality Act (Offner 1969, 145). It was also during

---

[5] Memo from Allen Rivkin, 7 December 1942, f. 22, Motion Picture Society for the Americas Records, Margaret Herrick Library, Beverly Hills.

Figure 4.5 *Donald's Better Self* (1938). Walt Disney Treasures.

the build-up to Germany's *Anschluss* with Austria, prior to the Munich Crisis of 1938. While there are no production documents available to scholars to confirm the contextual reasoning behind the cartoon, nonetheless, several conclusions could be drawn.

First, the cartoon advocates military action upon provocation. The Angel states clearly that he does not wish to fight and yet when the Devil takes action, the Angel takes to the skies, drops a water bomb on the Devil and ultimately kills him. Secondly, the document from 1942 states the method that could be used in animation in which the conflict between Good and Evil, the Allies and the Nazis, could play out. This cartoon utilizes these techniques. The inference is further confirmed by the fact that footage from *Donald's Better Self* is reworked into a propaganda film for the Canadian government: *Donald's Decision* (United States, 1942, no director's credit). When Donald is accosted by the Devil in the same manner, his decision to side with the Devil is implicated as aiding the Nazis. As the Devil Donald catches his attention by tapping the lever on the post box, it spins and makes the shape of a swastika (Figure 4.6).

Figure 4.6 *Donald's Decision* (1942). Walt Disney Treasures.

Animation and the Spanish Civil War

Alongside the rising Nazi threat in the 1930s, the civil conflict in Spain attracted significant attention in Hollywood. Documentary films such as *The Spanish Earth* (1937) and features such as *Blockade* (1938) passed commentary on the European conflict but were subject to heavy criticism because of the widespread desires to keep Hollywood neutral (*Motion Picture Herald*, 11 September 1937). Amid the neutrality crisis in Hollywood, Disney chose to take on 'The Story of Ferdinand' (*New York Times*, 27 July 1937, 24). The meaning of the story was not lost on the American public, attracting significant attention for its association with the Spanish conflict (*New York Times*, 23 October 1938, 165).

Ferdinand the Bull (1938)

Winner of the Best Animated Short Academy Award, *Ferdinand the Bull* tells the story of the little bull who, unlike all those around him, did not like to get involved in fighting. The short outlines Ferdinand's childhood, during which all his friends used to fight and he simply preferred to sit under his favourite tree, out of conflict and smell the flowers. Ferdinand grows into a big strong bull and all of his friends dream of fighting at the bull fights in Madrid. Men from the town come into Ferdinand's field to pick a bull for the fight. Ferdinand tries to keep out of their way but unfortunately gets stung by a bee and inadvertently impresses the men with his speed and strength. He gets picked for the fight and taken into town. In the ring, Ferdinand scares the men out of the fight by his sheer size but only smells the flowers the Matador has in his hands. The Matador pleads with him to take action and to fight, but Ferdinand stays peaceful and smells his flowers. The Matador cries out in desperation and Ferdinand has to be taken home, where he sits underneath his tree, smelling the flowers.

The short provoked considerable response within the American public. When the animation was produced, writer Munro Leaf claimed that he received letters from Leftists and Rightists, wanting to know 'where he gets off ignoring the Spanish Civil War like that' (ibid.). From this insinuation, it seems that Ferdinand was read as animated enactment of the United States refusing to live up to its responsibilities in Spain. Interventionist sentiment for the Spanish Civil War was rife in 1938. Following the bombing of Guernica on 26 April the previous year and the loss of American lives in volunteer forces fighting for the Loyalists, the American people campaigned actively for Roosevelt to apply the Neutrality Act towards Berlin and Rome, claiming that the lack of action constituted fighting for Franco's fascists (Dallek 1979, 141).

Importantly, the American people saw political undertones within animation, recognizing the ideology within the cartoon from the outset. The short begins with the narration, 'Once upon a time, in Spain ...'.

Forming the basis of a memorandum on how animation could contribute towards the war effort in 1942, Disney storyliner Robert Spencer Carr stated that 'the surface has not been scratched in the art of dramatic narration', highlighting the importance of dramatic devices of leading radio programmes.[6] Principally, Disney saw the pivotal role that narration had to play in the direction of the story and highlighted the way in which narrators could serve as educators. Narration is used to great effect in the wartime shorts but was used prior to the war in *Ferdinand*, drawing attention to the contemporary situation and Ferdinand's continued defiance against the Matador.

---

[6]   R. S. Carr, 'Ideas for a New South American Film Program,' 7 January 1942, p. 37, Motion Picture Society for the Americas Records, Margaret Herrick Library, Beverly Hills.

The memorandum also states that Disney needed to create a 'glossary of new characters to express today's new conceptions'.[7] It can be argued that with the character of Ferdinand, this was already accomplished in 1938. Ferdinand's primary characteristic is his pacificism. Despite provocation from friends and society, he remains unwilling to be taken into a war, preferring to sit and smell his flowers. This reflects exactly the stance taken in the Spanish Civil War by the American government. Ferdinand does not like to fight. When drawn into the arena, he does not take a stand against the brutality of the men nor does he withdraw. He remains neutral. Using a character such as Ferdinand to embody political isolationism allowed Disney to create similar feeling within the American audience during the Second World War, arguably with Donald Duck leading the charge for American intervention in Europe. While Ferdinand embodied American isolationism in Europe, Donald stood for intervention upon provocation. Following the trend of channelling political ideologies through the personalities of their characters, Warner Brothers' animation also provided its own response to the situation in Spain, using arguably its most popular principal character of the 1930s: Porky Pig.

Porky's Poultry Plant (1936)

Porky's Poultry Plant was released just one month into the conflict in Spain; however, due to the rapid turnaround of Warner Brothers shorts in comparison to Disney, their production turnover was a mere four weeks, putting the production period for this short at the outbreak of hostilities (Maltin 1980, 178). Notably, due to Frank Tashlin's direction, Porky is here portrayed as an adult pig, running his own successful chicken farm business. Porky is shown to be caring and considerate with his hens and reaches out to a baby chicken at the outset, ensuring that she gets her share of feed. The audience soon discovers that the farm business is in danger from an external enemy: the Hawk. The Hawk is identified as Public Chicken Enemy Number One by a 'wanted' poster. The external threat was significant to Tashlin, who even decided to name one of the kidnapped chickens after his first wife: Dorothy.

The Hawk flies high overhead and makes his play for the farm. Porky raises the 'Hawk Alarm' and the chickens flee for safety. All except one: the baby

---

[7]   R. S. Carr, 'Ideas for a New South American Film Program,' 7 January 1942, p. 37, Motion Picture Society for the Americas Records, Margaret Herrick Library, Beverly Hills.

chick which Porky sought to protect at the beginning of the cartoon. Porky sees the chick in danger and gets his gun, immediately mobilizing to protect his chickens. However, the Hawk takes to the skies and an aerial battle begins. Tashlin makes quick cuts in editing, to signify the danger and significance of the aerial conflict between Porky and the hawks. Porky climbs into his plane and begins attacking the Hawk, who calls for assistance from other hawks who fly and drop bombs on Porky in aerial battle formations (Figure 4.7). However, Porky is victorious and the chickens bury the hawks in the ground in exactly the same manner as Devil Donald in *Donald's Better Self* and *Donald's Decision*, signifying that Warners and Disney had similar ideas when it came to tackling an external enemy.

There are several techniques used within this animated production that can be studied in unison with the Disney cartoons. The first is the focus on aerial battle that forms the foundation for Porky's conflict with the Hawk. As in *Donald's Better Self*, aerial shots are used within the production, demonstrating that the principal threat to the short's protagonist is from the air. In *Porky's Poultry Plant*, the main threat to Porky's farm is from a bird of prey, echoing this aerial danger. This is epitomized by the way in which the Hawk acts throughout the animated short: with exactly the same mannerisms as an aerial bomber. The Hawk takes

Figure 4.7 *Porky's Poultry Plant* (1936). Looney Tunes Golden Collection.

to the skies like a plane taking off from an airfield and his allies fly with him in a plane-like formation. While their attack is ultimately harmless, the undertones and potential effects of an aerial attack upon 'civilians' are demonstrated in these cartoons. While Angel Donald drops a water bomb on the implied Nazi Devil Donald, the hawks drop egg bombs onto Porky. Furthermore, Porky alerts his chickens to the threat with an air raid siren, suggesting the imminent threat of the bombing of a civilian target, integral to the later fighting in Spain, for example, the intense bombing of Guernica, resulting in the loss of thousands of civilian lives. Applying the characteristics of weapons to the animated characters is used in *Donald's Better Self* and in the later propaganda shorts released during the Second World War, proving the existence of political commentary on the international situation as early as 1936.

However, one way that Disney remained more explicit in its commentary at this early stage was in its utilization of Technicolor. It was in 1932 that Disney first used the three-strip Technicolor process with the Silly Symphony Short, *Flowers and Trees* (1932) and the studios continued to use it to great effect. However, the significance of the red, white and blue at the end of *Three Little Wolves* was paramount to its overall political implication. Due to Disney's exclusivity on Technicolor and Leon Schlesinger's refusal to spend a lot of money on the quality of his cartoons, Warner Brothers' animated shorts were restricted to black and white. However, once Warner Brothers were able to utilize Technicolor, they did so to great ideological effect, the results of which will be discussed in Chapter 5.

Due to Porky's quick triumph over the hawks, an insinuation is also made regarding the nature of the enemy threat faced by Americans from the events in Europe. Porky works alone to defeat the enemy and yet is still able to fight off a school of eight hawks. A common American man is easily able to defeat his external foe. What is also of interest is the technique Porky uses to defeat the hawks. He uses strategies linked to the pride of the American nation: football. After the Hawk's attack of egg bombs proves unsuccessful, the enemies then turn to sport to try and outmanoeuvre Porky. The hawks get into a huddle and throw the chick between them like a football; however, Porky manages to catch the chick, sending the hawks flying to their death.

This makes the connection between Porky and America but also implies that America's national strengths will ultimately allow them to defeat their foes. The first of which is their moral superiority over their enemy; the second, the strength of their air force. In Robert Spencer Carr's 1942 memorandum on the ways in which animation could be of use in the Second World War, both of these strengths are mentioned, underlining the fact that these techniques were used in animation *before* the war.

Each of these cartoons uses similar techniques in order to get across their commentary on the action that should be taken by American citizens when they are faced with an external threat. They should take action, but only when provoked and only when there are innocent civilian lives at risk. This also insinuates a defensive type of warfare in order to keep the peace.

What Price Porky (1938)

The Warner Brothers cartoons continued to advocate such interventionist action and, in time, became significantly more direct in highlighting which countries they believed to be the biggest threats to the United States. This demonstrates that animation, as a medium, was subject to a freedom of interpretation not permitted for the live action feature. US involvement in world affairs became more direct following Roosevelt's 'quarantine speech' on 5 October 1937 (Dallek 1979, 148). Furthermore, the issue of a volunteer army force into the Spanish Civil War drew out 'American passion for action' against Franco's fascists (Tierney 2007). While a statement from the government read, 'The enlistment of American citizens in either of the opposing sides in Spain is unpatriotically inconsistent with the American Government's policy of the most scrupulous non-intervention in Spanish internal affairs,' FDR stopped the State Department from prosecuting those who volunteered and allowed for medical workers to obtain passports to provide assistance to the wounded.

This spirit of intervention, while against official government policy, played out in the animated world in a battle between Porky Pig and Daffy Duck, comically renamed as General Quacko, the Ducktator. The short begins in a simple farmyard setting where Porky is feeding his chickens. However, before the meal is through, a provocative duck steals corn from the feeding chickens. Porky confronts the army of ducks, sitting on the periphery of his farmland, asking if they could return the corn, as otherwise his chickens will go hungry. An armed guard watches over the leader of the duck army. Daffy wears a hat strikingly similar to the one worn by General Franco and also issues a threatening directive to Porky, stating that they should fight for their corn.

Newly hatched chicks form an army, trenches are dug out and battle begins. The battle is far from just a land conflict, as duck planes drop egg bombs from the air, taking off from carriers at sea, demonstrating a full-scale war, mobilizing all facets of military power.

Tanks are also utilized in the battle. Porky Pig, for the most part, remains in a dug out in 'no man's land' but is forced into battle when a grenade is thrown at him. He climbs out of his dug out and 'zips' it up, sealing the grenade inside. He is provoked into battle and fires corn at General Quacko's army. While he does not directly hit the forces, he inadvertently hits a nearby tree which topples over and restrains the Ducktator's army. While Porky and his chickens eventually win the battle and successfully capture General Quacko and his remaining 'men', the enemy forces do manage to keep the corn that started the fight in the beginning.

There are several techniques used within this animated production that draw comparison with the Disney shorts. The reference to air power is again, widespread, drawing attention to the aerial nature of the conflict in Spain. Egg bombs are dropped, as in *Porky's Poultry Plant*. The caricaturing and lampooning of the enemy that was widespread in the wartime cartoons begins here. General Quacko is explicitly framed as a fascist dictator as the short reveals armies marching and giving the fascist salute to their leader (Figure 4.8).

Figure 4.8 *What Price Porky* (1938). Looney Tunes Golden Collection.

Similar to the Disney cartoons, this short uses the character of Porky to convey a particular mindset in American society. Porky is reluctant to go to war and only really gets involved in the conflict at the very end of the short. He is provoked into forming an army by the aggressive directive of General Quacko. Porky makes no comment on the words; however, the chickens immediately mobilize. Much like *Donald's Better Self* and *Porky's Poultry Plant*, the short thus endorses military action upon provocation. The military action taken in this short, however, is far more widespread than evidenced in any other short of this period. Naval power, aerial power and land forces are all used to fight Daffy's army, suggesting the need for total mobilization of all armed units in order to fight the fascist threat.

This cartoon is unquestionably more violent than any other aired during the 1930s and the reference to the fascist threat is explicit and obvious. There is extensive death and destruction evident throughout and General Quacko is ruthless and unyielding with the direction of his own army and in the action taken against Porky's chicken army. The oppression of the fascist regimes in Europe is shown clearly in this cartoon, showing the beginnings of a propaganda campaign against fascism well before the United States became actively involved in the European conflict in 1941. Franco and Hitler are explicitly targeted in animation in the 1930s. While there is little explicit reference to Mussolini's Italy, the ruthless attitude of the puppeteer Stromboli in Disney's feature film, *Pinocchio* (1940) should not be overlooked to this end. Ruthless treatment in animation was specifically reserved for animated 'representatives' of the fascist powers in Europe.

Conclusion

The channels through which animation provides its commentary on the international situation were all utilized when cartoons were drawn into the full-scale propaganda battle conducted by Hollywood during the Second World War. The document produced by Disney storyliner, Robert Spencer Carr, in January 1942, used sporadically throughout this chapter, outlines these techniques explicitly. These techniques apply, in many guises, to the 1930s cartoons on the same subjects. Music, narration, use of celebrity, moral supremacy and the ridiculing of the Nazi state are all explicitly stated as ways in which the animated world could contribute towards the cause of propaganda. All of these techniques are used in the 1930s shorts. 'Music', writes Carr, 'plays a much more important part in an animated cartoon than in any other type of motion picture. ... The idea is that the music track on all these pictures should not be merely "appropriate" music – but should consciously be made part of the propaganda'.[8] As early as 1936, the Frank Churchill Depression anthem, 'Who's Afraid of the Big Bad Wolf', takes on new military undertones when the Pigs emerge victorious after a battle with the German Wolf. This becomes more explicit in the later production for the Canadian government. A battle cry against the Depression becomes a battle cry for the fight against the fascist threat.

The skill of narration allows for the audience to be guided in their thoughts on a picture. In Ferdinand, narration is used to alert the audience to the contemporary situation in Spain, in *Donald's Decision*, and the earlier *Donald's Better Self*, the Angel and Devil provide narration to Donald, our prototype for the common American man, so that the audience is made to draw the 'right' conclusions from the story's drama. Moral supremacy is subtly dealt with in the 1930s shorts, simply through the consistent involvement of innocents. Animation also provided its own viewpoint on the morality of war. Throughout, with its numerous references to armed conflict, often making explicit reference to aerial battle and the involvement of civilian casualties, animation enforces its moral code on audience. In *Donald's Better Self, What Price Porky* and *Porky's Poultry Plant*, Porky and Donald are provoked into battle by an external threat. Donald's 'better self' fights with the Devil Donald, with implications of a connection to the Nazis. Porky does battle with General Quacko, a ruthless 'Ducktator' who provokes Porky's chickens into total war on the land, air and sea. In all of these situations of conflict, both Disney and Warner Brothers animation make the case that war under provocation is justified. In most of these cases, an innocent is also involved, insinuating that in the case where civilians are drawn into the conflict, full mobilization is justified. Using personality animation developed during the 1930s, the Disney and Schlesinger Studios were able to develop characters which stood for intervention against the Nazi menace: the Practical Pig, Donald Duck and Porky Pig were among the first to physically take up arms against the fascist threat. These characters became 'celebrities' of the 1930s and through their actions in these animated productions, they provided their own models for social, political and military action, long before the outbreak of war.

---

[8] 'Ideas for the South American Film Program', Motion Picture Society for the America Records, pp. 6, f. 22, Margaret Herrick Library, Beverly Hills.

Their actions within the paradigm of the 1930s animated world allowed them to assume their propagandistic roles with ease during the Second World War. They became believable patriots, nationalists and educators.

By including caricatures of Hitler and General Franco, animation demonstrated awareness of the most dangerous figures to world peace. The image of Hitler caused fear in the animated world and the caricature of Franco sparks total war in Porky's farmyard. Disney gave his greatest villain, the Big Bad Wolf, a German accent and a swastika armband, transferring the hatred of a nation battling Depression into hatred for the Nazi state.

However, these techniques were not just utilized in the pursuit of interventionism or indeed, in directing the American people towards war with Nazi Germany, Mussolini's Italy and Hirohito's Japan. Using the nationalistic fervour developed through the shared experience of the Depression, these techniques were also transferred into the development of a nationalistic culture within animation based upon geography, national traditions and institutions and a shared sense of history. Upon the outbreak of the Second World War, this nationalism was channelled towards raising morale on the home front and in the service of fostering unity between North America and Latin America.

5

Animated Nationalism 1937–41

In his study of American culture in the 1930s, David Eldridge has made the argument for 'mass communication of radio, cinema and advertising forging national bonds' (Eldridge 2008, 23). Due to the social dislocation experienced by the American people following the Wall Street Crash, the ideology of the American Dream was called into question. People sought other ways to re-connect with their fellow Americans. Nationalism became a 'prominent characteristic of the changed American popular outlook' (Ekirch 1969, viii).

Nationalism, according to theorist Yehoshua Arieli, can be defined as the 'creation and maintenance of community life and destiny with a will and purpose expressed in the state and a unity embodied in the nation. Such unity is maintained by a system of symbols, values and notions' (Arieli 1964, 1). This was a concurrent trend within the production of movies in the late 1930s that held particular focus on America's national institutions, such as Warner Brothers' *Code of the Secret Service* (1939), American history such as Selzick's *Gone with the Wind* (1939) and military strength as found within Lloyd Bacon's *Wings of the Navy* (1939). Many of these films, alongside many of the 'interventionist' features, for example, Mitchell Leisen's *Arise My Love* (1940) were recognized as holding overtly propagandistic messages. However, in the current literature on this topic, there has been no case made for the inclusion of animation within this particular surge of nationalism in Hollywood towards the end of the 1930s.

The Walt Disney brand has always had a close association with American nationalism. As Stephen Fjellman has noted, the Walt Disney World and Disneyland theme parks across the globe are 'a concentrated distillation of one version of the United States and its view of the world … a combination of the mythical and the real' (Fjellman 1992, 21). Disney animation and its theme parks give a representation of the United States as 'it should have been' (Fjellman 1992, 31).

This association between Disney animation and nationalism crystallized in the years 1937–1941, as the United States drew closer to war. Characters that had drawn the American people together in the Depression, as proven in Chapter 3, came to unite the nation in its national identity. Animation, much like the live action features, provided a platform to showcase the most important elements of America's character through promotion of its rich history, geography, national institutions and traditions.

Distory: Animation celebrates America

An article in *Fortune* magazine in 1942 entitled 'Walt Disney: Great Teacher' tells of Disney's educational efforts during the Second World War. The article states that Disney's educational efforts are 'not only enlightening but exciting'. It goes on to claim: 'Enthusiasts who have seen his work in progress believe that he has set in motion nothing less than a revolution in the technique of education.' Disney, in the article, is labelled as an 'educator and propagandist'.[1] While this primarily refers to the educational films produced during the war, Disney actually started his work in the field of education before fighting commenced.

In Robert Spencer Carr's memorandum of 1942, the subjects of future animated productions were listed. One of the primary subjects listed was History.

> History of a hemisphere: The British made an all cartoon film called 'Atlantic' in which they attempted to show England's role as coloniser and organiser of the Atlantic world. ... My suggestion is that we make a much better, livelier film telling the true story of the colonisation and final independence of the Western hemisphere with special emphasis on how ... we Americans have always fought for our freedom.[2]

However, both the Disney Studios and Warner Brothers studios were producing films referencing US history before the outbreak of war, attempting to unite the American people behind their shared history. Stephen Fjellman refers to this concept of an animated past as 'Distory': describing it as the 'redefinition of the

[1] 'Walt Disney: Great Teacher.' *Fortune* magazine, undated article 1942, f. 404, Motion Picture Society for the Americas Records, Margaret Herrick Library, Beverley Hills.
[2] R. S. Carr, 'Ideas for a New South American Film Program,' 7 January 1942, p. 26, Motion Picture Society for the Americas Records, Margaret Herrick Library, Beverley Hills.

past as it should have been' (1992, 20); that is to say, the veneration of celebrated elements of America's past and the simplification of its tragedies.

Disney has come under attack for the 1946 production *Song of the South* (1946) for its glorification of slavery through the characters played by James Baskett and Hattie McDaniel (Brode 2005, 53). Its later production of the historical tale *Pocahontas* (1995) also came under similar criticism for being 'historically dubious' and for seemingly dismissing the harsher elements of treatment Pocahontas and her tribe were subjected to by the English settlers (Brode 2005, 265). These animated treatments of history were taking place as early as 1938 within Warner Brothers and Disney animation. It is impossible to escape the ideological implications of these shorts. While many of these cartoons do involve spoofs and gags, as was the nature of the medium, it cannot be denied that they do put forward their own interpretations of historical events. What is more, explicit connections can be made between what happens in many of these shorts and the wartime propaganda productions. This process took place in both the Warner Brothers and Disney cartoons of this era, clearing the way for the nationalistic propaganda films released during the Second World War. They forged an overtly positive outlook on American traditions. Important periods of American history are praised and simplified through the medium of animation.

Johnny Smith and Poker-huntas (1938)

Johnny Smith and Poker-huntas is a spoof animation, based on the story of the woman Pocahontas who became a well-known figure in American history for stopping the execution of the Englishman, John Smith (Woodward 1969). The cartoon loosely uses the narrative of the well-known tale as a vehicle through which to glorify elements of American history and culture. This animated short is also full of references to contemporary social and political culture.

When Johnny Smith first comes over on the Mayflower voyage, as he looks to land, his first sight is of a sign which reads, 'America: Free Parking' and another which reads, 'FHA Loans'. One of the most celebrated elements of the New Deal was the Federal Housing Association (FHA). According to Edsforth, the 'FHA made mortgage lending less risky and home ownership more secure', and opened the 'possibility of home ownership to millions of families' (Edsforth 2000, 193). This, in combination with the fact that, by the end of the short, Johnny Smith and Poker-huntas live 'happily ever after' in a secure home, seems to suggest the revival of the American Dream that had been lost after the Great Depression.

The America that Johnny Smith stumbles upon is a thriving metropolis with an equally thriving economy. This suggests that America, as a country, was successful in rebuilding itself and its national institutions following the depth of the Depression. While cartoons released within a similar timeframe such as *Porky's Road Race* suggest elements of failure in the New Deal, this cartoon's context is a celebration of America and its history and recognizes the successes of the New Deal.

Johnny Smith and Poker-huntas is narrated throughout by subtitles, much like many of the wartime animated shorts. These sometimes advance the narrative and on other occasions, address the audience directly. This self-awareness helps to guide the American public in their interpretation of the short's story. For example, the short opens with a dedication to the descendants of the Mayflower voyage, reminding the audience of their ancestry. This technique is also used in a later war short entitled *Scrap Happy Daffy*. The narration serves to remind the American public that they have a shared sense of history. Schlesinger admitted of the short *Johnny Smith and Poker-huntas* that he was happy to 'satirise' American history or well-known tales that people identified with (*Hollywood Spectator*, 24 June 1939, 11). This created a sense of unity between audience and animator. This unity was deeply embedded in a patriotic short released the following year.

Old Glory (1939)

Old Glory was first released over the Fourth of July weekend in the United States, just months before Hitler's invasion of Poland and Britain's declaration of war against Germany. It remains an astonishing example of the ways in which animation could present history through its use of colour and music.

The short was three hundred feet longer than the average Merrie Melody cartoon and was produced in a record nine weeks. According to an article in the *Daily Variety* of late June 1939, Schlesinger was under 'forced steam' from the Warner Brothers distributors to get the short out in time for the holiday weekend, doubling its patriotic impact (*Daily Variety*, 11 June 1939, 5). The short was also only the second of Porky's Merrie Melodies to be released in full three-strip Technicolor, further emphasizing its nationalistic impact as the utilization of red, white and blue throughout is particularly effective.

The short opens on the American flag, blowing in the wind. At the foot of the flag's pole, Porky Pig is reading a book on American history and is trying to learn his Pledge of Allegiance. However, he is struggling to remember the exact wording. Frustrated with his efforts, Porky falls asleep, throwing his book aside. Seconds later, the figure of Uncle Sam appears from the volume, and kneels down next to Porky, vowing to teach him why he needs to learn the Pledge of Allegiance (Figure 5.1).

Uncle Sam confides in Porky the importance of freedom and vows that the American homeland was not always as fortunate as it is now. Porky is shown the figure of Patrick Henry and is made to listen to his famous 'Give Me Freedom or Give Me Death!' speech at the beginning of the Revolutionary War. While Henry calls the American people to arms, the well-known song *Yankee Doodle Went to Town* plays in the background as the focus falls to the march of the men. Porky witnesses the signing of the Declaration of Independence by John Hancock while the British and American flags adorn the walls of Independence Hall.

After the Liberty Bell rings out in a powerful montage sequence, Porky watches George Washington sign the US Constitution. The key amendments flash out in bold subtitles for the audience to see. Uncle Sam explains to Porky that when George Washington signed the document, it laid the foundations for the US democracy. Following this, Uncle Sam looks to a nearby statue of

Figure 5.1 *Old Glory* (1939). Looney Tunes Golden Collection.

Abraham Lincoln. After his lesson in American history, Porky wakes up and is able to recite the Pledge with little difficulty.

Countless techniques are used within this short to forge an overwhelming sense of nationalism. First, Technicolor plays a major role within this short. The key historical figures throughout are wearing red, white and blue. Porky himself is even sporting his patriotic colours, wearing a red and white hat, blue jumper and white trousers. A comparison to the Pigs at the close of the *Three Little Wolves* short should be drawn here. Colour is also used to effect in the Treasury films to be discussed in Chapter 6. Without the use of colour, the patriotic significance of *Old Glory* is completely lost.

Secondly, as mentioned in Carr's Disney memorandum, this Warner Brothers' short uses history to great effect to unify the American people behind their forthcoming Independence Day. While Carr's ideas were put forward for Disney animation, the same features are infused within Warners' animation. Key historical figures such as George Washington, Abraham Lincoln, John Hancock and Patrick Henry are all animated in this short's narrative. They bring history back to life and give the short an educational direction. Through the use of the contemporary character, Porky Pig, history is also modernized making it appealing to adults and children alike.

Thirdly, the short also utilized another technique mentioned within the later 1942 Disney memorandum: animated posters. Carr writes: 'This term is used to describe those rapid fire, single scene presentations of disconnected ideas or tableaux.'[3] This is used to display the importance of those amendments in the US Constitution most at threat from the war against fascism in Europe: Freedom of Religion, Freedom of Press and Freedom of Speech.

The final technique used in this patriotic short is the ani-map. This is used to greater effect in the nationalist shorts in the period under examination that focus heavily on the geography of the United States, referencing its scope and natural beauty. However, it is also used within this short to 'place' the history in a specific geographical context. Carr's memorandum states the ani-map is a 'new, improved type. Not a flat geographic map but miniature landscapes in full colour, with tiny mountains, cities and rivers.'[4] While the Schlesinger Studios 'version' of the ani-map does not quite reach the proportions of the ani-map

[3] R. S. Carr, 'Ideas for a New South American Film Program,' 7 January 1942, p. 4, Motion Picture Society for the Americas Records, Margaret Herrick Library, Beverly Hills.
[4] R. S. Carr, 'Ideas for a New South American Film Program,' 7 January 1942, p. 2, Motion Picture Society for the Americas Records, Margaret Herrick Library, Beverly Hills.

envisioned by the Disney Studios, the foundations for its use are undoubtedly displayed within this short on several occasions. The most effective use of the technique demonstrates the spread of democracy from east to west, as the map of the United States changes colour accordingly (Figure 5.2).

Old Glory was an extraordinary cartoon, both for the extensive propagandistic techniques employed by the studios in order to forge a patriotic meaning and for the fact that for the first time, audiences read and fully understood the consequences of its narrative. The review for the cartoon from *Motion Picture Daily* states: 'There are no laughs in this cartoon and none are intended. It's a lesson in the significance of the Stars and Stripes, imparted in unusual fashion with the cartoon character, Porky Pig, awakened to the struggle that achieved liberty and tolerance' (3 June 1942, 9).

The fact that this cartoon was also re-released during the war is a testament to the propagandistic power of the message within its narrative. The techniques used within *Old Glory* to convey its ideology fit well within the thematic content of the wartime releases. *Hollywood Spectator* also illuminated the power of the message within this particular animated short. The review of the picture, which was part of a longer article on the Schlesinger Studios, recognized that *Old Glory*

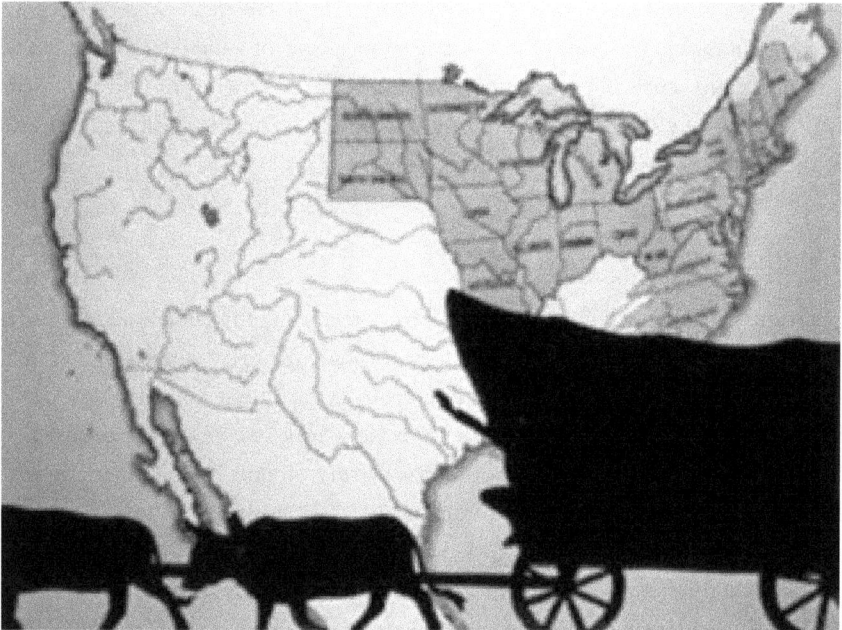

Figure 5.2 *Old Glory* (1939). Looney Tunes Golden Collection.

has the virtue of being amusing as well as inspiring: 'Certainly he [Schlesinger] has turned out a picture that every man, woman and child in the country should see' (*Hollywood Spectator*, 24 June 1939, 3).

Following the success of *Old Glory* and capitalizing on the national mood, Schlesinger announced plans to release further patriotic shorts in the *Daily Variety*, proving that there was a conscious decision to continue this nationalistic trend (30 October 1939, 87). Thus, the Schlesinger Studios began to release a series of newsreel and travelogue spoofs, showcasing the best of the United States. While there is no documentary evidence available to historians to prove a conscious decision by the Disney Studios to move in the same direction, the content of the shorts seems to suggest this was the case.

Idealistic geography and its historical consequences

As an early adaptation of the ani-map concept, many of the Disney and Warner Brothers' productions during this period showcased the best of American landscapes. Animated characters became physically involved with the land and worked and lived near America's famous landmarks, placing them directly within the cultural fabric of the United States. The Schlesinger Studios became involved in making a series of travelogue spoofs, each of which demonstrate the adventure and sense of history citizens could get from touring around America, while the Disney shorts allowed their characters to feature as dedicated citizens of the United States, making an honest living.

The Riveter (1940)

There are many points of interest for scholars regarding the Donald Duck short, *The Riveter*. First, much like some of the animated shorts released by Warner Brothers, this short seems to promote a pro-government and pro-New Deal message. The short is based in the city of New York (we can see the Chrysler building in the background) in which a steady stream of employment was facilitated through the WPA and notably, around the time that this short was released, employment in New York was steadily increasing (Blumberg 1979). Despite the differences and conflict explored between the government and the animated world during the late 1930s, this animated production seems to accept that things have improved for the average American.

Singing the popular song 'Heigh Ho' from *Snow White and the Seven Dwarfs* (1937), Donald rounds a corner on a New York street to find an advertisement for a riveter on a construction site and takes the job. The short centres on Donald as he struggles with the height at which he is being forced to work and with the endless pressures of his boss, Pegleg Pete. Donald is, in this short, a citizen of the city of New York. This is an interesting departure from the average Disney short as most of Donald's previous encounters had been based on the West Coast.

Donald Duck travels around the country in 1940 and 1941, looking for and finding employment, indicative of many men's employment patterns during the 1930s.[5] This assured identification with the figure of Donald as a well-travelled citizen of the United States. An article in the *New York Times*, published a few months after this short, emphasizes the importance of the character, Donald Duck, for America (23 June 1940, x4).

Window Cleaners (1941)

Window Cleaners sees Donald return to the West Coast as a window cleaner, as the short opens in a city, implicitly suggested as San Francisco by the appearance of the red Golden Gate Bridge. He is in employment, which is again suggestive of a change in the economic situation within America. Furthermore, his presence in both East and West Coast cities is indicative of the nationwide improvement in the employment situation (Gordon 1994). Working with Pluto as his sidekick, Donald is soon engrossed in his work. He asserts himself as being himself as proud of American history and as a patriotic, dutiful American by creating the silhouette of George Washington out of the water he uses to clean the windows. While there could also be a reference to Nelson here, Donald's pride at assuming this shape is suggestive of an American historical figure.

What is also of interest in this cartoon is the extent to which Donald shows his own ideology has changed. Just a few years earlier, he was frustrated with the politics of America; however, as war nears, it seems he is at peace with being in America, working diligently in American cities and taking pride in his nationality. As each of the animated productions throughout this chapter seems to prove, there is a definitive shift in the tone of the cartoon shorts in these years, which

---

[5] For more information on employment patterns during the Depression, see Wheeler, Mark (1998). *The Economics of the Great Depression*. Kalamazoo: W.E. Upjohn Institute for Employment Research and Rose, Nancy E. (1994). *Put to Work: Relief Programs in the Great Depression*. New York: Monthly Review Press.

mirrors the ideological focus of Hollywood in these years. While previously demonstrating a feeling of isolation from mainstream politics, animation unites itself with the presidency again through its identification with the nation.

At the beginning of the Depression, Donald is lazy and an honorary member of the Idle Hour Club. As the mood of the country changes, he accepts this communitarian ideology, (albeit reluctantly) as his continuous grumbles seem to suggest. His patience runs out in *Self Control*; however, through many of these shorts, he finds his patience through a re-discovery of what it means to be American. He works hard, despite his many obstacles, and is distinctly placed within famous American cities. What is more, this short demonstrates an unbearable frustration with Pluto. Pluto is lazy, exhibiting many of the qualities Donald himself demonstrated at the beginning of the 1930s. However, Donald is consistently aggravated by Pluto's unwillingness to help him. On the other hand, Donald's willingness to work literally shapes his patriotism, a quality that we see carried through into the war years.

While the Disney shorts engage with nationalism through the employment and situation of the character Donald Duck, the Warner Brothers shorts showcased the best of America through travelogue spoofs, engaging with American history through its geography.

Detouring America (1939)

Detouring America is a celebration of all aspects of American tradition through its exploration of geography. At the outset, the cartoon declares itself completely neutral in political orientation and denies the fact that it is trying to portray any state in a positive or negative light (Figure 5.3). The Production Code Administration had no problem with the content (the short was passed for exhibition without comment two weeks before its release), but its directors were aware that many of its caricatures and landscapes could be considered ideologically provocative.[6]

The narrator opens the tour in New York, referring to its 'ever changing skyline' and its 'mighty skyscrapers'. Much like the Disney shorts, the cartoon draws attention to the power of these cities and their iconic landmarks. The 'monarch of them all' states the narrator, 'is the Empire State Building'. The narrator attaches grandeur to such structures, making them a focus of American pride. The short then moves to one of the nation's 'most outstanding military

---

[6]   PCA Certificate Number No. 00179, Warner Brothers Archives, University of Southern California.

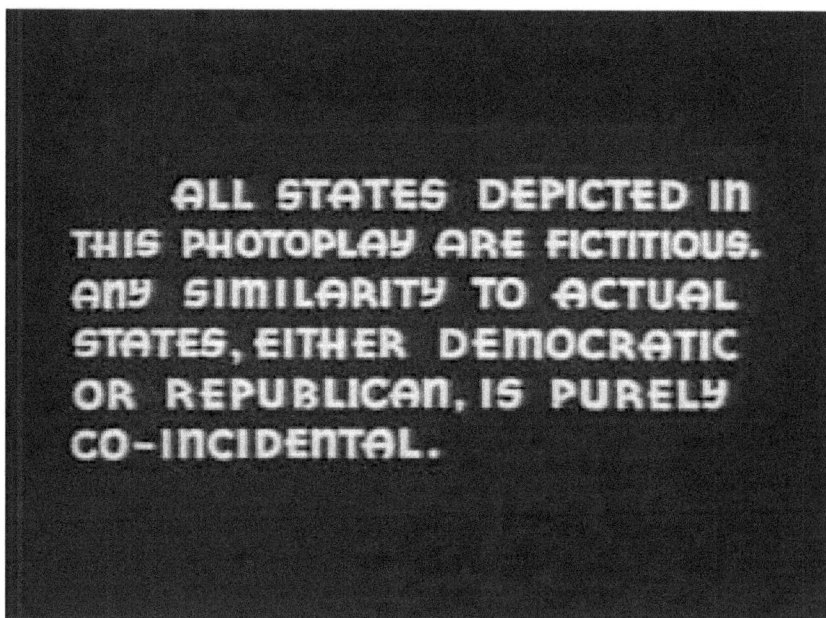

Figure 5.3 *Detouring America* (1939). Looney Tunes Golden Collection.

academies'. Given the structure of the building and its proximity to New York, it is likely the narrator is referring to the West Point Academy (Fleming, 1969).

The importance of discipline, obedience and strength are paramount in the narrator's description of this institution. The narrator also refers to the build-up of the armed forces in the United States, giving the impression of outstanding military strength. This short also provides gags surrounding the Everglades in Florida and a hitchhiking African American in Alaska. The Valley of the Giants in Oregon is also explored, referred to as one of nature's most 'breath-taking' sights. It celebrates the best of America by showing its most beautiful geographical assets, its awe-inspiring cities and military strength.

Aviation Vacation (1941)

Despite the fact that there is no mention of the US air force in this cartoon, patriotism is linked to air power from the outset. *Aviation Vacation* follows one particular plane on its journey across America. The plane and its hangar are adorned in red, white and blue. It is full of animated American citizens (notably people and not animals) and flies through California, which is shown to be uncharacteristically cold. The narrator, speaking to those aboard the plane as well as the audience of the cartoon, points out the faces of the 'famous Americans' carved into Mount Rushmore. The camera lingers on each of the figures for a few seconds at a time.

Each of the characters, as in the later war short *Scrap Happy Daffy* (1943), is accompanied by an American historical anthem, preserving the union of music with the medium of animation. This is even implicitly suggested as a technique in a further Disney memorandum of 1942, written by Robert Spencer Carr. While this was suggested for the Disney shorts, it seems the technique was being used in Warners' animation even before the war. Carr stated, that 'films could introduce these anthems, giving visual interpretations of the words'.[7] There is reference to a link between the music of the animation and what the audience is seeing on screen. This is, to an extent, evident here.

Aviation Vacation makes an explicit reference to the election of the previous year, providing the carvings of FDR and Wendell Wilkie as though they were also part of Mount Rushmore (Figure 5.4). While no particular candidate is

Figure 5.4 *Aviation Vacation* (1941). Looney Tunes Golden Collection.

[7] R. S. Carr, 'Ideas for a New South American Film Program,' 7 January 1942, p. 6, Motion Picture Society for the Americas Records, Margaret Herrick Library, Beverly Hills.

shown in a more favourable light, in combination with the later cartoons of this particular year, it becomes clear that the Schlesinger Studios and its characters had leanings towards Roosevelt's policies. Through the reference to 'real world' politics, a union is forged between the animated world and the real world, showing that the same political and social conditions are being experienced by animated characters and American citizens.

What makes America – National traditions

In the cultural study *Nationalism and American Thought*, Charles Alexander highlights the 'renewed interest in national values and traditions' within American society in the period under study (1969, 52). People became interested in what made America, *America*. This shift is referred to as a re-discovery of nationalism (Blumberg 1979, 184). However, what is perhaps most important is that animation and its characters became central to this celebration of American nationalism. Paraded like celebrities in front of their American audiences, cartoon characters were acknowledged as being as recognizable as their famous human counterparts.

Mickey's Polo Game (1936)

Mickey's Polo Game was one of the Disney Studios' first steps into the real world. While the shorts forming political, economic and social commentary discussed in Chapter 3 proved that the animated world was by no means immune to the pressures of Depression America, this animated short was the first to recognize that real people also existed within the animated world, again blurring the boundaries between the two. It is also the first time that animated characters are seen outside of their original contexts and, thus, suggesting their existence outside of their original, fantastical narratives.

The short begins amid a blur of red, white and blue, continuing to emphasize the power of Technicolor in transmitting a patriotic message to audiences. In combination with a brass band playing in the background, we are introduced to the nationally celebrated sport of polo. Equally as celebrated are the players introduced to us on the team. Mickey Mouse, Donald Duck, the Big Bad Wolf and Goofy ('The Goof') are paraded on the field and cheered by the audience in turn. As the attention draws to the audience, we see animated Hollywood movie stars and animated characters co-existing and interacting. The wartime shorts particularly capitalize on this link when acknowledging the existence of conflict within the fantastical landscape of the animated world.

Holiday Highlights (1940)

Connecting with a later war short *Fifth Column Mouse* (1943) with the song, 'Ain't We Got Fun', *Hollywood Highlights* makes further reference to the 'wonder' of living within the United States. The narrator introduces the 'well known holidays' of the year, starting with the New Year celebrations, moving to St Valentine's Day and then notably, George Washington's birthday. We see an animated George Washington and the cherry tree fill the screen. Much like *Old Glory*, this short celebrates American history and the important figures within it. Audiences see an animated interpretation of history as we see the child George Washington picking at the cherry tree and being reprimanded by his father.

The short animates Arbor Day, Mother's Day and Graduation month (during which the new graduate goes out to join the Bread Line) (see Figure 5.5). This could

Figure 5.5 *Holiday Highlights* (1940). Looney Tunes Golden Collection.

be interpreted as an explicit grievance with the unsolved unemployment problem as Congress pulled the funding for many of FDR's public works programmes in the early 1940s as the country drifted to war.[8] A further political commentary is offered when the short moves to discuss Thanksgiving. A calendar displayed to the audience denotes that Republicans and Democrats are to celebrate the Thanksgiving holiday on different days, a testament to the deep political divisions evident within society during the campaigning for the 1940 election between Wilkie and Roosevelt (*New York Times*, 31 August 1939, 6). Hoping to capitalize on the retail potential of having an earlier Thanksgiving, FDR moved the holiday forward by a week. Republicans were outraged by the move and began to refer to the later Thanksgiving as the 'Republican Thanksgiving' and the earlier as 'Franksgiving'. This shows that Warners' animators were willing, as early as 1940, to report on the country's political affairs. Much like many of the later military shorts, there is little ambiguity in this presentation.

The strength of America – Institutions of authority

In response to the growing threat from Europe, animation also began to assert America's authority and position in the world. This reflected a shift in cultural tradition and in America's foreign policy. Following the so-called 'quarantine' speech in October 1937, Roosevelt began to challenge isolationist sentiment within the country. He suggested that the nations of the world should unite and 'quarantine' the disease of 'world lawlessness' (Heale 1999, 45). Just three years later, following the outbreak of war in Europe and the surrender of France in 1940, opinion polls in the United States were showing an increase from 50 per cent to 64 per cent in favour of peacetime conscription. While facing pressure from isolationists in Congress, Roosevelt introduced the first ever peacetime draft in US history, passing a selective service law for all men between the ages of twenty-one and thirty-five (Dallek 1979, 249). This was swiftly followed by the introduction of the Lend-Lease scheme. Roosevelt justified Lend-Lease to the American people in a fireside chat on 17 December 1940, stating it was 'essential' to national security. The scheme was passed

---

[8]   See, in particular, Cochran, Thomas C. (1968). *The Great Depression and World War Two*. Glenview: Foresman and Young, Roland (1972). *Congressional Politics in the Second World War*. New York: Da Capo Press.

in March 1941 (Ambrose and Brinkley 1997). This shift towards military cooperation with the Allies against the Nazi threat was directly reflected within the animated world. Animation showcased American military strength and pride in its armed forces. Given the interventionist spirit of these cartoons, much like those discussed in Chapter 4, it is extraordinary that they were allowed to be put into production by the Hays Office.

The Fighting Sixty Ninth Half (1941)

The Fighting Sixty Ninth Half does not involve the audience in the war displayed within the animated world, unlike *Meet John Doughboy*, released just six months later. However, it does suggest that the characters within the animated world are more than ready to take up arms against any external threat.

The short opens in a forest, where two ants, one red and one black, fight over an olive at a leftover picnic. Unable to compromise, the ants mobilize their forces and go to war. There are many indications within this cartoon that perhaps the red ant forces are meant to depict the British. For example, their air force, the Royal Flying Ants air force featured seems suggestive of the Royal Air Force (RAF). The narrative also goes 'behind the lines' of the red ants, while the black ants are left to be the enemy forces.

In many ways, the type of warfare suggested within this short is indicative of the First World War. Trenches are built on both sides, surrounding the picnic, indicated to be a 'no man's land'. The ants are told by their general to go 'over the top'. The ant soldiers even use gas in their confrontation with the enemy. These references seem to imply that there is no difference in the enemy faced for America in 1941, than the one faced during the First World War. When the humans return to take away the rest of the picnic, all that is left for the ants to fight over, is a large slab of butter. The generals agree to hold a peace conference to try and split the butter, but neither can agree on the way that the slab should be divided as each wants a bigger piece for their country. Fighting breaks out once more (Figure 5.6) and the war between the two groups of ants continues. No resolution is offered.

This cartoon seems to offer a commentary on the futility of negotiations with the Axis powers. Released following the fall of France and a few months before the invasion of the Soviet Union, it seems to suggest that fighting is sometimes the only way that a conflict can really be resolved. This was in sharp contrast to the popular mood within Congress and shows direct alignment with the cases made for further intervention in Europe by FDR during this year.

Figure 5.6 *The Fighting Sixty Ninth Half* (1941). Looney Tunes Golden Collection.

Meet John Doughboy (1941)

Meet John Doughboy was released on 5 July 1941 and its timing could not have been more appropriate for the increasingly interventionist nature of Roosevelt's foreign policies and for its poignancy both in America and in the world. Released the day after Independence Day and just a short week following Germany's invasion of the Soviet Union, this animated short is a persuasive piece of propaganda, and yet is free from government intervention in its production. Its narrative calls for Americans to support the war and oppose anti-draft legislation.

The cartoon opens in a movie theatre where Porky is introduced to the audience as a draftee. Porky confesses that the theatre will show them some movies full of military secrets and asks for any fifth columnists to leave the audience. Following the highly publicized speech of Charles Lindbergh declaring that the United States was not in any danger of military attack, Roosevelt had grown increasingly wary of 'fifth columnists' and had become suspicious that some of Lindbergh's supporters were, in fact, fifth columnists trying to sow domestic discord (Dallek 1979). This was also reflected in a flow of spy movies released in Hollywood by the Schlesinger distributors, Warner Brothers, such as *Espionage Agent* (1939) (Dick 1985).

The curtain then falls upon an animated newsreel, which advertises America's Defense Effort, animating the conversion of iron ore into military weapons. The narrator states the importance of air power and the production of many different types of aircraft. The aircraft hangar that houses the planes is animated, and smiles at being able to play its part. The short also refers to the study of RAF planes in American factories, making an explicit link to the Lend-Lease scheme and the 'special relationship' between Britain and the United States. The spitfire is one such charge, which is shown to literally spit fire. This personification, used throughout the 1930s to allow understanding of complex concepts, is used here to a great effect. Most of the weaponry tried and tested in this short is shown to be 'alive'. For example, the anti-tank gun acts like an elephant. This is again used throughout the wartime shorts, proof that the blueprint for animated propaganda was in use prior to the attack on Pearl Harbor.

Animated men discuss their chances at being called into service. The cartoon glorifies conscription, referring to the 'outdoor life' and 'regular hours'. It even advertises that the recruits receive good meals. Describing the military equipment, the machine gun is transformed into a chicken. Even horses raised in South America are mentioned, who salsa their way across the battlefield. Incidentally, many of the spoof soldiers and the gags utilized in these animated newsreel spots seem to provide a foundation upon which the character of Private Snafu was later built.

A 'land-destroyer' more powerful than any other weapon ever invented is revealed to be Jack Benny, driven by Rochester. This demonstrates that much like the characters of Donald Duck and Mickey Mouse, their Hollywood colleagues in the entertainment industry were by no means immune from the seemingly inevitable fight against the Nazis. On the contrary, they are happy to do their part and 'assist' the armed forces. On another level, this also provides proof of the interventionist nature of Hollywood. Animation vindicates the worries raised by Gerald Nye. Giving an added edge of realism to the cartoon, more newspaper headlines are quoted.

The audience reads that President Roosevelt is testing the defence strength of the United States. Not only does this ally the president with Hollywood, but it also distinctly separates him from the heavily influential isolationist sentiment within Congress and the America-First movement. Despite their differences concerning economic and social policy at the end of the 1930s, animators were happy to validate the president's concern with events in Europe. Moreover, they were ready to rally behind America's armed forces, despite the fact that America was not even fully involved in the war against the fascist powers. As the armed forces are, as narrated in this short, at the president's command, the short also gives the impression of complete loyalty and obedience within the armed forces. According to the world of animation, there is no dissension within the country about their willingness to fight the war, despite the fact that the conflicts within Congress during 1941 on this issue were widespread.

The short then moves to an explicitly interventionist commentary, urging the audience for action, using the symbolic power of the Statue of Liberty. The narrator asks the audience, 'Are we safe from air attack?' while displaying a picture of the skyline in Manhattan, including Lady Liberty (Figure 5.7). The camera moves into the picture, animating the action within the shot. Aerial bombers move towards New York, but Lady Liberty shoots them down before they take action. 'Why isn't something being done?' the narrator asks the audience.

Using the power of the many shorts released in 1939 and 1940, showcasing the importance and symbolism of America's landmarks, this sequence clearly promotes interventionism. Given the number of times that the Statue of Liberty

Figure 5.7 *Meet John Doughboy* (1941). Looney Tunes Golden Collection.

is utilized in the wartime shorts as a symbol for the United States (see chapters 6 and 7) its use here is particularly important. This sequence proves unequivocally that animation was using these symbols before war even broke out. In Robert Spencer Carr's memorandum of January 1942, he refers to the need for the creation of an animated character to symbolize America, stating that this figure-head should be a 'cross between Lady Liberty and the Virgin Mary'.[9] This icon had already been created by 1941. The fact that Lady Liberty is also the first to take up arms against the enemy bombers also highlights the implied morality of the fight against Nazism.

Despite the power of this symbolism, there is much to be said for the use of narration in this short. Questions are directed explicitly towards the audience, inciting them into action. The power of narration is also mentioned in Carr's memorandum and is used extensively during the wartime shorts but here, it is used *before* the attack on Pearl Harbor. The audience are told how to interpret the images they are seeing. There is no room for ambiguity. This makes it all the more astounding that the Production Code Certificate for Meet John Doughboy is dated 11 July 1941, nearly a week after its premiere.[10]

Rookie Revue (1941)

Rookie Revue also spares no ambiguity in its overall interventionist message. Released just months after Nye's 'witch hunt' through Hollywood due to the explicit political undertones of its live action feature films, this cartoon can be read as an endorsement of the armed forces. It opens with a billboard advertisement for the army and the audience is led to follow the lives of the recruits at 'Fort Nix', described as typical of the army camps throughout the United States. The narrative of *Rookie Revue* claims that joining the army is an exceptional, patriotic thing for the average American to do. It is advocating intervention in the war in Europe. While its narrator does not offer the audience a question, it does seem to provide the answer: join the army to fight in case America's shores are invaded and its ideals come under attack. This question is also prevalent in the wartime animated shorts. Lady Liberty in particular is used

[9] R. S. Carr, 'Ideas for a New South American Film Program,' 7 January 1942, p. 37, Motion Picture Society for the Americas Records, Margaret Herrick Library, Beverly Hills.

[10] Production Code Certificates, Box No. 00179, Warner Brothers Archives, University of Southern California.

Figure 5.8 *Rookie Revue* (1941). Looney Tunes Golden Collection.

to convey the importance of American ideals when put against the fascist threat in the Disney short *Der Fuehrer's Face* (United States, 1943, dir. Jack Kinney).

Army life is followed through with a series of gags throughout. However, what is most provocative about this short is the appearance of a cartoon character that became very famous during the war. While many jokes are included as to the training of army recruits (many of which were reused during the SNAFU series) the overriding impression is of extreme military strength. The short showcases the various different types of bomb, anti-aircraft and anti-tank guns and aeroplanes utilized by the military. The ideal soldier is also pitted against the useless army recruit, who has his unnamed debut within this short. We see the undeniable blueprint for the army recruit Private Snafu (Figure 5.8).

Conclusion

As this chapter has shown, by the time America became involved in the Second World War, if not as early as 1938, animation was being read ideologically. Disney, Schlesinger and their audiences recognized the power of the animated medium to carry messages about what was going on in society. While Disney had an interest in the power and symbolism of his characters, for example in an 1939 interview he spoke of Mickey Mouse as being symbolic of American independence, Schlesinger did not particularly care for the content of his productions. All that concerned him was that his animation was successful, popular and profitable.[11] However, he changed the content of his shorts to adhere to audience response and demand. One cannot ignore the fact that the audience responded positively to these changes. The highest-grossing film of 1938 was the Disney full length animated feature *Snow White and the Seven Dwarfs*. People identified with the messages within Disney animation and as observed by *Hollywood Spectator* in 1939, animation was an expanding medium, growing in popularity every year noted by the increased orders for Schlesinger productions in 1939 (24 June 1939, 11).

What also seems to be of note in these particular animated shorts is the extent to which animation and the real world were developing a shared experience of life. This would be important during the War, as each world experienced the hardships of the conflict. However, the narratives of these shorts recognized and celebrated America's proudest achievements in these years. The Disney Studios and the Schlesinger Studios ensured that the best of America was recognized in the animated world. Many of these productions were narrated, proving the ideological power of narration referenced by Robert Spencer Carr during the war. They told their audiences exactly how to feel about what they were seeing on screen.

The techniques in which animation channelled patriotic feeling within society during the later years of the 1930s were invaluable during the war. They were a combination of the visual markers shown in the early 1930s productions and the sophisticated ideological narrative of the social and economic commentary seen in the mid-1930s productions. They also demonstrated the international awareness of the late 1930s, actively campaigning for intervention. This intervention was couched within a nationalist rhetoric banished from mainstream Hollywood features.

---

[11] See 'An Interview with Walt Disney,' *Fortune* magazine, 1 May 1939, p. 46 and 'Interview with Robert Clampett' (1970) *Funnyworld*, 12.

6

Animation at War: Disney, Warner Brothers and the US Government 1941–3

'Well you want to get this message over,' Walt said. 'I've given you Donald Duck. At our studio, that's the equivalent of giving you Clark Gable out of the MGM stable. Donald Duck is known by the American public. He'll open doors to the theatres. They won't be running a cartoon of Mr. Taxpayer; they'll be running a Donald Duck cartoon.'

Thomas 1976, 181

Animation was instantly mobilized for war. Just one day after the Japanese invasion of Pearl Harbor, Walt Disney received a call from his studio manager, informing him that five hundred army troops were moving onto the Disney soundstage at Burbank. They stayed there for eight months (Gabler 2007, 381). By the end of 1942, over 75 per cent of Disney's film output was for government work, making his studios the primary Hollywood contributor towards government training and propaganda films (ibid., 401). By the end of 1943, this number reached 95 per cent. From his work for the National Film Board of Canada, Disney had proved that he could utilize animation for the purposes of education.

Each of the films he had made in contribution, *Stop That Tank* (United States, 1942, no director's credit), an instructional film on the anti-tank rifle, *Four Methods of Flush Riveting* (United States, 1940, no director's credit) and *The Thrifty Pig* (United States, 1941, no director's credit) had all been enormously successful, receiving even the accreditation of well-known documentary filmmaker, John Grierson.[1] After the Japanese attack, the American government

---

[1] Accredited documentary filmmaker John Grierson was appointed as First Commissioner of the National Film Board of Canada in 1939. For more information on his position and the films produced for Canada during the war, see Evans, Gary (1984). *John Grierson and the National Film Board: The Politics of Wartime Propaganda*. Toronto: University of Toronto Press and Jones, D. B. (1981). *Movies and Memoranda: An Interpretive History of the National Film Board of Canada*. Ottawa: Canadian Film Institute.

was quick to capitalize on the effectiveness of the medium of animation as a channel for persuasion and for emphasizing the importance of patriotism and sacrifice in the wartime climate. As Bell et al. have argued, 'The US State recognised the potential for "direct propaganda films couched in the simplicity of animation"' (Bell, Haas and Sells 1995, 5).

The contribution of the Hollywood studios towards the propaganda cause during the Second World War has been well documented. Works such as Clayton Koppes and Gregory Black's *Hollywood Goes to War* and Bernard F. Dick's *The Star Spangled Screen* are seminal in painting an overall picture of the extent and nature of Hollywood's contribution to the war effort. Indeed, animation is mentioned in these works as having taken up the cause of nationalism as avidly as other studios (Taylor 2003). The contribution of the American motion picture industry to the US war propaganda effort was considerable. Koppes and Black paint a picture of unwavering loyalty to the US participation in the war, inferring that, 'Blatant morale building propaganda was a staple of its plot, speeches, and visual images' (2000, 2).

Despite the extensive role played by Hollywood in keeping morale high and sustaining unity at home and abroad in the face of enemies, much has been made of the turbulent relationship between Hollywood and the US government.[2] It has been argued that despite his enthusiasm for US participation in the war, Roosevelt did not set much store by propaganda itself. He created three conflicting departments, including the Office of Strategic Services (OSS), Office of War Information (OWI) and the CIAA, all with their own crossed aims, purposes and authorities, all of which desired the production of films to support their motives and objectives. Lowell Mellett, the head of the OWI's Bureau of Motion Pictures, and Nelson Poynter, the go-between of OWI and the studios, attempted to ensure smooth relationships between the Hollywood moguls and the federal government.

Objectives were issued to ensure that films were produced that ran in line with the government's most prominent policies. Films had to be related to the cause of fighting, the enemy, the United Nations, the solidarity of the home front and the fighting forces. By 1943, all studios except for Paramount, allowed the OWI to read all scripts before production (Koppes and Black 1977, 103). This level of control was extended to all studios, including even the Walt Disney

---

[2] See Winkler, Allen (1978). *The Politics of Propaganda: The OWI 1942–1945*. New Haven: Yale University Press and Culbert, David, ed. (1990). *Film and Propaganda in America: A Documentary History*. New York: Greenwood Press.

Studios, for their production of cartoon shorts. No production exhibited in theatres throughout the Second World War went without the approval of the US government, although as Colonel K. B. Lawton, chief of the Army Pictorial Division has stated, 'I have never found such a group of whole hearted willing patriotic people trying to do something for their Government' (Sklar 1978, 213). Using the framework laid out by the OWI, Hollywood's studios 'went to war with gusto' (Koppes and Black 2000). Determined to pick up the slack from where they had fallen behind Germany and Japan, whose propaganda agencies had been churning out material since its inception, Hollywood used the government's endorsement of its work to its full potential (Welch 2001). Similarly, the government capitalized on Hollywood's power and popularity to commission propaganda films for its own purposes, mobilizing the American people for war.

Disney was among the first to be approached. The day after Pearl Harbor, a navy official contacted the Disney Studios, offering a contract for twenty films on aircraft and warship identification at a total cost of ninety thousand dollars (Barrier 1999, 368). The Department of Agriculture, too, had offered Disney a contract for a film promoting Lend-Lease and even Frank Capra enlisted Disney's help to make the animated excerpts for his *Why We Fight* series (Gabler 2007, 388).

The first animated film to be made under government instruction after the United States declared war against the Axis powers was not in fact, Disney, but made by the Schlesinger Studios who distributed through Warner Brothers. While the Donald Duck short, *The New Spirit*, was the first to be released, Schlesinger's *Any Bonds Today?* (1942) was finished just a week after the attack on Pearl Harbor. An article in *Daily Variety* dated 14 December 1942 reported, 'Before the war began, Schlesinger pointed out he put Bugs Bunny in *Any Bonds Today* – an animated short for the Treasury bond drive and Secretary Morgenthau had written a letter of thanks' (7). Schlesinger mentions the desperation of the animated studios to acquire government work 'along lines being pursued by Walt Disney' (ibid.).

However, the issue at the forefront of the studio's production was *how* exactly they would translate their entertaining animated medium into a vehicle for the transmission of ideals. How could animation be used for the purposes of propaganda? The techniques utilized by the Disney Studios, and by Warner Brothers found their origins in the films of the 1930s. It is through comparison of the pre-war and war material that these similarities come to light.

Taxes to beat the Axis

The New Spirit (1942)

While FDR himself had little interest in the systematic use of propaganda, Secretary of the Treasury, Henry Morgenthau fronted the campaign to persuade Americans to help finance the war (Blum 1976). In the week of the attack on Pearl Harbor, John P. Sullivan, the Assistant Secretary of the Treasury, contacted Disney to make a film to encourage Americans to pay their income taxes. Due to the fact that the first set of payments for the film was due on 15 March 1942, the Disney Studios was given the deadline of 15 February, allowing the staff only a month to write the script, compose the music and complete the animation (Gabler 2007, 384). Disney agreed to produce the cartoon for eighty thousand dollars. Wilfred Jackson, the short's director, remembered the pressure the studio was under to produce the short in an interview with Michael Barrier in 1978. He stated:

> Our little crew working on the picture pitched in that first day and each of us kept on working until he was too tired to work anymore. Then he went home to sleep, whatever time of whatever day it was, and whenever he woke up he came back to work again, whatever time of the day, or night, of whatever day that might be. This caused some interesting problems for a director, who was also working that way, in coordinating the efforts of the various artists and technicians who actually made the cartoon. We had to invent a completely new approach, for us at Disney's – a production routine that would save every minute possible in each step on the way to the final answer print. (*Funnyworld Magazine*, 1978)

As it turned out, the Studios needn't have worried. *The New Spirit* was produced in record time and as Disney storyliner, Richard Huemer recalled, to great praise. He remembered, '[Morgenthau] was very pleased when we took the boards to him, very pleased. I remember that we tried to do it in the Baby Weems technique, limited animation. We actually ran Baby Weems for Morgenthau and he just shook his head and said, "No, I want the Blue Plate special." He wanted full animation. Which he finally got.'[3] Disney boasted to the treasury when the short was finally turned in mid-January that the turnaround on *The New Spirit*

---

[3] 'From This You Are Making a Living?' An Oral History of Richard Huemer. Interview with Joe Adamson, 1968, American Film Institute.

was the fastest in Disney history for an animated short and in turn, they had received the fastest ever service from Technicolor (Shale 1978, 28).

Audiences were immediately drawn into the patriotism of the cartoon by the memorable theme song, 'Yankee Doodle Spirit', written by Oliver Wallace. Wallace would later go on to write the immensely popular 'Der Fuehrer's Face', another theme tune to the Oscar winning short by the same name. The music plays over the opening credits, immediately drawing the audience into the musical foray of the animated world.

From their experiences in the Depression-era cartoons, it is clear that the Disney Studios had learnt the power of music. Robert Spencer Carr was placed as head of the Walt Disney Training Films Unit by Disney himself in March 1941 and was subsequently the lead contact at the studio for the films made by government contract (Gabler 2007, 383). In his memorandum on government work, dated January 1942, during the production period for the treasury short, he wrote of the importance of a musical score: '[Songs] are counted on to help the film short subjects suggested. The idea here is that the music track on all these pictures should not be merely appropriate music – but should consciously be made part of the propaganda.'[4] This was a conscious decision by the Disney Studios and evidently was used in *Three Little Wolves* to foster unity after the pigs victory over the Wolf as we hear *Yankee Doodle Went to Town* over their closing march as well as the well-known rallying cry for external enemies, 'Who's Afraid of the Big Bad Wolf'. After the song plays on the radio, Donald valiantly salutes his wireless and we see the American flag shining in both of his eyes. Disney makes use of colour throughout the short, much like Warner Brothers in *Old Glory*, to emphasize the importance of the red, white and blue of the flag (Figure 6.1).

What is also of interest in this cartoon is the reappearance of the wireless. The last encounter Donald Duck had with his radio ended in violence, as Donald was frustrated with its 'advice' and smashed it to pieces. From *Self Control* (1938), the audience immediately has an association with government in Donald cartoons where the wireless is shown. Naturally, this stems from Roosevelt's fireside chats but also from wartime advertising and newsreels on the radio. In this cartoon, the wireless acts as government as well; however, Donald shows a change in his character. There is patience and willingness in his demeanour now the country

---

[4] R. S. Carr, 'List of Suggested Subjects,' 1942, p. 6, f. 22, Motion Picture Society for the Americas Records, Margaret Herrick Library, Beverly Hills.

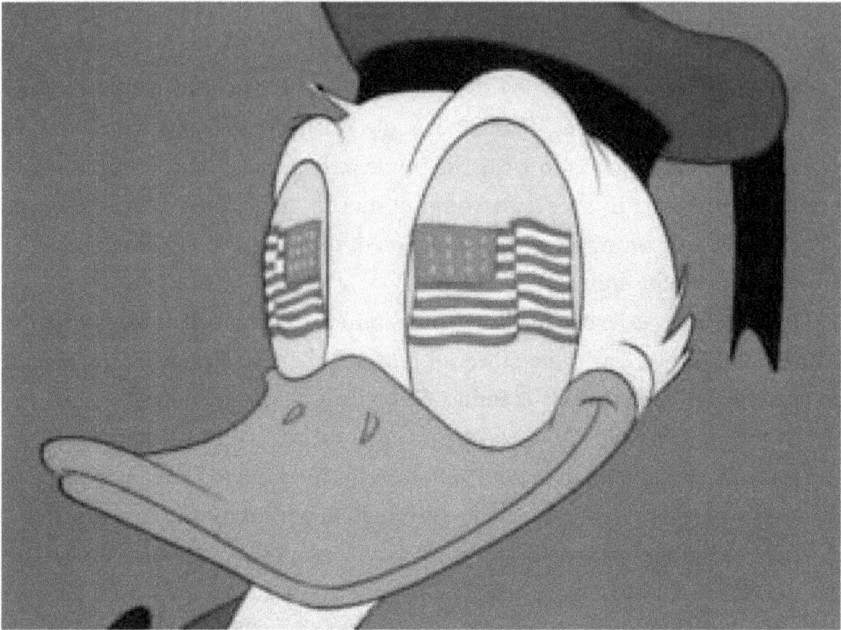

Figure 6.1 *The New Spirit* (1942). Walt Disney Treasures.

is at war and he is willing to listen. Much like *Self Control*, Donald engages in a dialogue with the voice on the radio, which states that 'our very shores have been attacked'. Donald is outraged, and throwing his hat on the floor, exclaims, 'That is not right!' After being told that he is needed by his country, Donald quickly retrieves his stash of weaponry and gets ready to attack.

The voice on the radio tells Donald that as a patriotic American, there is something he can do to help his country. He does not need to fight, but he does need to pay his income taxes. At first, Donald is reluctant and does not see why it is important but after hearing the clever tag line for the short, 'Taxes to beat the Axis', he is more than willing to pay his way.

The short then takes on many of the traits of Disney and Warner Brothers' earlier instructional films from before the war. Such ideas originated in the animation of the 1930s. For example, the animated mortgage roll in *Porky's Poppa* seems relevant here. Difficult and daunting prospects for the American audience are given animated form. This animated short simplifies a difficult and complicated process. In *The New Spirit*, the stamp, accounting pad and pen are all personified and help Donald to complete his income tax form. Even the mailbox that Donald rushes past when he is going to post his form is 'alive'.

However, moved by the 'new spirit', Donald rushes to hand deliver his income tax form and cheque to Washington. We also see a more developed version of Carr's 'ani-map', here. These were seen in primitive form with the nationalist location shots of the late 1930s cartoons and in the patriotic Warner Brothers short, *Old Glory*.

The New Spirit then moves to a darker montage sequence, in which the voice from the radio transforms into a more general narrator. We see the chimney of a munitions factory chirp out steam. Similar to the early 1930s cartoons, personification is utilized to great effect here. These dull mundane objects associated with the munitions industry are transformed into animated creatures and are thus made more endearing to the American public. The chimney even wears Uncle Sam's hat. We see the guns produced in these factories used against enemy ships.

The Disney Studios continued to use simple symbolism from the early 1930s cartoons to deliver these messages. For example, no caricature or enemy is utilized at this stage for the Japanese. Only their flag is used to represent their nation. Interestingly, there were no plans for an ideological treatment of the Japanese nation. The primary source documents simply suggest that Nazism as an ideology was the only political system that would come under direct scrutiny from Disney's animation. The narrator of the short also makes reference to the threat from the air, naming them the 'birds of prey'. There is an allusion here to the interventionist shorts of the late 1930s, which portrayed threats to the animated characters as birds from the air. Even the menace from under the sea is animated as the Nazi U-Boats are made to look like great white sharks.

The short concludes with a slow pan to the sky, in which the American flag is emblazoned in the clouds, associating the United States with moral righteousness and to a certain extent, heaven. This association was also made during the cartoons of the 1930s, particularly evident in the battle for Donald's conscience that took place in *Donald's Better Self* and the more potent, *Donald's Decision*. The Angel embodied the spirit of the United States and the Devil was associated with Nazi Germany, or in the case of this short, the Axis powers.

The New Spirit is an astonishing cartoon, and in many respects can be seen as an amalgamation of all of the techniques used in the 1930s shorts to convey ideology: music, colour, Donald's character and the ani-maps. The subtlety of ideological narrative, however, is reserved for the later propagandistic shorts.

The New Spirit was an incredibly effective cartoon.[5] As Gabler states, 'By one estimate, over thirty-two million Americans eventually saw the film at nearly twelve thousand theatres and of these viewers, according to a Gallup poll, thirty-seven per cent said that the film had had an effect on their willingness to pay taxes and eighty-six per cent felt that Disney should make shorts for the government on other subjects' (Gabler 2007, 385).

This statistic in itself proves that animation was viewed as an effective medium for propaganda by the American people. Trade press reviews of *The New Spirit* seem to recognize the techniques used by animation in this short in order to convey meaning. The review states that the short 'serves its purpose well', and adds that 'colour, music and entertainment combine to convey the idea with graphic effect' (*Motion Picture Daily*, 29 January 1942, 4). Bosley Crowther of the *New York Times* described the film as 'the most effective of the morale films yet released by the Government' (27 January 1942, 25).

The American people were thus incredibly receptive to animated propaganda and yet the same techniques were used to convey ideology in the 1930s. The only thing that had changed was the fact that America was now at war.

One who was not happy with the finished product was Disney himself. As Wilfred Jackson recalled, 'I do not believe I have ever seen Walt so completely frustrated when viewing one of the cartoons I directed for him' (*Funnyworld Magazine*, 1978). The animation in *The New Spirit* fell far short of the quality he was used to delivering in his productions. By his own admission, after spending too long on *Pinocchio* and *Fantasia*, he had to concede that the wartime productions worked to a different quantity and quality scale than his peacetime productions. His animation was not going to be perfect. Disney also lost an enormous amount of money making the film. As he explained to *Motion Picture Daily* after the treasury short's premiere, '[At] Radio City Music Hall, the booking on one of the regular short subjects had been reduced from two weeks to one to make room for the income tax short. The same thing is happening all over the country, with the result that about fifty thousand dollars in bookings will be lost completely' (10 February 1942). He also lost money in the production of extra prints of the film and through all the overtime put in by his staff to get the film out to their tight schedule.

---

[5] Congress was unfortunately not receptive to the film. John Taber of New York stated publicly before the House, 'They have hired him to make a moving picture that is going to cost $80,000 to persuade people to pay their income taxes. My God! Can you think of anything that would come nearer to making people hate to pay their income tax than the knowledge that $80,000, that should go for a bomber, is to be spent for a moving picture to entertain people?'

While seemingly bitter about the costs of the production at the time, Disney later recounted to Hollywood reporter, Hedda Hopper that he 'didn't expect to [receive full payment]'. He explained, 'We were in war and I wanted to do what I could. The guys who went to battle were lucky to come out with their lives. This was war – this was something we could do and we did it.'[6]

Any Bonds Today? (1942)

Donald Duck was not the only cartoon character to get involved in campaigning for the treasury. Bugs Bunny first appeared in Schlesinger's cartoons as early as 1938 with the popular Warner Brothers character Porky Pig (Maltin 1980, 241). He was first sketched by animator Ben Hardaway and later appeared with adversary, Elmer Fudd in *Elmer's Candid Camera* (1940). He took on his more popular form as late as 1940.[7]

While Bugs Bunny's personality evolved far too late for him to capture the imagination of the American people in Depression, unlike his animated predecessor, Porky Pig, he quickly became a star in his own right. Steve Schneider describes this progression as running alongside Warners' take on personality animation as it evolved 'to a different and eminently hipper level'. He argues, 'The turnabout could not have been more extreme: where cartoons had been soft and frolicsome, Warners' made them hard and brassy and confrontational' (1994, 21). However, it was exactly this confrontational style which made Bugs Bunny the perfect host for a war bond cartoon.

Unlike the dialogue with the 'Government' evidenced in *The New Spirit*, *Any Bonds Today?* capitalizes on an explicit relationship between Bugs and the audience and is thus able to build on foundations of the 1930s cartoons to make a direct connection to the audience. The self-awareness evident in the Schlesinger animated shorts of the 1930s that we witness in *Milk and Money*, *Porky's Poppa* and even in the early politicized Bosko cartoons, such as *Bosko in Person*, is used to great effect in this wartime animation to create a new dynamic (Cohen 1985, 36). Unlike the Disney shorts, these characters could be blunt in their patriotic pleas. It was the way that they had been developed.

However, for all of the differences in the characteristic approach to the war bond cartoon, *Any Bonds Today* and *The New Spirit* utilize many of

[6] 'Interview with Walt Disney', 19 January 1962, Hedda Hopper Papers, f. 599, Margaret Herrick Library, Beverly Hills.
[7] See *A Wild Hare* (1940).

the same techniques. Exploiting the impact of American history used in *Old Glory*, Bugs walks towards the audience against a backdrop of George Washington hoisting the American flag through the clouds. Similar to the closing scene of *The New Spirit*, the idea of the United States representing moral righteousness through the power of religious imagery is exercised. Without any need for introductions, Bugs bluntly tells the audience that the 'tall man with the high hat will soon be coming down your way'. He then puts on Uncle Sam's hat and begins to dance. He continues with a musical interlude, singing 'Any Bonds Today?'

Again, similar to *The New Spirit*, this short uses music to effect as Bugs launches into a musical rendition of the Irving Berlin song *Any Bonds Today?* As stated by Carr, music is of the utmost importance in animation and for arguably the first time, Warner Brothers utilizes an explicitly Disney technique in order to convey ideology specifically linked to animation. Previously, the Warner Brothers cartoons only utilized songs from Warner Brothers' films (Maltin 1980, 220). Towards the end of the cartoon, Bugs slips into a performance of *Any Stamps Today*, as Al Jolson. While the reason for the parody is unknown, especially given Al Jolson was considered a Hollywood 'has been' by the time of the war, audiences at the time did not mind the racial stereotyping evident in this cartoon and in fact, 'responded well to its overall message' (*Hollywood Reporter,* 1 May 1942, 550). The cartoon later includes Porky Pig, dressed in naval uniform, alongside Bugs and Elmer Fudd (in an army uniform) all singing the rest of the song together, asking the American audience to 'buy their share of freedom', against a staged backdrop of bombers and naval ships (see Figure 6.2).

Any Bonds Today? should be noted for employing the patriotic techniques of the Warners' cartoons of the late 1930s and early 1940s discussed in Chapter 5 through its use of colour, American institutions and American history. Clampett connects these patriotic markers to the animated world as in *Old Glory*. However, there is a subtle difference between the integration of the cartoon characters and the battlefield which is of interest here. While Donald involves himself directly in the war effort by filling out his tax form and marching over to Washington, the Warner Brothers cartoon characters, Bugs, Porky and Elmer simply 'put on a show' to the American people regarding their involvement in the war. This highlights the differences in animation techniques used by the different studios. Warner Brothers' characters remain self-consciously animated, they are not *real* and, in this wartime setting, they do not yet exist as characters *at*

Figure 6.2 *Any Bonds Today?* (1942). Looney Tunes Golden Collection.

war. However, as the conflict continues, Warner Brothers integrated the Disney style of character involvement into their productions to create a real connection between the animated world and the real world.

Spirit of '43 (1943)

Despite the conflict surrounding payment for the first treasury film, *The New Spirit*, Disney was approached to construct its sequel, *Spirit of '43* within six months (Shale 1978, 34). While he was opposed to reusing footage from its predecessor, Morgenthau and Lowell Mellett, head of the domestic branch for the Bureau of Motion Pictures, only agreed to give Disney twenty thousand dollars to make some new scenes to be tagged onto the beginning of *The New Spirit*.

The short opens on the chimneys for the munitions factories audiences witnessed in *The New Spirit*. However, the camera then pans to Donald, who is busy counting dollar bills in his hands after having just received his wage. The narrator then tells us that in the mind of the average worker, two separate personalities live side by side. Out of mid-air, a thrifty Scotsman (which interestingly provided the prototype for the later animated character Scrooge McDuck) tells Donald to save his money. However, Donald's money literally burns a hole in his pocket and he is tempted into spending it by 'The Spendthrift'. This character is simply a Donald Duck dressed in expensive clothing. This 'version' of Donald puts his arm around his real-life double and takes him to the 'Idle Hour Club', where posters tell him to relax and spend his money. While Donald is contemplating how to spend his money, the Scotsman pulls him away from the Idle Hour Club and presents him with a calendar, showcasing the date 'March 15th' – the deadline for income taxes.

The calendar then presents all subsequent deadlines for payment of American income taxes. The narrator puts the need for extra taxes down to 'Hitler and Hirohito'. Noticeably, the enthusiastic fervour of wartime Donald felt during *The New Spirit* has disappeared. 'Taxes are higher than ever before,' notes the narrator.

The Scotsman Donald asks the real Donald if he 'wants to forget our fighting men?' to which Donald is outraged and replies, 'No, Sir!' The spendthrift continues to tempt Donald away from the 'correct' path and the two literally fight over Donald's conscience until the spendthrift tumbles into the 'Idle Hour Club'. The 'camera' pauses and the swing doors of the club are revealed as the Nazi swastika (Figure 6.3).

Startled, Donald then looks towards the Scotsman Donald, who has crashed into a wall, revealing the American flag. Donald contemplates his choices as narrated, 'Spend for the Axis or save for Taxes?' Disney also transforms the spendthrift into a comical Donald Duck version of Hitler with a swastika tie, black hair and short black moustache. The figure is also smoking a cigar, the smoke clouds from which also spiral into swastikas. Donald walks up to the spendthrift Hitler and hits him back into the Idle Hour Club, leaving a 'V' sign outside the door where the swastika once was. This was associated with the 'V for Victory' campaign throughout the United States.

The key concept of this cartoon is the battle for Donald's conscience. This conflict, between Good and Evil, is taken directly from the 1930s cartoons, also featuring Donald Duck. *Donald's Better Self* and *Donald's Decision*, and, indeed, *Mickey's Pal Pluto* reference this fight over Donald. The short personifies these ideals, the spendthrift is transformed into a Nazi, Scotsman Donald is transformed into democracy, and the sway of Donald's own ideology is reflected

Figure 6.3 *Spirit of '43* (1943). Walt Disney Treasures.

in his eyes which feature a swastika and a US flag. In the early 1930s, in the Pluto cartoon of similar storyline, this technique was used to convey the differences between the 'selfish' 1920s ideology of individualism and the 'selfless' ideology of FDR's new America: community. As the ideological premise of these cartoons changed, so too did the ideological associations made with the Devil and Angel characters. The Devil becomes a smoking truant, an aggressive Nazi and then is transformed into Hitler, cast as the ultimate Disney villain. It is also of interest that 'Hitler' Donald smokes, which is exactly what the Devil Donald in *Donald's Better Self* tries to persuade Donald to do while he is off school.

It is also worth noting the reference to the Idle Hour Club. In the cartoon *The Wise Little Hen*, released in 1934, Donald and Percy Pig are the charter members of the Idle Hour Club. At the time, this was associated with 1920s individualism. Those who were not willing to work under Roosevelt's new system of government were frowned upon. Especially those who wished to reap the benefits of other people's work, as Donald and Percy try to do with the Hen. Donald, as the audience knows, is opposed to working hard and does try to 'cut corners' wherever he can. Over the course of the 1930s cartoons, he complains constantly when forced to do something he does not want to do. In fronting the treasury campaign, he is transformed into the ultimate patriotic citizen. However, as the war deepens and the sacrifices demanded of him seem to get bigger and bigger, he is tempted back to his old ways. The reference to the Idle Hour Club ultimately ties Nazism with 1920s individualism. Donald must find his new 'community' spirit in order to help the United States fight the war. Naturally, Donald does the right thing and saves his money for his taxes. The film was as effective as its predecessor. In a review of the short on 4 February 1943, the *New York Times* described *Spirit of '43* as a 'thoroughly agreeable inducement to a tough task'.

Der Fuehrer's state – The animation of Nazi Germany

Unpublished minutes from a meeting between Robert Spencer Carr, Joe Grant and government representative, Allen Rivkin, reveal that Disney's plan for contribution towards the war propaganda effort did not begin and end with the film produced for Morgenthau at the treasury. In fact, they did not even end with the films well known now to scholars of the period, which were made as an extension of the contract with the treasury.[8] On the contrary, this document lays out provisions for the handling of other proposed subjects for propaganda and the way in which the Disney Studios believed animation could convey these subjects to audiences effectively. To scholars, this proves that Disney already had a well-developed plan for how animation could handle ideologically sensitive subjects.

While plans were in motion for the animators to consult with anthropologist Dr Hooton in order to ridicule Hitler's racial theory, the Disney Studios also planned to showcase Hitler's life 'starting with Hitler in the Munich cell, writing *Mein Kampf*, realising his German countrymen had inferiority complexes'.[9] The studio planned to realize Hitler's inner circle through a 'conference of stooges'. This conference was to animate a 'Minister for Pure Blood Strains who would draw the perfect Aryan'. Disney even planned to show the German people trying to adhere to the fuehrer's order … peroxide stocks in pharmacies go down to such a level that the Army starts beefing'.[10]

---

[8] The films now known as *Education for Death*, *Chicken Little*, *Der Fuehrer's Face* and *Reason and Emotion* were made with financing from Reader's Digest and from the treasury.

[9] 'Memorandum from Allen Rivkin,' 7 December 1942, f. 22, Motion Picture Society for the Americas records, Margaret Herrick Library, Beverly Hills.

[10] 'Memorandum from Allen Rivkin,' 7 December 1942, f. 22, Motion Picture Society for the Americas records, Margaret Herrick Library, Beverly Hills.

This lampooning of the Nazi state and its ideology began as early as 1936 and was heavily developed during the Second World War into a powerful ideological treatment. Carr, Grant and Huemer also envisaged a production entitled 'Hitler the Anti-Christ'. This was thought of as a 'powerful appeal for the defeat of Hitler on religious grounds'. Grant suggested that the short should 're-enact atrocities, show bombed churches, imprisoned priests, teaching of atheistic heresies to little children'.[11] While this inevitably plays on much of the religious imagery found in *The New Spirit* and *Spirit of '43*, the reference to religious morality, one could argue, also has its roots in the battle for Donald's conscience.

However, while most of these productions were intended for domestic audiences, many of these ideas were presented for release in South America, as part of an extension of Disney's contract with the OIAA. The document containing the outline for these productions acts as a belated blueprint of the ways animation had already channelled ideology in the 1930s. It also contains a subtle reference to the part the Disney Studios saw itself playing in the war. Carr writes:

> Exposing Goebbels' technique of spreading lies, doubt and suspicion among Good Neighbours. We show how ideas can be more dangerous than bombs. We show South America being shelled by Axis radios, show the 'propaganda bombs' landing and bursting like real bombs, throwing harmful rumours far and wide. Backed up with sufficient facts about Axis propaganda activities in South America, this should be an effective counter stroke.[12]

This suggests that the Disney Studios, despite only having been at war for five weeks, saw itself as fully mobilized and a part of a propaganda war with the Axis powers. It also demonstrates that they envisaged this animated war of ideas to be the way in which they could contribute towards the war effort. It is also of interest that this is viewed by the Disney Studios and by the government as an example of 'good' propaganda. Lampooning the Nazi state; ridiculing Hitler's personality; elevating the religious and moral superiority of the Allies; exposing the lies, executions and oppression of its people; and undermining the ideology at its core were seen as the most effective way to turn the South American people away from their temptation to endorse Nazism.

---

[11] R. S. Carr, 'Direct Propaganda Films,' 7 January 1942, p. 15, f. 22, Motion Picture Society for the Americas records, Margaret Herrick Library, Beverly Hills.
[12] R. S. Carr, 'Direct Propaganda Films,' 7 January 1942, pp. 16–17, f. 22, Motion Picture Society for the Americas records, Margaret Herrick Library, Beverly Hills.

Many of the films within this document were not made into either animated shorts or feature films. However, much of the ideology, technique and content did make its way into the films that were made under contract with the government. Indeed, many of the techniques used in these films had been tried, tested and read in a political context in the 1930s.

Der Fuehrer's Face (1943)

Perhaps the most famous of Disney's wartime contributions was the Donald Duck short, *Der Fuehrer's Face*. Originally to be released under the title *Donald Duck in Nutziland* but changed due to the popularity of the short's title song, written by Oliver Wallace, the short won an academy award in 1943 for Best Animated Short Film (Shale 1978, 62). The story was first intended for the treasury short and was developed by Huemer and Grant. However, it was eventually rejected by Disney as it did not lay the focus on taxes.[13] There is no mention of government involvement in the picture under the title cards, unlike the treasury shorts. Despite the notation of government funding in the archival documents, the American public would not have been aware that the short was made under the government contract. Audiences simply believed that they were going to be viewing another Donald Duck cartoon.

The short opens with the title tune. Disney was capitalizing on the unification of the American public behind a popular song. Gabler argues that the song became an anthem for Hollywood's battle with the Nazi threat, as one and a half million copies of the song were sold (2007, 390). In combination with the music, the shot fades in to show the comical goose-step of the Nazi elite, marching in a marching band. The short, for the first time, includes animated versions of Goebbels, Goering, Tojo (caricatured heavily with yellowing skin, buck teeth and large glasses) and Mussolini. The camera pans to Donald, who is sleeping in a tiny house. In sync with the singing Nazi elite who are marching on the street outside his house, Donald even gives the Hitler salute in his sleep, ridiculing the severe indoctrination of the German people into the Nazi ideology. Donald's alarm goes off and the cuckoo in the cuckoo clock in his bedroom pops out a caricature of Hitler himself, ridiculed for his chirping 'Seig Heil!' Donald jumps out of bed and salutes the three Axis leaders in pictures

---

[13] *'From This You Are Making a Living?'* An Oral History of Richard Huemer. Interview with Joe Adamson, 1968, p. 116, American Film Institute.

on the wall of his bedroom. He sleepily tries to climb back into bed, but hands come through the window and splash cold water onto his face so he is not allowed any further rest.

Complaining, Donald dresses in his uniform, exclaims he is hungry and goes in to his safe to retrieve his breakfast: a grey-looking coffee bean, which he dips in water before putting it back into the safe; a piece of rock hard bread, that he hacks at with a saw and 'essence of eggs and bacon'. While eating his breakfast, a sword comes through Donald's window, providing his morning reading material: Mein Kampf (Figure. 6.4). The marching elite parade straight into his house and when they emerge, Donald finds himself carrying a snare drum and marching with them, out into the street.

The short then fades to a shot of a Nazi munitions factory where Donald Duck works. Swastikas adorn the chimneys of the factory against a threatening red sky. A voice over explains to the people of Nutziland that it is 'their privilege to work forty-eight hours a day for the Fuehrer'. With knives to his back and his arm thrust into the air, Donald marches into the factory. Echoing the treasury shorts, even the chimney in the factory is dressed in Nazi uniform. Donald

Figure 6.4 *Der Fuehrer's Face* (1943). Walt Disney Treasures.

gets to work, screwing the caps onto artillery shells. While he is working at immense speed, pictures of Hitler appear on the assembly line, which Donald has to salute as he is working. The work becomes too much for Donald and he soon resumes his grumbling. However, at first grumble, he is threatened with seven knives to his throat. Overtaken with the speed at which he is expected to work, Donald soon descends into an exhausted delirium and shouts, 'I can't stand it! I'm going mad!'

After experiencing an abstract world in which he is stamped upon by an iron boot and made to salute as an iron prisoner, Donald wakes up and rubs his head. The shadow of what appears to be a man saluting is upon his bedroom wall; however, Donald is in his stars and stripes pyjamas. He gets ready to salute but his attention is drawn to the window, in which there is a gleaming miniature Statue of Liberty. Donald kisses the statue and states how glad he is to be a citizen of the United States (Figure 6.5).

Following the release of *Der Fuehrer's Face*, Theodore Strauss of the *New York Times* described Donald Duck as 'one of this country's No.1 propagandists'. The article quotes Disney's view of animation being used for 'educational purposes'.

Figure 6.5 *Der Fuehrer's Face* (1943). Walt Disney Treasures.

Disney stated that, 'The war has taught us that people who won't look at a book will look at a film. … Mass education is coming. It's coming because it's a necessity. Democracy's ability to survive depends on the ability of its individuals to appreciate their duties as citizens and to comprehend the complex problems of the changing world we live in' (7 February 1943, x3). This film was viewed in contemporary society as the film that solidified Disney's commitment to the war effort as a citizen of the United States. Moreover, the short cemented Donald's position as the figurehead of the Disney Studios for the propaganda war against the Nazi threat.

There are several techniques of interest within this film. However, what is most pertinent is the use of the character, Donald. Donald Duck, who fought the Depression by reluctantly adhering to the ideology forced upon him, came directly into contact with the new threat to the United States: the Nazis. In this film, however comical, Donald is subjected to torture, both physical and psychological, at the hands of the Axis powers. He leaves the comfort of US society and becomes a part of the conflict.

As in other animated productions, the swastika is used as a well-known symbol of the Axis powers to ensure that the American people are well aware that Donald is no longer in the United States. It should be noted that as in *Donald's Decision* and *Spirit of '43*, swastikas are everywhere in the animated version of Nazi Germany. The bushes, windmills, clouds and even the pulley on the blinds in Donald's bedroom are all swastika shaped. While this is undoubtedly ridiculous and unrealistic, in the animated world, anything goes.

However, this short also uses many other sophisticated persuasion techniques only possible within the animated medium. *Der Fuehrer's Face* uses Donald as something of a 'test subject'. Much like in the shorts *Moving Day* and *Self Control*, we see the effect of a political change, not on the real victims, but on Donald himself. Everything the American public may imagine the German people were going through, we see happening to Donald. The audience is told that the average Nazi is impoverished and under constant threat. The short satirizes and exaggerates these ideas by the invisible man holding a knife to Donald's back and throat as he goes about his everyday life. Donald hides his coffee bean in a safe. We learn his bread is hard, not because he tells us but because he cuts it up with a saw. His only source of protein is sprayed into his mouth like a perfume. The American people are educated on the hardships being experienced by the German people because Donald cannot stand to live in the horrific conditions of the Nazi state.

Donald is exhausted from his forty-eight hour day, implicitly suggesting that the average German is forced to work constantly and that their consistent surveillance to Nazi ideals (implied by Donald's salute of Hitler's picture on the production line) actually diminishes their productivity. The cartoon also capitalizes on the nationalistic symbolism of the late 1930s in this short to exemplify Donald's patriotism. Lady Liberty, associated with the city of New York and with American democracy, is perched on Donald's bedroom window. Donald is dressed in American flag pyjamas. This animated short uses the unifying power of these symbols to provide a stark contrast to Donald's early morning awakening in 'Nutziland'.

Der Fuehrer's Face is also the first Disney cartoon to provide developed caricatures of the Axis power elite. While Hitler's first caricature was provided in *Stop That Tank* (1942), Disney had previously left figures such as Goebbels, Goering, Mussolini and Hirohito untouched. The American public were used to negative caricatures of the Japanese, as they were widespread in the Hollywood film industry following the bombing of Pearl Harbor. In films such as *Remember Pearl Harbor* (1942), *A Prisoner of Japan* (1942) and *Danger in the Pacific* (1942), the Japanese are often stereotyped and typified by their cruelty. However, little had been shown of the other Axis powers. Their forms appear ridiculous in this short, making them comical to the American public, lessening the impact of their threat. Similar to the way in which the Big Bad Wolf and the villainous Pete are easily defeated by the pigs and Mickey Mouse, the Nazi threat seems defeatable in *Der Fuehrer's Face*. While other treatments of the Nazi menace are more ideologically based, the entire regime is ridiculed in this short. This is a lighter propagandistic treatment before the Disney Studios began to use its skill in animation to undermine the underlying ideology of Nazism.

Education for Death (1943)

Education for Death was a true first in Disney animation. Based on the book written by George Ziemer and published in 1941, the short follows the education of a young Nazi boy named Hans and his ideological journey into becoming a German soldier. For the first time in Disney history, the short embraces a wholly dark and conservative tone. Caricatures are used, but there is little room for humour. The short is narrated throughout, from the birth of the child until his indoctrination into the German army.

The audience sees a young German couple registering the birth of their child in an intimidating German court. The man who registers the birth of the child is faceless and the shot is consumed by his frightening shadow as he snatches the child's birth certificate from the parents. The narrator informs the audience that the couple first has to prove their 'pure blood' status and the name, Hans, has to be approved by the government before his birth can be registered. As a reward for his birth, the child is given his own copy of *Mein Kampf*. The narrator tells the audience to follow the child's journey. We are taken inside a Nazi version of the fairy tale of *Sleeping Beauty*. The narrator tells us that the wicked witch is democracy, the beautiful princess is Germany and the 'brave handsome knight' is Hitler himself. At one point during one of his outbursts, the Prince even sports devil horns. He hoists Princess Germania onto his horse with difficulty as she is quite large; however, they eventually ride off into the distance. Despite the brief comical interlude of this sequence, the narrator tells us that the moral of the story is simply that 'Hitler got Germany on her feet again and took her for a ride.' We are then transported into the German schoolroom, in which children salute a picture of Hitler in armour. Hitler is now shown to be Hans's idol. In the next scene, Hans becomes ill and the audience sees Hans's mother tending to him by his bedside. She is worried for his safety for, as the narrator tells us, the unkempt are taken away and never heard from again. The faceless Nazi soldier knocks on her door, coming for the ill child. Hans, we are told, recovers and we are once again shown the school room, where the children are saluting Hitler, Goering and Goebbels.

The Darwinist principle of 'survival of the fittest' is animated on the school blackboard, showing a rabbit getting eaten by a fox. Hans expresses sympathy for the rabbit but soon changes his mind when he is ridiculed by the teacher. The short then moves to a montage sequence of German soldiers holding flaming torches against a red sky and marching. The short even shows the mass book burnings carried out in 1933 and 1934 and the replacement of the Bible by *Mein Kampf*. Statues of Jesus Christ are replaced with a Nazi sword. Hans then evolves into a German soldier from a Nazi youth. The soldiers march forward but a montage transforms these soldiers into gravestones. They are also pictured in shackles, forced into service until their death (Figure 6.6).

Politically striking and ideologically disturbing, *Education for Death* had an immense impact on American audiences (*Motion Picture Daily*, 6 January 1943, 9). They noted upon the worrying absence of their familiar characters, Mickey Mouse, Donald Duck and the Three Little Pigs and the 'grim' use of

Figure 6.6 *Education for Death* (1943). Walt Disney Treasures.

humour. In the Carr memorandum of January 1942, it is stated that animation could use 'personification', 'word visualisations' and 'narration' in order to convey its ideological message.[14] These are used to effect in *The Wise Little Hen*, *The Country Cousin* and *Ferdinand the Bull* and to a certain extent, Warner Brothers' *Porky's Poppa*. They are used again here.

Hans's story is narrated to us throughout. There is no room for interpretation by audiences. Even the most comical moments of the short, such as the caricaturing of Hitler and Germany in the story of *Sleeping Beauty*, are translated seriously for the audience. In the absence of subtitles, the German spoken by Hans's parents, the faceless soldier, the teacher and even Hans himself is translated for us by the narrator. This is particularly striking in the case of the soldier and the teacher as they are shown to shout and gesticulate violently for a fairly simple message, mocking the many newsreels of Hitler's speeches to the German public. However, as the soldier is threatening to take away the child from his mother and Hans himself is ridiculed in front of the class, the comical impact of these sequences is minimal.

---

[14] R. S. Carr, 'Methods of Presentation,' 7 January 1942, pp. 4–7, f. 22, Motion Picture Society for the Americas records, Margaret Herrick Library, Beverly Hills.

Hitler's complicated rise to power and fight for the restoration of a 'great' Germany is animated to the audience through personification. The idea of democracy, associated with the cause of the Allied powers, is personified by a wicked witch, providing a true inversion of animation's traditional enemy associations. Hitler, the knight in shining armour of the ideal of fascism, comes to the rescue of Princess Germania. These complex ideas are given physical form, allowing the audience to see their impact. As the next shot is the indoctrination of young Hans, the editing of this short works alongside this personification as an 'happily ever after' for the twisted Nazi fairy tale.

Word visualization was suggested by Carr to be used as follows: 'Word visualisations [are] animated reincarnations of the good old fashioned lantern slide, by which phrases sung or spoken are literally illustrated in sync. For instance, if our commentator says, "Hands across the sea," we simply show a pair of hands clasped across the sea.'[15] While this was intended for use to simulate the unity between the Allied powers, this is used in the final montage sequence of *Education for Death* to show the true limitations of the fully indoctrinated Nazi soldier, Hans. As he 'sees nothing but what the party wants him to see and says nothing but what the party wants him to say and does nothing but what the party wants him to do', Hans is shown blindfolded, with a muzzle upon his face and a chain around his neck. As the audience had seen the development of Hans from a small child, this image is particularly disturbing.

These montage sequences are particularly in keeping with Carr's ideological message regarding Hitler being depicted as the 'Anti-Christ'.[16] The sequences towards the end of the short, showing the supersession of religion by Nazism are particularly effective. The colour of the film also changes in sequence from a godlike white to a devilish red. Again this also references Devil Donald's personification as Nazism, depicted in *Donald's Better Self*, *Donald's Decision* and to a certain extent, *Spirit of '43*. These links were very simple but powerful enough to convey ideological messages. *Der Fuehrer's Face* mocked the Nazi regime, *Education for Death* followed a young child and his journey through the Nazi system and yet Disney delved still further into the ideology of Nazism.

[15] R. S. Carr, 'Methods of Presentation,' 7 January 1942, p. 4, f. 22, Motion Picture Society for the Americas records, Margaret Herrick Library, Beverley Hills.
[16] R. S. Carr, 'Methods of Presentation,' 7 January 1942, p. 15, Motion Picture Society for the Americas records, Margaret Herrick Library, Beverley Hills.

Reason and Emotion (1943)

As the Motion Picture Society for the Americas records reveal, Walt Disney began the storyboarding process for *Reason and Emotion* as early as June 1942. The short was produced at the recommendation of figurehead Walter Wanger who wished to see an animated version of the 1941 book *War, Politics and Emotion* by Geoffrey Bourne.[17] He deemed a psychological treatment was necessary in order to pre-empt a 'complete understanding of the Nazi threat'.[18] *Reason and Emotion* was Disney's first journey into the realm of the psyche. The short opens on a set of scales, portraying the balance between 'Reason' and 'Emotion' within a person's brain. It begins with a baby boy, in which we are told, Emotion is alone in controlling his movements. Emotion is personified as a little red-headed child inside the baby's brain. He is dressed in a leopard skin loin cloth, encapsulating his relationship to the primitive. When the child grows older, the audience sees that Reason has now joined Emotion in the man's head. This relationship takes the form of a car, in which Reason is driving the man's actions inside his head, while Emotion is made to sit in the back seat.

On occasion, Emotion tries to take over, for example, when the man sees a pretty lady on the street, but unfortunately, Emotion's attempts end in failure. A similar journey is made inside the lady's head. Emotion wants the lady to eat whatever she wants, while Reason insists she stick to her diet, otherwise she will get fat.

The short then takes on a more sombre tone. We see headlines of newspapers stating the seriousness of the current international situation. They refer to Axis and Allied victories, the drafting of soldiers and even the appearance of a 'fifth column' within American society. The average American, John Doe, is listening to the wireless in his living room. While listening, many different viewpoints try to battle for his attention. These take the form of ghostly figures, which sit on his chair, pulling at his ears and tagging on his arms. The man is an emotional wreck, with bags under his eyes and a pale-looking face. Inside his head, we see Reason and Emotion battling with one another but Emotion has the upper hand.

---

[17] 'Letter from Walter Wanger,' 2 June 1942, p. 3, f. 409, Motion Picture Society for the Americas Records, Margaret Herrick Library, Beverly Hills.
[18] 'Letter from Walter Wanger,' 2 June 1942, p. 3, f. 409, Motion Picture Society for the Americas Records, Margaret Herrick Library, Beverly Hills.

However, the narrator tells both Reason and Emotion that their squabbling is great for Hitler as he tries to destroy Reason by playing upon Emotion with fear. The short then cuts to a shot of Hitler at a microphone, speaking to an audience of German people. We then get a shot of the inside of a Nazi 'superman' where Reason and Emotion are again at odds. As Hitler speaks to the German people, Emotion is taken aback with fear (of the Gestapo) and sympathy for Hitler's plight, as he explains he 'didn't want to go to war'. When Reason attempts to calm Emotion by telling him that Hitler is lying, Emotion hits Reason on the head with a club. As Emotion gains the control through Hitler's further speeches, instilling Pride into Emotion, Reason becomes smaller and smaller in the mind of the Nazi. Inside the Nazi's head, Hitler's control over Emotion becomes more widespread. He locks Reason inside a concentration camp. We then venture outside of the Nazi's head and the marching feet of a Nazi soldier leads us through a heavily bombed Germany. The narrator explains that Emotion is now the Master of Reason. Churches and houses are completely destroyed. We return to the battle between Reason and Emotion in the mind of John Doe. He explains that the two must work together in order for the Allies to be successful. The shot pans out to transform John Doe into a bomber pilot who, now Reason and Emotion are working together, can 'do the job he [*sic*] set out to do'. The animated production finishes with a shot of the American air force flying proudly in formation in the clouds.

In a 1947 article in *Hollywood Quarterly*, Charles Palmer described the process utilized in *Reason and Emotion* as 'solidifying the intangible' (1947, 27). However, on closer analysis, it seems that all the Disney animators utilized here was their already tried and tested technique of personification of an ideology. The abstract ideas of Reason and Emotion are simply caricatured to the extreme and given physical form. Emotion is portrayed as an untrained caveman, guided by his primitive instincts; Reason as an unmistakeably British character obsessed by social rules and regulations. These characters are then placed in different locations – one in America and the other in Nazi Germany. In America, the two characters are at odds with each other inside John Doe's head. Recognizing the pressures of the war on the ordinary American's emotions, the narrator explains that Reason and Emotion must not fight as this is 'good for Hitler'. In Germany, Emotion is taken in by Hitler's pleas to the nation and eventually beats Reason with a club and locks him away. After telling his story, the narrator tells the pair in the American's head that they must work together to fight the war. Given the nationalities of the two ideological characters, this could also be indicating the relationship between Britain and America during the war; America driven by Emotion; Britain, by Reason.

Reason and Emotion also uses the 'animated poster' technique exercised in *Old Glory* during the Hitler speech sequence, to illustrate the effect particular 'emotions' displayed on screen have upon the Emotion caricature. The combination of all of them within the mind of the average Nazi; fear, sympathy, pride and anger lead to the imprisonment of Reason and the widespread destruction within Germany (Figure 6.7).

By highlighting the ideological differences between the average American and the average Nazi, *Reason and Emotion* again taps into the battle for control exemplified in many of the Donald Duck short subjects. In some ways, therefore, scholars can view *Reason and Emotion* as its most advanced treatment of the ideological battle between the Angel and the Devil.

Since the release of this cartoon, it should also be noted that the concept used in *Reason and Emotion* can also be seen at work during the hugely successful Disney–Pixar film *Inside Out* (2015) although undoubtedly with no sinister undertones.

Figure 6.7 *Reason and Emotion* (1943). Walt Disney Treasures.

Chicken Little (1943)

Chicken Little has already attracted the attention of scholars for its references to the battle with the Axis powers. Richard Shale has commented that *Chicken Little* rivals *Education for Death* in its grim, unhappy ending (Shale 1978, 65). It was the fourth and final film to be produced as an extension of the contract with the Coordinator of Inter-American Affairs and along with *Reason and Emotion, Education for Death* and *Der Fuehrer's Face*, was financed by Reader's Digest and the government.

The short opens on the traditional animated farmyard setting. We are introduced to our characters by a narrator, which seems to further differentiate many of the government cartoons from those under normal commercial release. With the exception of *Der Fuehrer's Face*, all of the government releases were narrated to ensure that there was no ambiguity in the ideology they were transmitting to their audiences.

The protagonist in the story, Chicken Little, is identifiable as a small middle-class American child. By the narrator's admission, he is not particularly intelligent. The audience is also introduced to the villainous character: Foxy Loxey. Foxy vows to get through the compound's defences to serve his 'culinary interest' in the community. This is not an insubstantial feat, particularly given that the narrator emphasizes the heavy fencing surrounding the compound, the locks and even the farmer's shotgun. Foxy then states that he's 'not a fox' for nothing and cunningly calculates that there is 'more than one way to pluck a chicken'. He then reaches for his psychology book and reads.

Speaking on the production of *Chicken Little*, animator Ward Kimball confided that originally, 'Foxy's book was meant to be *Mein Kampf* but this was "watered down" for the version that reached the screen.'[19] However, reading from *Mein Kampf* all the same, Foxy says, 'To influence the masses, first aim for the least intelligent.' Surveying the animals in the farmyard, Foxy aims for Chicken Little. He blows a puff of cigar smoke in his face, tips a watering can over him and drops some wood on his head to simulate a thunder storm. Foxy then pretends to be the 'Voice of Doom' following the storm and tells Chicken Little that the sky is falling and he must run for his life. Panicking, Chicken Little dashes off to tell Henny Penny and the other animals. Cocky Locky, the group's leader, however, is not fooled and declares that it was only a piece of wood that

[19] *Walt Disney Treasures: On the Front Lines: The War Years.* DVD (2004) Audio commentary.

fell on Chicken Little's head. Foxy reads some more of his book aloud, which tells him to undermine the leaders of the masses. Taking on the voice of one of the hens as they play cards, Foxy whispers through the fence, making them doubt the judgement of Cocky Locky. He states, 'Now in my opinion, Cocky Locky displays some totalitarian tendencies.'

Foxy's whispering campaign reverberates throughout the community. With the seeds of deceit spread throughout the farmyard, Foxy then tells Chicken Little that he was born to be a leader. Foxy undermines Cocky Locky in front of the farmyard community, ensuring that they look to Chicken Little as their leader and tells him to relay the message that the animals should seek shelter in the cave. The animals flee the safety of the farmyard community and are taken right into Foxy's lair. The narrator assures the audience that all turns out all right; however, Foxy takes charge of the narrative as he sucks on chicken bones, which gives way to a sinister bone graveyard (Figure 6.8). The narrator exclaims, 'This isn't how it ends in my book,' to which Foxy retorts, 'Don't believe everything you read.'

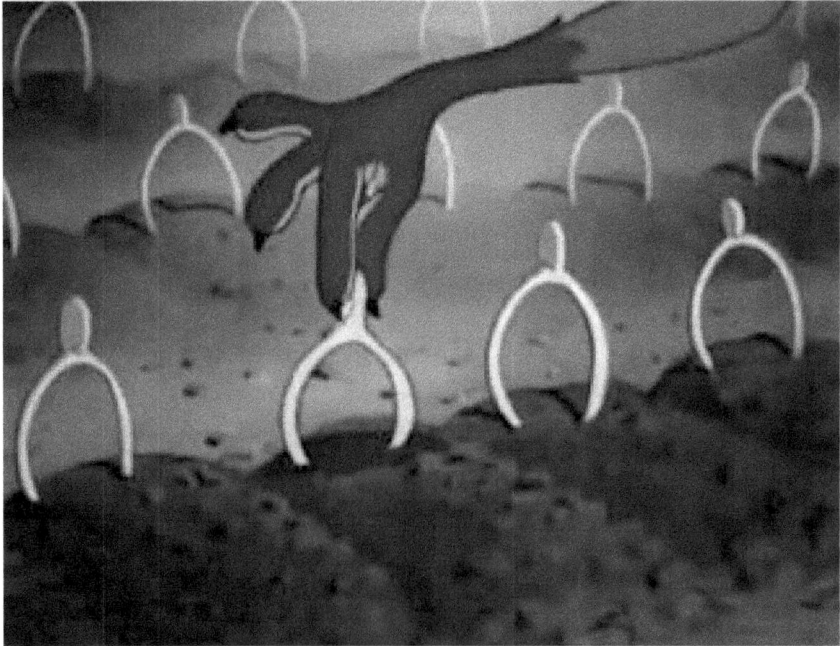

Figure 6.8 *Chicken Little* (1943). Walt Disney Treasures.

In terms of its sombre tone, *Chicken Little* is comparable to *Education for Death* in that it is one of the only Disney shorts to end on a negative note. The premise behind it is comparable with the 1933 short *Bosko the Musketeer*, in relaying the physical power of an idea and the effect it can have upon society. This short dealt with the power of confidence and the 'New Deal 32' ideology. However, unlike these productions which simply give the idea a physical form in the animated world, Foxy actually puts the idea into practice, using 'psychology' to manipulate the farmyard community. This ultimately sends them all, except Cocky Locky, to their death. This was particularly shocking for the audience, who expected a happy ending from the fairy tale world of animation and unfortunately, the manipulative Fox is triumphant.

Disney educates: The informational & advisory short subjects

Food Will Win the War (1942)

Disney was approached by the Department of Agriculture within weeks of the Japanese bombing of Pearl Harbor to produce a short film stressing the abundance of American agricultural output. The film was to propagandize Secretary Wickard's slogan 'Food Will Win the War'.[20] Its purpose was also to link the Department of Agriculture's efforts with the Lend-Lease scheme, showing how the extensive food output of the United States could contribute towards the victory of the Allies and most importantly, the defeat of the Axis powers.

The short opens with an explicit reference to the 'V for Victory' campaign as wheat grain in the shape of a V even precedes the opening credits (Figure 6.9). The audience then sees an animated shot of the earth, which the narrator explains is 'aflame'. Using the multi-plane camera, the short focuses on a war-torn landscape, ripped apart by conflict. The narrator draws attention to the victims of this barren wasteland, explaining that there is hope for Europe: the hope of American agriculture. The shot fades to an extensive map of the United States, in which its sheer size in comparison to Europe is emphasized. This is done through highlighting of the European countries which would comfortably fit within the borders of the United States.

---

[20] 'Walt Disney: Great Teacher' *Fortune* magazine, 14 May 1942, p. 154, Walt Disney Publicity Ephemera, Box 9, Collection 280, folder 9–22, University of California Los Angeles Archives.

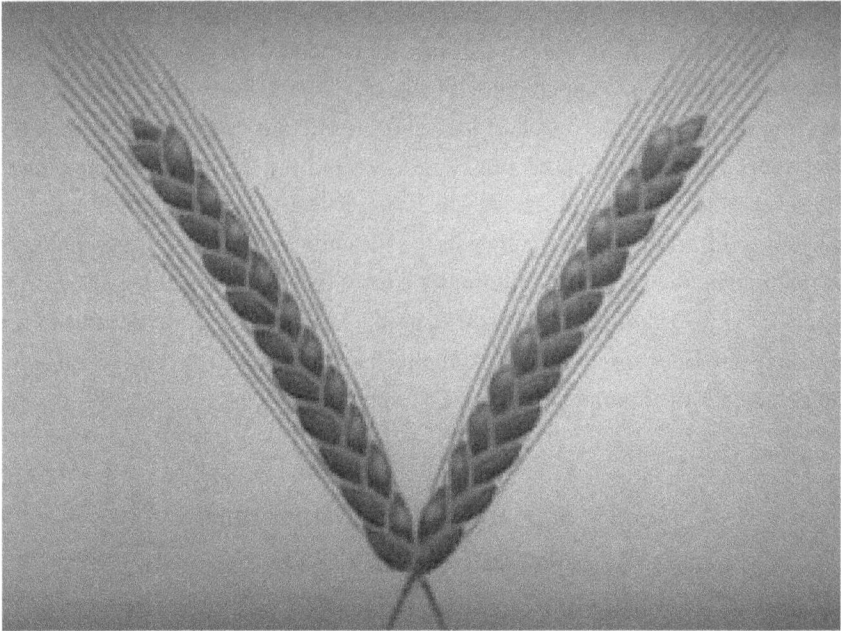

Figure 6.9 *Food Will Win the War* (1942). Walt Disney Treasures.

The next shot features the cusp of a globe, on which the farmers and their wives stand, poised for battle. The narrator explains that their number is twice as many as the Axis powers have soldiers. A montage of farming production methods follows, accompanied by extensive battle rhetoric from the narrator. Animated production statistics are also displayed, in which the annual sum total of US production of various crops are compared with the sizes of cities and global landmarks such as the pyramids of Egypt and Niagara Falls. Many of the comparisons are also linked to the Axis powers. For example, the number of bushels of corn grown into one ear would stretch from London to the Black Sea, which 'hangs right over your head, Adolf', explains the narrator.

In the middle of these statistics, there is also reference to the fact that the United States produces food with enough power to 'bowl' over the Axis powers. This is displayed literally as the skittles animated are caricatures of Hirohito, Mussolini and Hitler. A girl grown fat on the oils produced by the United States would 'black out Berlin'.[21] The Three Little Pigs then feature as part of a feature

---

[21] According to the same article in *Fortune* magazine, in this particular sequence, Disney requested to have the girl sit on Hitler's head but the Secretary refused.

on bacon. The pigs are marching forward playing 'Who's Afraid of the Big Bad Wolf' on their instruments and waving the American flag. A naval sequence follows in which U-Boats are signed with the Japanese flag and the swastika, the fronts of which are shaped like sinister skulls. The short closes with an insignia featuring a blue eagle, adorned with white stars on a red background, signifying the fight for the 'freedom of speech, freedom of worship, freedom from want and freedom from fear'.

This short lends from many of the ideological devices of the 1930s cartoons, even to the extent that footage from *Three Little Wolves* is utilized in *Food Will Win the War* to create the same nationalistic effect. The Three Little Pigs, leading the charge of the one hundred million American pigs willingly sacrificing themselves to the Allied powers for bacon could be interpreted as sinister; however, the resolve of the pigs marching forward waving the American flag diminishes any doubt in the mind of the audience. The only difference is the white peace flag of the 1936 short is replaced by the U S flag (Figure 6.10).

The position of America has changed from a reluctant interventionism to a fierce nationalism. Reference to the Wolf is again made, but simply through

Figure 6.10 *Food Will Win the War* (1942). Walt Disney Treasures.

the music played by the pigs on their instruments as the narrator links this shot with the next, stating, 'And who is afraid of the Big Bad Wolf? Not the farmer of the United States.' Again, this puts the Axis powers in the position of the Wolf, indicative of the narrative of the 1930s short *Three Little Wolves* and the pre-war Canadian Short *The Thrifty Pig*. Much like Donald Duck, the pigs were now central to the wartime narrative of the Disney Studios.

While lending itself to the device of caricature in the skittles sequence, *Food Will Win the War* also extends the boundaries of the hyperbolic animated universe to demonstrate the relative impact of the agricultural industry on the Axis powers. The bowling ball literally knocks down Brandenburg Gate. While Carr's 1942 memorandum describes this technique as a 'word visualisation', similar techniques are utilized to effect in the Depression films of the 1930s such as *Porky's Poppa* (1938). These cartoons are able to give a complicated idea a presence within the animated world, showing its physical effect. In a similar vein, as in the treasury films, the weapons of the Axis powers are personified, stressing that they are a direct threat to the beloved Disney characters of the animated world. Carr refers to this technique as 'personification' using the example that 'Hitlerhito' could be a 'two faced monster', however the personification of villains within the animated world simply reinforces a dialogue already current within the animated productions. Ideas and weapons and even real-life personalities are not a threat in the animated world unless they are given an animated form, Pegleg Pete, the Depression, the Wolf, Hitler and the other Axis leaders are all given a presence within the confines of the animated world so they are *physically* a threat to both the characters and therefore, by extension, the audience.

Out of the Frying Pan Into the Firing Line (1942)

As well as the films for the Department of Agriculture, Disney was also called upon to make films for the Conservation Division of the War Production Board. These were simply informational films, to advise American citizens of the ways in which their conservation at home could aid the war effort.

The film opens on a frying pan, where Minnie Mouse is cooking eggs and bacon. Pluto can smell the food cooking from the other room and pushes his bones away, ready for the grease the eggs and bacon are cooked in. Minnie goes to give the grease to Pluto; however, the narrator tells her, as a 'housewife of America', that the fat must be conserved. The narration is, similar to *Self Control* and *The New Spirit*, coming from the wireless in the kitchen, indicative of authority and instruction. Pluto, much like Donald, is hesitant over the sacrifice he is being asked to make for the war effort. The audience is then shown a montage sequence, demonstrating the ways in which fats can be utilized for the war effort. We follow the glycerine through a funnel, through which it is transformed into droplets which further transform into bullets. The bullets are numerous enough to circle an animated globe six times.

Following further explanation from the narrator, the audience see fat dripping from the bacon into the pan. These droplets also transform into bombs underneath American squadrons. This plane goes on to successfully bomb an enemy submarine. In another montage sequence, the fat from french fries powers death charges to crush Axis submarines. The narrator explains that Pluto's fat will give some boy at the front some extra cartridges. Pluto looks to the wall, where there is a picture of a saluting Mickey in his army uniform (Figure. 6.11). Minnie asks Pluto if he still wants the grease but he turns away from it and, instead, brings Minnie the correct container in which to store it. The narrator describes *how* the audience need to conserve their fats.

Figure 6.11 *Out of the Frying Pan Into the Firing Line* (1942). Walt Disney Treasures.

When Minnie has enough, Pluto balances the can of grease on his nose and trots down the street (adorned with war saving posters) taking it to the local approved meat dealer. Pluto is meant to receive money for the fats but instead takes sausages from the butcher. The scene fades into what we believe is the American flag, but when the camera pans out, it is simply Pluto's tail, from which the flag is hanging, as he makes his way home to Minnie.

While this is simply an informational film as opposed to carrying an explicit propagandistic message, ideology is still forged throughout the narrative. When the film opens, the audience hears the first few bars of *Yankee Doodle Spirit*, written for the treasury film starring Donald Duck. This not only serves as a reminder of the patriotic duty of each American citizen, as demonstrated by Donald himself, but also forges a patriotic link between animated characters, showing that they all belong to the same world, are aware of each other's experiences and are in the fight together. Minnie hums the song herself while she is cooking bacon until the narrator interrupts her. There is also an association to the Allied powers over the end of the short, as a few bars from the British national anthem, *God Save The King* are played.

Secondly, in the absence of Donald, Pluto (another reluctant receiver of 1930s communitarian values) plays the part of the selfish individualist who must convert his way of thinking for the war. Pluto is desperate for the grease from Minnie's bacon and eggs, but, after hearing the narrator, is convinced of the need to conserve the fats for the war effort. What finally sways his ideology is the picture of Mickey, hanging on the wall of Minnie's kitchen. Again, this serves as a reminder that while he and Minnie are doing their bit on the home front, they are helping their 'boy' out in the field. Incidentally, this is the only shot of Mickey in army uniform throughout the series of wartime shorts. With the popularity of Donald, he was the face of Disney's war campaign. However, this short confirms to the audience that Mickey, too, has gone out to fight for America. Minnie has also remained an absent fighter in the war against the Axis powers until this short. She is referred to as a 'housewife' of America and represents those left on the home front. Her partner, Mickey, has left her at home with the dog and yet the short stresses that her role in the war is also significant.

Thirdly, *Out of the Frying Pan* continues the trend of showcasing authority through the wireless. Since *Self Control* and its indications of the frustration the American public were experiencing through Roosevelt's fireside chats, it is apparent that a link is made between the wireless and the government. This is built upon further in *The New Spirit*. What is interesting about this film is that authority is directly applied from the wireless into the animated world. Minnie is all set to give Pluto the grease from the frying pan until she is stopped in her tracks by the narrator of the short, the voice coming from the wireless.

Conclusion

The wartime shorts that the Disney Studios made for the government are of interest to scholars for several reasons. First, for the first time in Disney history, their content was explicitly propagandistic. These films were financed by the government with the specific purpose of making the American audience feel a certain way about paying their income taxes, saving grease for bullets and fighting the Axis powers. Hitler is portrayed as both the devil and a ridiculous figure to be made fun of. Because of the flexible medium through which animation proved it could operate, it could both educate and persuade.

The cartoons of Warner Brothers and Disney did not draw the attention of the Hays Office for producing such content during the 1930s but was the first to be called upon to do so during the Second World War. During the war, Disney animation proved itself an effective ideological medium. For financial necessity and for his own patriotic drive, Disney needed the government contracts. However, this relationship worked to profit both parties. The American government needed the products and characters of his studio to fight the war alongside the American people.

Secondly, Disney characters were further confirmed as national symbols. The characters of Mickey, Donald, Pluto, The Three Little Pigs and the Big Bad Wolf all assumed these roles during the 1930s. They fought the Depression, became community idealists and witnessed the rise of Nazi Germany alongside the American people. However, they were called upon to act in these roles *for* America and *with* America during the war. By doing so, they validated their own importance within American national culture. If even the fantastical world of Disney was going to war, then so too should the American people.

Hitler and the Nazis were introduced to the animated world in the form of the Big Bad Wolf and the Devil, the ultimate Disney villains. In the 1930s, when the United States was not yet at war with the Axis powers, the threat was concealed behind these 'acceptable' animated figures. However, in a wartime setting, it was now acceptable for the real characters to make their way into the animated world, representing the fact that they too were a threat to the safety of Donald and Mickey. Furthermore, because of the nature of animation, these characters could embrace an exaggerated form of patriotism without appearing ridiculous.

Animation, by nature, was ridiculous. Therefore, it was of no object for the American public to see the American flag glowing in Donald's eyes. Or even to see him run all the way from California to Washington faster than the speed of light, simply to get his taxes paid. These studios produced overt, hyperbolic propaganda for the war and were not subjected to the same constraints as the live action movie. What is more, the American people recognized the symbolism in these characters. Reviews and responses within the national press prove that these characters had become more to American audiences than simply cartoon personalities. They represented, as Carr wrote, 'a glossary of new characters to express today's new conceptions'.[22] They were not just cartoons but in themselves, represented ideas and symbols. As written in the *New York Times* as early as 20 May 1942 – even before the creation of the OWI – these characters were seen as 'ambassadors of goodwill' and a 'growing force within our midst' (17).

However, what is most important about these cartoons was not their content, but their place within the journey of animation in the 1930s and 1940s. These shorts represent the culmination of Disney and Warner Brothers' contributions to forging ideology through its short subjects, not the extent. The lengthy memorandum, written by Disney's key contact with the government, Robert Spencer Carr, less than a month after the United States joined the war, outlines all the different ways in which animation, as a medium, could ideologically contribute. This should be analysed, not as a wartime document, but documentary proof of all the lessons learnt by the Disney Studios and by animation, in general, throughout the 1930s. The Studio already knew how to put messages across through animation. This is evidenced by identical ideas, narratives and even reused footage to transmit the same effect. This document simply proves their plans to put their skills to government use during the war.

---

[22] R. S. Carr, 'The Creation of New Symbols,' 7 January 1942, p. 37, Motion Picture Society for the Americas records, Margaret Herrick Library, Beverly Hills.

7

Animation at War: Disney, Warner Brothers and Wartime Entertainment 1941–5

Despite the explicit nature of the cartoons Disney produced under contract with the government, animation's contribution towards the war effort did not end with its Treasury productions, instructional films or even psychological propaganda films surrounding the Nazi regime. Animation, in keeping with the stringent traditions of Hollywood during the Second World War, was responsible for the production of many more ideologically focused films. These productions fell into line with many feature films of the period in their characterization of the Nazi elite and in the racist and bestial stereotyping of the Japanese.

Unlike the other nations fighting, whose homelands had been directly affected by the outbreak of war, America perceived no direct threat to their safety. While the bombing of Pearl Harbor by the Japanese on 7 December 1941 was undoubtedly carried out on American soil, the attack was in the middle of the Pacific, miles away from their homeland. Therefore, Americans, unlike other nations, required the movies to highlight this danger in order to fully endorse US interventionist policy and most specifically Roosevelt's 'Europe First' policy. Films such as *Hitler's Children* (1943) and *This Land Is Mine* (1943) brought the perceived danger from the Nazi regime closer to home by threatening the values that the United States held most dear.

However, Roosevelt's concentration on defeating Hitler's armies did not exempt the Japanese from treatment in Hollywood's propaganda machine. After Pearl Harbor, the Japanese were portrayed as a cruel, remorseless race in productions such as *Thirty Seconds Over Tokyo* (1944), *Bataan* (1943) and *Purple Heart* (1944). On the other hand, the Allies were venerated for their strength and courage in productions such as MGM's *Mrs Miniver* (1942) and *Journey for Margaret* (1942).

Warner Bros led the way in telling the story of the common man, the most famous of which was the endearing Rick Blaine in Michael Curtiz's *Casablanca*

(1943). *Casablanca* subtly undermined the isolationist cause by showing the conversion of the hero to interventionism as Rick is persuaded into the line of duty. It also hangs the promise of refuge in the United States through its narrative, allowing the American audience to take pride in the freedoms of their country and strengths in a time of crisis (Schindler 1996, 70). When the population developed a desire for more escapist entertainment, Warner Brothers amalgamated American pride and musical optimism in *Yankee Doodle Dandy* (1942) and even sold first night tickets for war bonds (*Life Magazine,* 14 June 1942, 65).

The full extent of Hollywood's contribution to the war is well documented, but what is most clear from the literature is the simplistic nature of the narratives in features. Those Germans who worked for the Nazi Government were incurably bad and Germans who supported Hitler were misled. The Japanese were sinister and monstrous and their antithesis was exemplified in the American ideal of democracy and freedom. Furthermore, the characters used to personify this ideal often changed form. While actors such as James Cagney, Humphrey Bogart, Fred Astaire and Errol Flynn were often cast in the role, Hollywood also enlisted the help of the fantastical to wage war on the enemy and sustain morale and unity on the home front. Among the conscripted were Captain America, Superman, Tarzan and Sherlock Holmes. It is here, within the realm of fantasy, that animation was used by the US government as a weapon of propaganda.

Following the establishment of the OWI in 1942 by former journalist Elmer Davis, the department issued a decree to all motion picture production studios.[1] The OWI explained that its purpose was 'to coordinate the dissemination of war information by all federal agencies and to formulate and carry out, by means of the press, radio and motion pictures, programmes designed to facilitate an understanding in the USA and abroad of the progress of the war effort and of the policies, activities and aims of the government' (Blum 1976, 31).

Central to the purpose of the Motion Picture Division was the idea that the studios in Hollywood had to produce motion pictures with central storylines or theses falling under the following headings: why we fight, the need for total war

---

[1] For further information on the establishment of the OWI, see Koppes, Clayton and Black, Gregory D. (2000). *Hollywood Goes to War.* London: Tauris Parke and Winkler, Allen M. (1978). *The Politics of Propaganda.* New Haven: Yale University Press and Culbert, David (1990). *Film and Propaganda in America,* Vol. 3. New York: Greenwood Press.

to bring victory and any film that focused on the 'four freedoms'; the enemy, including negative representations of same and the fifth column element; the United Nations as a union of democratic societies with a common anti-fascist goal; the home front, particularly the union of the civilians contributing towards the war effort through the payment of taxes and purchase of war bonds and lastly, the fighting forces. The union of the components of the various strands of the armed forces was to be emphasized, as well as the union of the various different nationalities in the United States. Fatalities and sacrifice were also to be handled by the motion picture industry (Koppes and Black 2000, 69).

It should be noted that there are a significant number of animated shorts released in this period that feature Donald Duck, Daffy Duck or Porky Pig during wartime; however, the author has chosen to reference and analyse the cartoons that are of interest, due to their utilization of techniques from the 1930s in order to transmit a particular political message.

Donald gets drafted – The entertainment shorts of the Disney Studios

While on the surface, these subjects seemed too solemn to be handled within the realms of the animated world, the Studios rose to the challenge, producing films that coordinated with each of the required topic areas. Disney himself was not keen on producing overtly propagandistic films and detested the idea that his studio was no longer its own boss, with over 98 per cent of his studio output geared towards the production of government war films in 1943 (*Motion Picture Daily*, 11 March 1943). Nonetheless, his strong focus on the development of personality animation throughout the 1930s allowed his characters to fit into this new world of conflict, while still satisfying the entertainment and morale boosting needs of his keen audience.

In an article in *Daily Variety* in 1942, Disney revealed that he believed 'keeping them [American audiences] laughing during war time was paramount' (7 October 1942, 47). However, the presence of many of the ideologically focused animation techniques within the cartoon shorts produced during this period proves that while entertainment was definitely a consideration, Disney was also happy to keep in line with government requirements and produce animation with an ideological focus. Central to this development, again, was the character of Donald Duck.

Donald Gets Drafted (1942)

Donald, who showed his overwhelming patriotism by fronting the war bonds campaign for the Treasury, was also the first cartoon character to be drafted into the US Army. In this extraordinary cartoon, audiences saw Donald suffering for the very first time in his line of duty. This allowed them to understand the 'sacrifices' made by soldiers on the front lines and the terrible conditions they were often forced to live in. However, as Donald was willing to make these sacrifices, audiences responded well to the cartoon and its overall message.

The short opens with the traditional image of Donald's face, except Donald's usual sailor hat has been replaced with an army hat, immediately alerting the audience to the fact that Donald is in a completely different place physically and perhaps, psychologically, now the country is at war. Engaging its audience with music at the outset, *Donald Gets Drafted* opens with a song regarding the strength of the army. The lyrics state, 'The army's not the army anymore, it's better than it's ever been before.' The short's narrative instantly boosts the morale of the audiences through exhibiting confidence in America's forces.

The combination of this song with the fade in to Donald's conscription notice also implies that Donald's influence on the army is going to be a positive one. Donald salutes the audience, marching down the street to the tune of the music, showing his excitement and willingness to take up this new military challenge. He wanders down the street, looking at all the posters of exciting things he will be able to do once enrolled in the army. Many of the posters show the friendly nature of all the soldiers and generals within the forces. Donald is also thrilled by the pictures of pretty women on the arms of many of the soldiers. He arrives at the conscription office and salutes the general. He states to the general that he wants to be in the air force. Donald wants to fly straightaway but is told that he must pass his physical examination first. Noticeably the office holds many maps and flags of the United States, underlying the patriotism of Donald's conscription.

Going into the back of the office for his physical examination, Donald is quickly prodded by the army doctors who assess his general level of health and test his psyche. He is told he must guess the colours of the cards put in front of him, which state the colour on the card clearly. When Donald inexplicably gets one of the colours wrong, he is told that 'it's close enough'. The audience sympathizes with Donald's stupidity but are pleased that he is still able to do his patriotic duty. Donald is then stripped bare and measured for his army uniform. He is dressed in a uniform that is far too big for him, but soon shrinks to size and is stamped with a blue 'Ok'.

The location switches to an army camp, where Donald is shown to be frustrated by the fact that all he does is march. The army sergeant, Pegleg Pete, demands that he 'get in step'. Donald, however, enthusiastically marching, accidentally steps out of line. Pete announces that he's going to give Donald 'special training'. He announces that Donald 'ain't no soldier' and that he is 'hopeless'. Donald is furious and is told he needs to learn discipline. Pete demands that he does not move a muscle, which proves particularly difficult for Donald when ants begin to crawl all over him, making him want to scratch. When the ants become too difficult for him to bear, Donald begins to fire his gun everywhere. His punishment is peeling potatoes, while the music concludes, 'The army's not the army anymore.'

There are several points of interest within this cartoon. The first, naturally, relates to the character of Donald. In this year, Donald has already shown his willingness to contribute to the war effort by rushing to pay his income taxes. When he receives his draft notice, Donald is excited by the possibilities of the army, particularly the glamour associated with the air force, as demonstrated by the posters. However, his experiences in the army prove that being drafted does not automatically qualify him for the glamorous lifestyle, vindicated by his position at the end of the short, as he is left peeling potatoes as a punishment. However, Donald does not run away from his position. While he does complain about his plight (he peels his complaint word 'phooey' out of the leftover potato peel), he keeps loyal to his draft notice and tries desperately to obey the commands of his sergeant, Pegleg Pete.

Another point of interest in this cartoon is that the animated world directly reflects the real world. While the Treasury film was meant to instruct people on the necessity of paying their income taxes, *Donald Gets Drafted* shows the direct impact of the new conscription legislation introduced in American society from 1941. Due to the speed at which this film was made and released, the conditions of the army are displayed before American audiences so they were able to see the reality of life in the forces, before many of them had heard about it from friends, neighbours or even loved ones. While no mention of the identity of the enemy is made in this film, Donald is nonetheless signing up to fight and the valiant patriotism of his act of conscription is heavily suggested.

The music relays the pride experienced by Donald in being allowed to fight for his country. The first half of the animated short takes on the traits of many of the nationalistic shorts of the late 1930s, such as *The Riveter* and *Window Cleaners* by showcasing famous American landmarks and cities. Donald is in New York when he gets drafted into the army. The office he enters to sign up is full of posters of famous American landmarks, maps of the United States, army crests and American flags.

Donald Gets Drafted thus fulfils many of the required aims of the OWI, by glorifying the fighting forces and through the suggestion of total war implied by Donald's conscription into the army. It also demonstrates that every person involved within the war effort is of vital importance. While Donald does not prove himself a particularly effective soldier, he is still given an important role in preparing food for the soldiers. His position is integral to the winning of the war.

Sky Trooper (1942)

Sky Trooper was released soon after Donald's initial conscription into the army, and audiences see that he finally makes it into the air training base he has dreamed of since enrolment. Bombers emblazoned with red, white and blue stars and stripes, zoom past Donald's window as he longingly looks outside. He is in the kitchens, peeling potatoes. He cries out that he wants to fly and even carves a plane out of his potato skin. Absent minded as ever, Donald accidentally peels Sergeant Pete's hat into the shape of many aeroplanes. Noticing his enthusiasm, Pete teases Donald and releases thousands more potatoes. He tells Donald that once he has finished peeling all those potatoes, he will be allowed to fly. Thrilled, Donald gets to work.

Finishing quickly, he reports to the Air Sergeant's office. Donald is subjected to a series of ridiculous tests to judge his suitability to fly, including pinning the tail on the aeroplane while he is blindfolded. Spotting a sign for parachute troops, Pete calls Donald who boards the plane with the other troops. Donald excitedly puts on his pack, not knowing that he is carrying a parachute. Once the soldiers line up to jump off the plane, Donald exclaims that they must be on the ground, clueless that he is going to have to parachute off the plane at great height. Scared of heights, Donald clings on to Sergeant Pete to stop himself from leaving the plane. However, Pete eventually loses his own grip and the two cling to the weapon aboard the plane. They explode into the general's headquarters and are both sentenced to potato peeling. A large potato is stuck onto Donald's nose and he squeals, 'Am I mortified?!'[2]

Noticeably, as the horrors of the war have not truly set in for the United States, the tone of the animated shorts is still quite optimistic. In this short, while it does not have a particularly positive ending, Donald is able to go up in an aeroplane for the first time in his life. This dream of flying is what attracted him to the forces and it is fulfilled here. There is also no evidence of suffering, unlike the later short *Fall Out, Fall In*. Here, his only suffering is his need to fulfil his dream of flying. He is not put through any physical duress, apart from the ridiculous tests he is made to do by Sergeant Pete. The continuation of old gags found in the 1930s cartoons also signals the retention of normalcy, for example, the play on Jimmy Durante's nose at the end of the short.

Fall Out, Fall In (1943)

Audiences next encounter Donald in a wartime setting in the 1943 cartoon, *Fall Out, Fall In*. Again, the short opens with Donald wearing his US army hat, instantly alerting the audience to the military nature of the cartoon. The wartime setting of animated shorts was now seen to be normal. While the constraints of the war on the home front were anything but ordinary, the charting of Donald's exploits in the army came to be part of a regular cinematic context for cinema goers.

Noticeably, the enthusiasm and patriotism of 'The Army's not the Army any more' is absent from this animated production. As with the Treasury short subject *Spirit of '43*, the Disney Studios recognized that the initial enthusiasm for the war was rapidly fading, given that the Allies were bogged down in the North African Offensive in Europe. As the conditions of the war changed for the American people, so too did the experience of the animated characters living the war *for* the American audiences.

The short opens on the army, participating in a military drill. Donald is shown at the end of the company, struggling to keep up with the quick pace of the men

---

[2] 'Am I mortified?!' was the well-known catch phrase of comedian Jimmy Durante who was enormously popular with Hollywood audiences during the 1930s. For more information on Jimmy Durante, see Fowler, Gene (1991). *Schnozzola: The Story of Jimmy Durante*. New York: Viking Press.

he is fighting with. Donald, while at the back of the company, enthusiastically charts that they are five miles from the army camp. His tail even drums the back of his army pack in time to the march he is participating in. In a flash, we soon discover that the army company is now ten miles from the camp. Again this demonstrates that the army training that Donald is participating in is in the United States. The journey that Donald takes with the rest of the soldiers showcases some beautiful animated landscapes, tapping into the national pride of the audience, animating the best of the country they are fighting for. Again, this was a tried and tested technique utilized in the late 1930s to instil nationalism into audiences.

Donald shows that the journey is tiring him but still continues to march. The company hits bad weather and Donald plods on through the rain and snow, charting the number of miles they have all travelled on the back of his comrade's pack. The company then reaches the desert, where Donald's white fur is catastrophically exposed to sunburn (Figure 7.1). When the company finally halts, Donald collapses with exhaustion, however, soon gets to his feet when dinner is announced. He pulls his pack open, revealing many pictures of Daisy

Figure 7.1 *Fall Out, Fall In* (1943). Walt Disney Treasures.

Duck and assembles his cooking utensils. However, the sergeant tells him that he must fix his camp first. Noticeably, to enhance the feeling that Donald is training with and fighting alongside men, Donald's sergeant is a faceless voice who gives Donald his orders.

While the other soldiers help themselves to food, Donald fixes his camp but finds that his tent is not secure and will not protect him from the elements. Donald is still trying to fix his tent, having had no food or water when the rest of the company is asleep. Fed up, Donald covers himself with a small blanket. He is interrupted by the snoring of his comrades who make the noises of drums, rifles and trumpets as they sleep. Donald sports huge shadows under his eyes by the time the company is ordered to begin marching again in the morning.

In this short, Donald leaves the comfort of the training camp and experiences the rough terrain and terrible conditions of the army company out in the field. While the company does not participate in any combat, Donald seriously suffers with exhaustion from the terrible conditions he is made to experience. Donald's enthusiasm for the army life rapidly wavers throughout the short, particularly when he is unable to put up his tent and is denied any food or sleep until he does so. What is more, the formerly selfish member of the American citizenship has to learn to tolerate the bad habits of others, which Donald discovers through the snoring of his comrades. He eventually has to literally bury his head in the sand, in order to get some peace and quiet.

True to the historical context under which it was released, *Fall Out, Fall In*, is an accurate reflection of the rigorous nature of army life.[3] Donald struggles day by day. And yet, true to the struggles of the Allied powers, on no sleep and no food, Donald is ready to carry on marching with his company when called to order in the morning. While he complains to himself about his situation through his traditional grumble, 'Phooey', he never complains to the sergeant or to any of the other soldiers in his company. Donald thus exemplifies the perfect patriot in this cartoon. Despite his failed attempts, all his actions are to attempt to keep him in line with the community of soldiers. His actions are all for the greater good and his tribulations throughout the short demonstrate the OWI inspired sacrifice.

---

[3] For more information on the day-to-day life of an US army recruit, see Ambrose, Stephen E. (1998). *The Victors: Eisenhower and His Boys: The Men of World War Two*. New York: Simon & Schuster and Wells, Mark K. (1995). *Courage and Air Warfare: The Allied Aircrew Experience in the Second World War*. Essex: Portland.

Victory Vehicles (1943)

In an interesting twist on the regular Disney personalities fronting the US war effort, *Victory Vehicles* was the first ever Disney cartoon with Goofy as the leading personality. An association is immediately made with the Allied 'V for Victory' campaign on the title page of the short as the car featured is adorned with patriotic stickers, including the blue 'V for Victory' symbol. In an attempt to induce the audience to action with another war spirited song, the animation opens with a convincing ditty aimed at reducing the amount of fuel consumption by the general public. The lyrics state, 'Who needs a limousine that's always out of gasoline. Jump on your pogo stick and laugh your cares away.'

The short opens with the familiar narrative of the educational wartime shorts. It charts the development of towns and cities since the invention of the motorcar and the subsequent highways. However, the narrator explains the problems that come from a heavy reliance upon cars and gasoline. This is demonstrated by the technique of the ani-map. The ani-map charts the various journeys needed to be made by different people and the struggles they face with a gasoline shortage.

The narrator then explains that thousands of people tried to come up with a solution to the gasoline shortage, inventing different kinds of vehicles that operated without gasoline. Many of these blueprints are shown to the audience; some are nothing more than bathtubs with wheels. Goofy demonstrates these ideas for the audience, representing the patriotic spirit of the many citizens who submitted ideas to the government. One of these ideas, for example, involves Goofy cycling on a wheelbarrow to transport his building materials around site. This would be to no avail, were it not for the fact that his actions are part of the 'Victory Housing Project', shown in the background of the animation in red, white and blue. Many of the other ideas showcased by Goofy pass into the realms of the ridiculous; however, the presence of red, white and blue throughout the animated short indicates that all the ideas are done in the service of the country and are motivated by patriotism. Goofy even plays the part of an exhausted air raid warden (again, his patriotic motives are indicated by the presence of a red, white and blue emblem on his armband and on his helmet.) Even his idea of moving himself along by holding a magnet close to his helmet is proved in the interests of patriotism. Goofy attracts a heap of scrap metal to his person with the magnet and crashes into a red, white and blue sign, reading 'Beat the Jap with Scrap!'

The narrator explains that not all the ideas were as successful as the ones demonstrated by Goofy but then reveals that the answer to society's gasoline shortage lies primarily in an object regarded by many as a children's toy: the pogo stick. Indeed, the pogo stick's association with the national effort is also demonstrated. The toy is light with a white light, places on a blue pedestal with red ledges for the feet of the one riding it. Goofy emerges from his house with the stick, labelled as a defence worker, automatically linking him with the war effort. Despite riding a pogo stick, explains the narrator, Goofy is able to continue with his normal day-to-day tasks. For example, we see Goofy reading his newspaper while on his pogo stick. Goofy arrives at work, invigorated by his morning exercise and ready to start a day's work.

As Goofy makes his way on the highway, the narrator suggests that the country could save on concrete if everyone took to using the pogo stick for transportation instead of their cars. The saving on concrete, he enlightens the audience, could be dropped on Tokyo or Berlin. The narrator then explains some further benefits of the adoption of pogo sticks and the audience witnesses the entire animated world utilizing them for transport.

What is of particular interest in this cartoon is not its basic premise of replacing motorcars with pogo sticks. It is simply the evidence of the extent to which total war has hit the animated world. Much like *Out of the Frying Pan Into the Firing Line*, the link is made between the animated home front and the war in the Pacific and Europe. The patriotism of each idea, as mentioned, is demonstrated by the recurrence of red, white and blue throughout the short. The narrator's references to Tokyo and Berlin as well as the sign 'Beat the Jap with Scrap' links the home front's efforts directly to victory on the battlefields.

This short also promotes the OWI directive on the unity in the civilian war effort, the 'total' nature of war and on the purchase of war bonds. The backgrounds in *Victory Vehicles* all show evidence of involvement in the war effort, showing the commitment of the animated world to the cause of the Second World War. Goofy's encounter with the newspaper salesman shows a poster for the sale of war bonds in the background. A shot in the centre of Goofy's town shows the Rationing Board and a poster in a shop window for citizens to 'Sign up and Serve'. Everything within the animated world is geared towards the war effort, making it an accurate reflection of the nature of the home front in 1943 America.

Commando Duck (1944)

While many of the 1942 and 1943 Disney cartoons featured a direct attack on the Nazi regime and its ideology, no such treatment was placed upon the

Hirohito regime. Similar to the situation within Hollywood, an effort was made within animation to separate the German people from the evils of the ideology of Nazism. However, the Japanese were simply depicted as a cruel, barbaric race of people, led only by their animal instincts. Their appearances were ridiculed and caricatured throughout animation. Interestingly, while the Warner Brothers cartoons featured extensive caricaturing of the Japanese race, the Disney Studios only really depicted the Japanese race through the last battle themed short of the war: *Commando Duck*.

In previous shorts, the threat from the Japanese was secondary to that faced by Hitler's Nazi regime, reflective of Roosevelt's 'Europe First' policy.[4] However, with the threat of the Axis powers in Europe fading quickly during 1944, the enemy in the Disney cartoons shifts to the Japanese. Donald fights the Nazis in his dreams in *Der Fuehrer's Face* (1943); however, in the final years of the war, when the American army focused its strategy on the Japanese, Donald is put directly into the Pacific war zone.

The short opens aboard an aircraft. Donald is heavily burdened with weaponry and equipment but having seemingly conquered his fear of jumping from planes, he receives his war assignment to find an enemy airfield with pride but also demonstrates his fear for what is about to happen to him. He jumps from the plane and lands safely, launching his emergency boat. Visibly displaying caution, Donald sets sail on the river. On the banks, however, the audience sees two Japanese snipers aiming for Donald. They are hidden in trees but upon hearing their accents and seeing them bow to each other, they are immediately identified as the Japanese enemy. The short then shows many Japanese rifles pointed in Donald's direction.

Donald is soon under fire but manages to escape being hurt. He paddles away quickly, only to come across a dangerous waterfall. He throws a rope over a nearby rock to try and pull himself to safety. However, in the bushes, we are given our first shot of a Disney animated Japanese soldier. The soldier manages to shoot at the rope holding Donald to safety. Donald's raft fills with water and eventually bursts on him. He runs quickly to escape the cascading water. Upon reaching the edge of a cliff, he catches sight of a Japanese airbase.

---

[4] Roosevelt's 'Europe first' policy sparked controversy in American society. Due to the attack on Pearl Harbor, many wanted to see the Japanese as the first target of the armed forces during the war. However, in combination with Churchill, Roosevelt believed that tactically, attacking the Axis powers through mainland Europe was the better course of action. The policy was widely reported; see, for example, A. O'Hare McCormick, 'First Blow in Europe', *The New York Times*, 18 June 1942, p. 20.

In a saddening twist, Donald looks at the oncoming water cascade, full of dangerous rocks heading towards him, accepts his fate, and salutes, ready to die for his country. However, the force of the water cascades him upwards, leaving him hanging from a nearby tree. The water falls down the cliff edge, destroying the enemy air base. Donald happily sends out the message that he has 'washed' away the base.

In its depiction of the Japanese enemy, this Disney cartoon was relatively tame by comparison to its Warner Brothers counterparts. However, there are several things of interest. Firstly, with regard to the Japanese, no attempt is made to separate the Japanese people from the soldiers as is accomplished in the earlier Disney cartoons with the German enemy. While only one Japanese soldier is shown, all are depicted as equally stupid. The brutality of the Japanese is only shown in so far as he is responsible for Donald falling to his death; however, no blood is shed and Donald is ultimately not hurt by the soldier's actions. On the contrary, with hindsight, the Japanese soldier is ultimately responsible for the destruction of his own airbase.

The short also showcases the height of Donald's contribution towards the American war effort. From undergoing rigorous training, fighting the Nazi threat within his dreams, paying his taxes while at home, peeling potatoes for the soldiers, Donald is finally able to assist in destroying the enemy for his country. His actions are direct and under command. However, notably, to maintain his goodness and morality, Donald is never shown actually destroying the enemy or even pointing a gun. In this way, Disney characters maintain a level of innocence kept out of the live action films.[5]

Bugs, Daffy & the Japs – Warner Brothers' contribution to the war effort

The Warner Brothers producer Leon Schlesinger was somewhat resentful of the fact that Disney was awarded all of the government contract work. However, this did not stop the Studios from producing some of the most ideologically focused animated shorts of the entire wartime period. Unlike Disney, due to the harsh

---

[5]   While the Disney cartoons were clear to show the fact that their animated characters would never hold a gun to an animated man or woman, Donald was no stranger to toting weaponry and threatening to use it against another. In the 1939 short, *Donald's Penguin* (1939) Donald holds his penguin up at gun point.

and anti-realist nature of Warner Brothers' animation, the productions of the Schlesinger Studios developed licence to handle harsher and cruder subjects, notably in their depiction of the Japanese threat. However, again, this animation capitalized on techniques used within the 1930s. Many of the stereotypes for the Japanese and for war subjects during these animated shorts were laid upon the foundations of the short subjects that handled international relations in the 1930s. Furthermore, the shorts handling the American armed forces and the importance of the Allied ideology lent heavily from the patriotic material of the late 1930s.

The Ducktators (1942)

The Ducktators provided an explicit commentary on the rise of Hitler and his relationship with the Axis powers. Its closest Disney counterpart is, arguably, *Der Fuehrer's Face*, as both use simple animated concepts in order to relay complex ideas to the audience. However, unlike Disney, who animates the men Hitler, Mussolini and Tojo, *The Ducktators* leaves the dictators in their animal form. The threat they pose is therefore restricted to the animated world.

Far from taking place in 'Nutziland', or the animated version of Nazi Germany, *The Ducktators* is strictly confined to the traditional farmyard setting of the animated world. Warner Brothers' animation, in its anti-realist stance, in this way, separates the conflict of the animated world from the real world. As the impact of Hitler's rise to power grows, so too does the impact on the farmyard setting. The short opens in the same way as many of the 1930s Looney Tunes shorts, showing an idyllic farmyard landscape. We are shown many of the geese and ducks waiting to smoke their cigars as 'Mr. and Mrs. Duck were expecting.' We hear the chirps of an unhatched egg and Mrs Duck rushes to see her newborn hatchling. The egg, however, is black and rotten, indicating from the outset that perhaps something is amiss with this newborn. The parents crowd around the egg, waiting for it to hatch. The father duck asks the mother duck, 'Was ist los?' signifying the first diversion from the traditional Warner Brothers' cartoon: the animals are German. The egg finally hatches and a baby Hitler chick is born (Figure 7.2).

Instantly recognizable as the animated duck form of the German leader, the chick is a ridiculous character. In showing the hatchling Hitler as inherently evil and 'rotten' due to the black egg, *The Ducktators* deals with a sophisticated ideological concept. It implies that the Axis leaders were born evil. There is no

Figure 7.2 *The Ducktators* (1942). Looney Tunes Golden Collection.

room for the middle ground of social conditioning in the animated world. This is also in keeping with the straightforward portrayal of the Nazis and the Japanese in Hollywood during the war. There is no such thing as the good Nazi or the good Japanese. Disney, however, does make these distinctions. The mother and father of the child Hans in *Education for Death* seem innocent in comparison to the Nazi soldier who threatens to take their child away when he becomes ill.

The narrator then tells us that time passes and with his artistic efforts spurned, the Hitler chick finds talent elsewhere. We see the grown up Hitler duck giving a speech on a 'soft soap' podium in the barnyard to some eager geese, stuffing their faces with corn. The narrator states that there were 'some gullible ones who listened'. While this does imply a negative portrayal of the German people, the narrator quickly diverts attention from the German citizens to the 'most gullible goose'. This is a caricature of Mussolini (Figure. 7.3). Mussolini is importantly viewed as a Nazi. Their shared ideology of fascism is broken down simply into Nazism through the display of a swastika armband on Mussolini's arm.

Demonstrating its self-awareness in a way that always separated Warner Brothers' animation from Disney, a disclaimer appears from the management, apologizing to 'the nice Ducks and Geese who may be in the audience'. Breaking

Figure 7.3 *The Ducktators* (1942). Looney Tunes Golden Collection.

the fourth wall between the confines of cinematic narrative and the audience, Warner Brothers also shields itself from any offence it may cause with its crude caricaturing.[6] If the caricaturing of Mussolini and Hitler brought the action of the animation too close for comfort to the real world, the Warner Brothers' animators step in to remind the audience that they are *only* watching an animation. Due to the realist nature of Disney animation, this extra layer of audience-directed narrative never exists.

Watching the developments of the Ducktators unfold, the Mussolini goose appears ever more ridiculous, shouting 'Tutti Frutti and all kinds of whipped cream and nuts!' to one tiny chick who is held in place with a ball and chain and made to applaud when Mussolini goose holds up a sign reading, 'Applause'. We also see the animated version of the Nazi storm troopers, who literally take a storm with them as they march through the yard. High above the farmyard,

---

[6] The 'fourth wall' is a cinematic term used to describe the effect when the presence of the audience is acknowledged within the narrative of a film production. This is usually done in mainstream film by an actor or actress looking directly at the camera, showing an awareness of its existence. For more information on the 'fourth wall', see Bordwell, D. and Thompson, K., eds (2002). *Film History: An Introduction.* New York: McGraw-Hill.

we see the Dove of Peace, watching sorrowfully at the militaristic marching movements of the duck storm troopers. We are then taken to the farmyard peace conference, where Hitler duck signs the treaty in front of many other ducks and geese. The treaty is put into a letter box labelled, 'For filing sacred pledges', which at its base, is a 'Treaty tearer upper'. The Treaty comes out as confetti.

Through its natural simplification of everyday objects and concepts, this short's narrative showcases physical objects to simplify complicated concepts. To explain Hitler's intentions at Munich, which is obviously under scrutiny here, *The Ducktators* simply shows Hitler putting the peace treaty into a shredder straightaway, demonstrating that he never intended to stick to his 'sacred pledges'.[7]

From the West, explains the narrator, comes another power. The newest addition to the *Duckators* is a caricature of the Japanese prime minister, Tojo. Similar to the Disney interpretation in *Der Fuehrer's Face*, Tojo's appearance is heavily caricatured as he makes his way across a nearby pond to join the other two ducktators. So there is no mistaking his nationality or his ideological allegiance, Tojo, like Mussolini, is also wearing a Nazi swastika armband and carries the Japanese flag. To signify his plans for expansion, while swimming over the pond, the Tojo duck sticks a sign on what he believes to be an island but what turns out to be a tortoise, which reads, 'Japanese Mandate Island'. He even tries to trick the tortoise into thinking he is Chinese, by pointing to a simple badge on his torso which reads, 'I am Chinese, Made in Japan.'

Frustrated, the Dove of Peace decides to take action against the Axis powers. He leads the charge against the three ducktators, which breaks out into total war within the farmyard. Amid the conflict, he passes a poster, reading 'Buy United States war bonds'. A soldier within the poster hops out into the farmyard and begins shooting at the ducktators. This constitutes the first indication of US involvement in the fight. Interestingly, while this is a man involving himself in a barnyard re-enactment of the Second World War, the distance between the real-life conflict and the animated conflict is maintained as the man returns to the poster at the end of the short.

---

[7]   The Munich Conference was held in September 1938. Hitler made demands upon Britain, France and Czechoslovakia for an annexation of the Sudetenland in northern Czechoslovakia. When an agreement was made for the land, British Prime Minister, Neville Chamberlain stated that the Munich Agreement would bring 'peace for our time'. Just five months later, Hitler went back on the Agreement and invaded the rest of Czechoslovakia. The Conference was believed, at the time, to have been very successful and its outcome had a positive effect on America's economy. See 'Stocks Here Leap in a Dramatic Day', *The New York Times*, 29 September 1938, p. 7.

Following the victory of the Dove of Peace over the ducktators, the audience is addressed once more through a textual narrative. Showing the three heads of the ducktators on the wall of Peace's cabin, the text reads, 'If you would like to make this true, all you have to do is buy war bonds.' The man from the poster who contributed towards victory is shown once more and the audience are encouraged to purchase war bonds.

As well as the ideological concepts already mentioned, there are a few other points of interest within this particular animated short. Firstly, with the exception of the soldier who leaps from the war bonds poster to shoot at the ducktators (which is not even shown to the audience) there is no Allied involvement whatsoever in the conflict that unfolds within the barnyard against the dictators. In their place, what develops is an interesting one-sided interpretation of the morality play we encounter in the Disney cartoons *Donald's Better Self* and *Donald's Decision*. The Dove of Peace is instantly recognizable as morally right and his position far above the farmyard setting also implies a link to heaven. The Allied powers, clearly defined at this point within the war, find their voice only through the Dove of Peace. This in itself can be seen as explicit ideological commentary. The Dove of Peace does not want to fight the Axis powers and only fights when provoked, suggesting that the Allies were forced into war.

Furthermore, if one compares the treatment of the Nazi threat here to, for example, *Education for Death* and *Der Fuehrer's Face*, a serious distinction can be made. The Warner Brothers cartoons, anti-realist in nature, ridicule the Nazi threat and their Allies. Donald is afraid of the Axis powers and is physically threatened by their presence on a day-to-day basis. While the dictators in each of the Disney treatments warrant ridicule, their position as animated men makes the physical threat of their presence seem more substantial. The dictators in *The Ducktators* are all farmyard animals and never seriously threaten the position of any of the other animals. There is no battle and weapons are fired not in conflict but in chaos.

Fifth Column Mouse (1943)

While many of the wartime Warner Brothers cartoons simply dealt with lampooning the Nazi, Japanese and Italian threats, equally many dealt with themes inherent within Hollywood movies of the time, for example, spies and infiltration of the enemy. As Blum has argued, in the absence of a direct threat to the homeland of America, false threats had to be created in the movies, particularly in support of Roosevelt's 'Europe First' strategy (1976, 15). *Fifth Column Mouse* was one such cartoon.

It opens in an idyllic community, where mice live together in harmony. They are even singing the popular 1920s song 'Ain't We Got Fun.' One of the mice spots the cat observing them at the window and fears for their lives. He is told not to worry as they are safe inside. However, the cat soon finds his way in to disrupt the mice. An authoritative mouse rises up and cries 'The cat! Lights out!' As though mimicking an aerial bombing, the mice are plunged into darkness and run for their lives into their hole. Tricking one mouse by holding up an artificial mouse hole, the cat manages to trap him. He implores that he will not hurt him and tempts him with cheese. The cat whispers that the mouse can have all the cheese he wants and then whispers a temptation to him in German.

The animated short instantly identifies the enemy cat as German. Similar to the Disney characterization of the Big Bad Wolf, this association thus has the power to carry to all subsequent cat and mouse variations. Indicatively, once the cat has finished giving his demands to the mouse, the mouse gives a Nazi salute to the cat, making the instant connection with Hitler's regime (Figure 7.4).

Figure 7.4 *Fifth Column Mouse* (1943). Looney Tunes Golden Collection.

The mouse is released from the cat back into the community where he attempts to convince his peers that the cat is not as bad as they think he is. An association with Nazi propaganda methods can be made here. The mouse speaks in song, almost attempting to hypnotize the mice to accept his point of view. He gestures wildly, inducing the mice into a trance which can easily be compared to the power of Hitler's spoken word.[8]

In the next shot, we see that the fifth column mouse was successful in his vendetta as the mice are acting as slaves to the cat, clipping his nails, grooming him and fanning his face. When browsing the menu for his evening meal with many mice waiting to tend his every need, the cat announces that he wants a 'fat tender mouse' for dinner. Fleeing in fear, the mice retreat to the hole. However, they soon group together and under leadership, decide to 'get rid of that cat'. The mice, in soldier formation, march out for their final battle with the cat. Helmets are placed upon their heads and they develop secret weapons in mass community projects. Indicative that the battle they face is on a scale with the one faced in the barnyard against the ducktators, a clear shot of the 'V for Victory: Buy War Bonds and Stamps' is visible, with the animated human soldier replaced by a mouse soldier in similar dress. Due to the clear connection made to the war against the Axis powers through the propaganda posters, his German accent and the methods he uses in order to trick the mice, an immediate association is made between the cat and Hitler.

Having built a large animal contraption to rival the cat, the mice easily manage to scare off their enemy. Once victorious, the mice sing of the fact that they 'did it before and they did it again'. Through music, animation is able to forge another layer of meaning complementing the short's content. The reference to a previous battle is made. While on the surface, this could refer to a previous dual the mice fought with the cat, due to the associations made between the cat and Nazi Germany throughout, it seems clear that the short is actually referring to the First World War fought against Imperialist Germany from 1914 to 1918, which roused similar nationalistic sentiments among the German nation (Carr 1991).

Tokio Jokio (1943)

Tokio Jokio is now widely regarded as one of the most racially offensive animated shorts ever made (Cohen 1997, 54). In stark contrast to Disney animation,

---

[8] For more information on the Nazi regime and its propaganda methods, see Welch, David (1983). *Propaganda and the German Cinema*. New York: I. B. Tauris.

Warner Brothers were not afraid to use offensive caricatures of the Japanese. While live action films lent themselves to explore the bestial quality of the Japanese threat, animation took up the cause of exaggerating and playing upon the supposed stupidity of their enemy in the Pacific.

Several advanced propaganda techniques are used in the making of *Tokio Jokio* which separates it from many of the other animated shorts of the period. While still operating within the paradigm of the animated world, framed typically by the opening shot of Porky, Daffy and Bugs, the short does not open in a rural or stereotypical city setting. The audience is exposed to static, and the narrator announces that the footage has, in fact, been captured from behind enemy lines. Adding this fourth wall to the narrative, enabling the familiar self-aware connection with the audience facilitates the feeling of truth from within the exaggerated framework of the animated world.

The cockerel who opens the news swiftly transforms into a buzzard, caricatured to look like the Japanese prime minister, Tojo. Again, the character of the buzzard already has negative connotations for audiences of Warner Brothers' cartoons. In *Porky's Poultry Plant*, it was the buzzard that threatened the peace of Porky's farm and that launched an aerial attack against him, provoking a terrible conflict between them.

Using text credits to separate the scenes of the animation, much like an official newsreel, the narrator explains that the audience is now to witness the Japanese air raid siren which contributes towards the defence of its civilians. The shot pans to the right and we see that the siren is simply the cry of a Japanese man, being prodded by another Japanese man with a needle so he winces in pain. Both men are heavily caricatured with glasses and buck teeth. Not only does this give the impression of Japanese stupidity, but it also creates the impression that Japan's civilian defence is easily penetrated. This idea is continued with the Listening Post, as another caricatured Japanese man simply listens to a post; the aeroplane spotting division (a man who paints spots on planes) and the fire prevention headquarters, a village which is now up in flames.

The next section of the short deals with 'Incendiary bombs' and the audience are shown a Japanese man who is instructed not to approach the bomb for five seconds. The connection between Nazi Germany and the Japanese regime under Hirohito is made here, as the man's watch reveals a swastika symbol. Using the simple iconography of the early 1930s cartoons, animation is able to forge a meaning without explaining the inner details of the alliance between Japan and Germany. *Tokio Jokio* also makes light of the lack of resources within Japan, hoping to boost morale by drawing a comparison with the United States. The 'club' sandwich, as prepared in Professor Tojo's cooking class, consists of a stack of ration cards, finished with Tojo hitting himself on the head with a club.

Interestingly *Tokio Jokio* also draws a direct comparison with US culture with its references to headline 'poisonalities' and sports. These make references to ice hockey, polo and American football. Poisonalities, as presented in this manner on a newsreel, draw comparison with the glamour of Hollywood. The best of the US culture was celebrated in the patriotic shorts of the late 1930s and to a certain extent, in the patriotism of the Bugs Bunny Treasury short by its references to history. By invoking such memories within the confines of the animated world, *Tokio Jokio* restores morale to the United States while at the same time, ridiculing its enemy. Its headline 'poisonality', Admiral Yamamato, has his sights set on the White House, however, the editors note that the only room reserved for him is one containing the electric chair.

Using the powerful symbol of the White House and its relationship to the president, animation plays on the emotional connection of the American people to their ideology in order to make an equally powerful and suggestive response to Japan's aspirations. This suggestion of the use of lethal force is interestingly one of the most sinister treatments of the enemy broadcast by Hollywood during the war period. While many of the war films such as *Bataan* (1944) do involve heavy violence against the Japanese threat such a suggestion has been rendered 'off limits' for treatment by animation. However, this was not the first time that animation had suggested the use of lethal force. *What Price Porky*, another Warner Brothers cartoon released in the 1930s authorizes the use of violence against an aggressor. Therefore, it can be concluded that this violence was not just confined to the wartime productions.

Reaching outside the confines of Japan to its neighbours within the Axis, *Tokio Jokio* reveals a donkey caricature of the radio personality William Joyce, who broadcasted a Nazi propaganda programme to people of the United States and Britain.[9] The donkey reveals that the fuehrer has just received a postcard from a friend, vacationing abroad, revealed only to be Rudolph Hess who abandoned the fuehrer and fled to Scotland (Read 2004, 685–7). The postcard shows a caricatured Hess in a concentration camp. The message reads, 'Wish you were here.'

---

[9] Lord Haw-Haw's activities were well known to the American people and were widely recorded in the press. See, for example, 'Lord Haw-Haw Now in Open', *The New York Times*, 28 September 1942, p. 7.

This allows audience to take away the impression that the fuehrer himself is low on allies, isolating him and demeaning his worldwide influence. Elsewhere, in Rome, Mussolini sits in his ruined capital, playing with a yo-yo. Interestingly, this shot gives the first indication of the impact of the Allied forces in the Mediterranean. Considering the historical context of this short, while animation did not accurately predict the outcome of the war, the short certainly is suggestive of the direction of the troops. During the period of production for this short, the Allies were emerging victorious in the North African campaign (Brighton 2009). Following this, in hindsight, were the invasions of Sicily and Italy, pre-empting the Italian surrender in September, through which Rome was negotiated to safety from the Germans (*The New York Times*, 12 September 1943, e4). While the ruins of Rome never actually came to pass, the short is shockingly accurate in its assumption of the proximity of Italian defeat which happened only months after *Tokio Jokio*'s release in May 1943.

While criticizing the military might of the Axis powers, *Tokio Jokio* also pokes fun at the production of Japanese submarines. The audience are shown a submarine half-finished at the bottom of the ocean. Japanese engineers are still constructing the vessel underwater. It is still being painted but is finished three weeks ahead of schedule. Swiftly moving to ridiculing the air force, Japanese planes are launched into the air with a large catapult aboard an aircraft carrier. The power of *Tokio Jokio* lies primarily in its ability to capitalize on powerful US symbolism and channel it into evoking hatred within the audience for their enemy as well as ridiculing their defence efforts, lampooning the enemy, ensuring that they do not provoke fear within the audience. It is also of interest that this animated short leaves the traditional animated world of animals. It is a direct caricature of the Japanese state. Humans are animated. The implication is that these ridiculous figures are the direct enemy of the audience. Warner Brothers' continuous narration and 'notes' for the audience forge this connection from the outset. The threat here goes beyond that experienced by the geese and ducks from the ducktators. This justifies both the threat of the electric chair (a decidedly human punishment) and criticism of the strength of the Japanese military.

Scrap Happy Daffy (1943)

This short, much like the Disney shorts *Victory Vehicles* and *Out of the Frying Pan Into the Firing Line*, draws a direct link between the contributions of the characters in the animated world to the conflict against the Axis powers in the real world. Daffy Duck draws the audience in with music, forging a connection between his efforts and their own, singing, 'We're in to win, so let's begin to do the job with junk.' He goes on to sing that this action will 'conquer freedom's foes'. This is directly in line with the directive from the OWI regarding the sort of pictures to be made in Hollywood to contribute towards the war effort. While Daffy sings his song, there is a direct utilization of the Disney technique in *The New Spirit*, which features Donald dancing in front of the mirror to *Yankee Doodle Spirit* (Figure 7.5).

This demonstrates the interchangeability of the studio's techniques during the war period. As each was promoting similar messages, the techniques they used to channel this ideology were readily used and reused between animated media. However, Daffy's reflection is altered upon the lyric, 'freedom's foes' to indicate the three Axis leaders. Once Daffy is finished listing all the many bits of junk that American people can save to help the Axis powers, he addresses the rear end of a horse, which quickly fades to a shot of Hitler's head. This constituted one of the first effective uses of editing within animation in order to convey a political message. Tashlin, well known as a director for shooting his animated

Figure 7.5 *Scrap Happy Daffy* (1943). Looney Tunes Golden Collection.

shorts as though they were live action, borrows from a well-known technique within the live action feature film to create effect in the animated world (Barrier 1999, 464–5).

The shot to Hitler unfolds as he reads a newspaper. The headline is 'Mussolini in Scrap Heap, now let's junk Hitler'. Again, this short requires placing within its specific historical context. The animated productions provide an explicit commentary on the direction and promise of the war, simply through the use of animated newspaper headlines. However, this technique was used in the 1930s to convey a sense of historical context to the cartoons. Many of the Porky Pig and Disney shorts feature headlines discussing Roosevelt. However, this is developed during the war to great effect.

Daffy becomes one of Carr's new 'symbols' for the war effort by fronting the scrap campaign in the animated world, as advertised in the newspaper and witnessed in the reality of the animated world. While such symbolism was not attached to the Warner Brothers' characters within the 1930s to the same extent as the Disney characters, their potential to become symbols for national unity was recognized and built upon. The short also shows the physical effect of home front initiatives such as the scrapping campaign on the Axis powers.[10] The caricatured Hitler is so enraged by Daffy's campaign, he demands that all Nazi scrap piles be destroyed and eats his carpet in frustration. As his message finally reaches the German navy, a bomb is fired at Daffy's scrap pile but as the German navy is seemingly out of ammunition, the only firepower that emerges from the bomb is a goat who goes to work to eat all of Daffy's scrap pile. Daffy quickly locates the goat who is wearing a swastika round his neck. After a duel, Daffy emerges beaten and tired. However, leaning on the nationalistic techniques of the 1930s to inspire a similar fervour in wartime, reference is made to the Mayflower voyage of 1620. Daffy's Uncle Gillingham sings 'Did I cry spinach when I stood a duck on Plymouth rock?' Daffy draws on the history of his ancestors and thus the history of the United States in order to give him the strength to win his fight with the Nazi goat.

Furthermore, Daffy's Uncle Gillingham appears before Daffy as an apparition in the clouds. Showing similarity with both the Disney Treasury films and with the Warners' Treasury film *Any Bonds Today*, the moral righteousness of the American is emphasized through the appearance of an animated figure in

---

[10] See 'Campaign Widened for Scrap Metal', *The New York Times,* 14 September 1942, p. 23 and 'Industry will Push Campaign for Scrap Metal', *The New York Times,* 25 October 1943, p. 23.

the clouds. Consequently, a connection can be made between Daffy's Uncle Gillingham and heaven. Drawing on further from American history, many of Daffy's relatives who fought in significant battles, coach Daffy on his mission to defeat the goat. This sequence closes with a caricature of Abraham Lincoln who tells Daffy that, 'Americans don't give up.'

These apparitions firmly situate Daffy as an American citizen with a solid family grounding in most of the seminal events in American history. Not only does the animated world recognize the depth of the commitment and the historicity of the Second World War, Daffy is made a *part* of that history. The caricatured Duck forms of many of the major personalities in American history forging a real connection between Daffy's personal history and the history of the American people. This shared history is thus used as a tool to bridge the gap between the animated world and the real world, as was the case in the 1930s cartoons. Daffy announces to the audience that he is an *American* duck and takes on the form and uniform of a superhero, ready to conquer the Nazi goat. Daffy, while flying after the goat, is hit at many times by Nazi soldiers aboard a submarine but the bullets simply fly off his new superhero costume.

Scrap Happy Daffy, while originally taking on the guise of a simple education film showing the merits of saving scrap metal actually translates a deeper ideological meaning which was noticed by its American audience. Daffy, thus far pushed into the background by the overriding popularity of Bugs Bunny, took on his own symbolic significance following this cartoon (*The New York Times*, 22 July 1945, 43). Through his experience with the goat and his fierce protectiveness over his position as Salvage Warden, an important link is made between the work being done on the home front and the battle American armed forces faced on the front lines. As previously mentioned, Daffy also finds strength from within his American heritage. Through references made to pivotal points in American history, Daffy embraces the kind of patriotism discovered by Porky Pig in *Old Glory*.

Bugs Bunny Nips the Nips (1944)

Much like the focus of the 1944 Disney cartoon, *Commando Duck*, following the successful invasion of occupied France in 1944, the direction of the principal enemy in the animated world noticeably shifted. While *Tokio Jokio* showcases the stupidity of the Japanese race and explicitly refers to the depth of hatred between the two nations, *Bugs Bunny Nips the Nips* depicts the Japanese as a ridiculous, beatable foe, well within the animated character's strength to defeat.

The cartoon opens on the Pacific Ocean, where Bugs is inexplicably inside a crate, singing. Upon spotting an island, he quickly swims to shore. He remarks how peaceful and beautiful the island is; however, he soon comes under gun fire and seeks cover in a haystack. He comes face to face with a Japanese soldier, whom he addresses with his famous catchphrase, 'What's Up, Doc?' Unlike the caricature featured in the Disney cartoon *Commando Duck*, a full caricature of a Japanese man is displayed.

The apparent ruthlessness and cruelty of the Japanese is highlighted as the soldier immediately swings for Bugs Bunny with a knife. Bugs runs for cover and the soldier throws a bomb down the rabbit hole after him. In order to save himself from execution, Bugs poses as General Tojo. In an interesting twist, the Japanese soldier whispers to the audience that he recognizes Bugs Bunny for who he really is – a cartoon character. His cover blown, Bugs pretends to take to the sky, hotly pursued by the soldier; however Bugs ties his enemy's plane to a tree so the Japanese soldier has to parachute from the plane. To 'help' the soldier on his way, Bugs gives him some scrap metal, ensuring he is weighted down sufficiently to have a 'happy landing'. Later, Bugs does battle with a Sumo wrestler and manages to fool him by dressing as a geisha. However, he soon spots an army of Japanese soldiers heading in his direction. Disguising himself as an ice cream man and selling bombs, disguised within ice cream cakes, he soon eliminates the threat, while dealing out fond insults to the soldiers such as 'monkey face' and 'slant eyes'. Happy with his work, Bugs declares that he hates the peace and quiet of Japan. In the distance, heralded into shot by the blowing of trumpets, he spots an American warship. He calls for help quickly but soon changes his mind about leaving the island upon sight of a pretty lady.

Using Bugs Bunny as a point of unity for the American people, the upcoming confrontation with the Japanese is played out in the animated world. Reflecting the militaristic tradition of Hollywood in 1944 with films such as *Thirty Seconds Over Tokyo* (1944), Bugs emerges in this animated short as the militaristic hero. He is assertive and decisive in each of his encounters with the Japanese men. Here, it can be deduced that not only does animation lean on techniques from the 1930s, but also takes from the cinematic traditions of the Second World War in order to put across its ideological message. In forming a line of resistance against the Japanese threat, Bugs presents himself as a civilian soldier, fighting the war in the Pacific.

Animator Bob Clampett reflected on Bugs Bunny in an interview with animation historian Michael Barrier, stating that, 'Bugs Bunny was a symbol of American resistance to the fascist powers. ... In both instances [the war and the Depression], we were in a battle of our lives, and it is most difficult to comprehend the tremendous emotional impact Bugs Bunny exerted on the audience back then' (*Funnyworld Magazine,* 1970). Bugs Bunny was not viewed simply as a comical character highlighting the weaknesses of the Japanese. He took on a greater symbolic meaning to the American people which, according to Clampett, was emotional and significant.

Russian Rhapsody (1944)

Russian Rhapsody is unique among the wartime animated shorts in that it opens with a physical commentary of the war. Through the use of a narrator, the short refers to the German army's failure to capture Moscow in the winter of 1941–2 (Overy 2004, 493–5). Moscow, however, remained important to Hitler and to Stalin in terms of its symbolic meaning for the Russian people (Service 2004, 423–4). Its importance is thus highlighted within the narrative of this animated short. It is highly significant that this short was released in 1944.

Confident of success against Germany, the lack of progress of Hitler's armies against Stalin's Red Army drives this animated short. A heavily caricatured Hitler screams at the German people, telling them the importance of Moscow. He states that he will send 'the best bomber in the Reich' in order to ensure that the job is done properly. However, as an unseen civilian comments, the only person that satisfies Hitler's criteria is Hitler himself. Much like *Plane Daffy*, such a twist in the narrative only serves to highlight Hitler's present isolation with the Nazi regime. He no longer even trusts his best pilots to do the job for him. Furthermore, as newspaper headlines state, the importance of Moscow warrants the personal attention of the fuehrer himself. However, while in the air, Hitler's plane is attacked by 'gremlins from the kremlin' who all work together to ensure Hitler is removed from the plane and the threat from Moscow is removed. The short also includes an animated version of Stalin, the first in any animated short over the war period.

Given the fact that Russia did not officially join the side of the Allies until June of 1941 when they were invaded by the Wehrmacht, its absence from treatment within animation is of interest, particularly since animation willingly passed comment on the Communist threat during the Cold War (DelGaudio 1997).

This short is particularly interesting for historians as it gives an interpretation of sorts, from America's point of view, on a conflict they were not directly involved in. The war on the Eastern Front between Germany and Russia thus receives its first treatment in animation with *Russian Rhapsody*. Again, it is of interest that in order to convey its ideological treatment, many of the techniques mentioned within Carr's memorandum are utilized within this Warner Brothers' cartoon.

The 'ani-map' is used on the short's opening in order to establish a sense of time, place and location. In addition, the cartoon does not lose the self-awareness evident in ideologically charged 1930s animation such as *Bosko in Person*, and to a certain extent, *What Price Porky*. After the Hitler makes a particularly animated speech, referring, among other things, to 'sauerkraut in dein delicatessen', a human hand holds a board up for the audience which reads, 'Silly, isn't he?' establishing a shared bond and experience between the animators and the American people. Crucially, by discouraging the realism demonstrated by the Disney cartoons and maintaining its own levels of exaggerated and crude humour, Warner Brothers forges its own self-contained pantomime out of the fuehrer's mannerisms.

Plane Daffy (1944)

Following over ten years in the animation business, Leon Schlesinger sold his studio to Warner Brothers on 1 July 1944 for seven hundred thousand dollars.[11] *Plane Daffy* was one of the very first cartoons to be released through Warner Brothers Productions and is also the last ever cartoon Tashlin ever completed for the studio before he left in September 1944.

Released on 14 September, *Plane Daffy* focuses on the activities of the animated air force. The commanding officers of the animated air force are waiting on the return of Number Thirteen, Homer Pigeon, who, it is revealed by the narrator, is not 'doing his duty'. He is seen lying on the lap of a voluptuous woman, Hatti Mari, who is an Axis spy and a stereotypically morally ambiguous femme fatale. The woman tips alcohol down Thirteen's throat, trying to get some information out of him. He quickly tells all about the fleet's proposed movements.

---

[11] 'Acquisition of Leon Schlesinger Productions', Memorandum from Warner Brothers Cartoons Incorporated. Document Reference USC/WB/DOC 7704, Warner Brothers Archives, University of Southern California.

The woman switches on the television in the corner and the narrator states that Thirteen has told all to 'you know who'. The television shows Hitler with his hand to his ear, gladly taking in all of the information. Realizing he has betrayed his country, Thirteen takes a gun offered to him by the woman in order to commit suicide. Back at the air force base, the commander concludes that Homer has been tricked by the 'queen of the spies' and shows the officers what they are up against. While they are taken aback by her beauty, Daffy arrives and announces he is a 'woman hater' and that he will not be fooled by her charms.

Setting off, however, he is quickly taken captive by the spy. She seduces Daffy with an explosive kiss and asks him to hand over his military secrets. However, rather than be a traitor to his country, Daffy eats the paper containing the secrets. Hatti Mari shoves Daffy in an X-ray machine, anxious to get to the secret. Under the machine, the secret is revealed to be 'Hitler is a stinker'. On a nearby television screen, Goering and Goebbels conclude that 'everybody knows that', and shoot themselves in the head upon receiving Hitler's disapproving glare (Figure 7.6).

This animated short is worthy of interest from scholars for many reasons. The first is simple. *Plane Daffy* was the first wartime cartoon to link Nazism to promiscuity. Hatti Mari, incidentally a reference to the First World War German spy Mata Hari, is brazen in her seduction of both Thirteen and of

Figure 7.6 *Plane Daffy* (1944). Looney Tunes Golden Collection.

Daffy.[12] Wearing sexually revealing clothing and drinking alcohol, her persona links the Axis powers to sexual and moral ambiguity. Here, the Carr memorandum of 1942 written for the productions of the Disney Studios also seems to apply. In opposition to the creation of a 'Pan Americana' who is described as a 'noble female figure, subtly suggesting both the Virgin Mary and the Goddess of Liberty', Warner Brothers created the Axis equivalent.[13] Hatta Mari seems representative of the ideology of the Axis powers. Hatta is violent and promiscuous, which again seems to target the anti-religion angle the Disney animation proposed in the Carr document. She is deceptive and cunning, in stark contrast to the frankness and honesty demonstrated by Daffy.

Also of interest to scholars is the depiction of the Nazi elite. Untouched in such detail since perhaps the Disney treatment in *Der Fuehrer's Face*, *Plane Daffy* not only caricatures the Nazi elite but also makes a statement about the stability of the Nazi regime at that point during the war. In 1944, as the Russians moved through Poland, the British continued its heavy bombing campaign in Berlin, causing the morale of the German people to reach new lows.[14] This short articulates that low morale is depicted within the Nazi elite. When the military secret, 'Hitler is a stinker' is revealed, both Goering and a green-looking Goebbels agree with the statement. The short thus puts across the message that there is disunity among the leaders of the Nazi state, making the enemy look all the more defeatable for the American audience.[15]

The short also gives a somewhat shocking commentary on the importance of loyalty to the state in the animated world. Thirteen shoots himself once he realizes that he has allowed himself to be tricked into spilling military secrets to Hatti Mari. The dishonour of betrayal is too heavy a burden for an officer in the air force, even in the animated world. This explicit reference to suicide within these cartoons needs to be taken seriously as a form of commentary on the military context of the time. While the Allies were confidently making advances into

---

[12] American audiences would have immediately recognized the caricature of the German spy. Famous 1930s actress Greta Garbo played the German dancer and spy in a successful film adaptation of her life entitled *Mata Hari* in 1932. See 'Greta Garbo Gives a Brilliant Portrayal', *The New York Times,* 1 January 1932, p. 31.

[13] R. S. Carr 'The Creation of New Symbols', p. 37, f. 22, Motion Picture Society for the Americas records, Margaret Herrick Library, Beverly Hills.

[14] See 'Berlin Gets First US Bombing', *The New York Times,* 5 March 1944, p. 1.

[15] The depiction of the faltering loyalty of Goering and Goebbels in this short is ironic, considering that these two members of the Nazi elite were in fact, the most loyal to Hitler. Goebbels and his wife committed suicide after Hitler himself had passed away, after poisoning their own children. Goering, too, committed suicide at the Nuremberg trials after being sentenced to death by hanging. See 'Guilt Is Punished', *The New York Times,* 16 October 1946, p. 1.

occupied Europe during the year this cartoon was under production, nonetheless, the officers within the animated armed forces still remain on their guard. Duty and honour to their country are as important as ever and complacency is viewed as a weakness punishable by death. The scenes in *Plane Daffy* are shocking even when analysed in the context of the explicit nature of modern animation.

Herr Meets Hare (1945)

Released just four months before Hitler's death and the surrender of Berlin on 7 May 1945, *Herr Meets Hare* shows a 'final battle' between the animated symbol for the United States, Bugs Bunny and the Nazi high command. The short opens with a radio transmission discussing the end of Germany and pondering over the whereabouts of 'Fatso' Goering. The short then cuts to an overweight Goering in traditional dress, marching through the 'Black Forest' in Germany. We then see Bugs, burrowing his way through the woods. He is held at gunpoint by Goering and asks the way to Las Vegas. Soon discovering he is no longer in America, Bugs is spooked and runs away from Goering. Goering soon begins to share with Bugs his unhappiness with the Nazi state, calling his fuehrer a 'schwein'. Bugs quickly styles his hair like Hitler and paints on a moustache to scare Goering who flees the scene on sight of the Hitler-Bugs and dresses in his military uniform, adorned with medals and the swastika. After dressing and dancing to the Wagnerian opera *Tannhauser*, Bugs is captured by Goering. Proud of his catch, Goering takes Bugs Bunny to the fuehrer. Before Hitler can pass judgement, Bugs pops out of the bag, dressed as Joseph Stalin and the pair flee in fear.

Herr Meets Hare was one of the last significant war cartoons to be released by the Warner Brothers studio. Unlike Disney, who thereafter focused mainly on their production of feature animation, Warner Brothers continued to make short subject animation their strongpoint. However, despite their differences, there is a noticeable link between the two studios' contributions to the animated propaganda effort during this particular animated short. During Goering's marching scenes, the music accompanying his movements is uncannily similar to Oliver Wallace's *Der Fuehrer's Face*. Indeed, reference is made to a lyric of the song as Goering states, 'I kiss right in der Fuehrer's Face.' This demonstrates recognition of Disney in Warner Brothers' animation, as a celebration of their work over the war years.

In this short, Warner Brothers also shows recognition of the fact that the war, soon to be over, was ultimately a war of ideologies. Goering and Hitler run scared

Figure 7.7 *Herr Meets Hare* (1945). Looney Tunes Golden Collection.

at the sight of Bugs dressed as Stalin. While the alliance of the United States and the Soviet Union does constitute an uneasy ideological and cartoon hybrid (demonstrated by Bugs, the symbol of America, dressed awkwardly as Stalin, the head of the Soviet Union) (Figure 7.7), it is ultimately the combination of these two ideologies that allows the Allies to triumph over the Axis powers. Through the union of Bugs and his own caricature of Stalin, this short demonstrates an awareness of these ideologies and the role they had to play in the Second World War. It also uses caricature in order to simplify the difficult political consequences of the alliance for the American people, a technique used throughout the 1930s when dealing with complex subjects.

Conclusion

By the time of the Japanese surrender in September 1945, the ability of animation to deal with advanced political subjects was extraordinary. Building upon the work carried out for the Treasury and in Disney's case, through its work for the OIAA, these animated studios were able to make an explicit case for the continuation of the war against the Axis powers by making animated shorts in line with the OWI's directives for Hollywood. Each film produced by each of the animation studios showed an awareness of the international situation. It did this by making its characters, narrative and music embrace the key concepts of nationalism, freedom and determination to bring the United States to victory.

For audiences, following the antics of their favourite animated characters, most of whom had come to hold a particular emotional significance to them, was a source of comfort. The connections made between the real world and the animated world are most explicit in the shorts explored in this chapter, they demonstrate a shared experience of war. Donald fights in the US Army with animated human soldiers. Donald, Daffy and Bugs Bunny all take up arms against the Nazi elite. The fight is taken from the animated world straight to the enemy in the real world. This enemy, as the War continues, becomes easier to defeat for the cartoon characters, and therefore, seems easier for US audiences to overcome.

Following the war, animation was seen as an important idealistic forum in which these characters could overcome obstacles difficult to face during the real world. Walter Wanger's article of 1950, entitled *Donald Duck and Diplomacy*, suggests that these characters and, indeed, Hollywood, had taken on a special international importance during the war and that this should thus be recognized on an international scale (1950, 452).

It is impossible not to read these cartoons ideologically. They did not have the subtleties of many of the 1930s animated productions. The explicit propagandistic messages of each of the shorts studied in this chapter, and many more besides, made it impossible for the audience *not* to notice the ideological messages woven into their narratives. However, such cartoons did not represent animation's only commentary on political, social and economic conditions. During the war, these studios simply used the techniques they had used throughout the 1930s in order to forge meaning to audiences. Essentially, the only thing that had changed was the historical context.

8

Conclusion: That's All Folks

And yet, as he said this, Disney's eyes darkened and he pointed to a series of
identical plaques in the trophy jammed anteroom of his office. The plaques
all read, 'For the Best Children's Picture.' For an instant, the old frustrations
seemed to return as he spluttered, 'They persist in giving me that blasted award
every year. I don't make children's pictures. Why do they do it?'

Davidson 1964

On the surface, the animated shorts released by Disney and Warner Brothers'
Schlesinger Studios looked innocent enough. Donald Duck, Mickey Mouse,
Minnie Mouse, Pluto, Goofy, Porky Pig, Daffy Duck and Bugs Bunny were
all colourful creations, stumbling around comically in a fanciful caricatured
version of reality. Due to their comical misdemeanours, childlike fighting and
grossly exaggerated romances, their cartoons were categorized as harmless
by the Hays Office. Disney's reputation for producing outstanding quality
animation did not alleviate him from Hays pressure, for the shorts produced by
the Schlesinger Studios, too, did not fall at the hands of 1930s movie censorship.
And yet, these productions developed into a highly politicized medium by the
Second World War.

The main obstruction to scholars wishing to engage in an analysis of Disney or
Warner Brothers' animation in this period is the lack of primary source material
surrounding production. The Warner Brothers Archives hold little by way of
information on the formation of plotlines and gags of the animation produced
by the Schlesinger Studios and the Disney Archives are closed to all but internal
researchers. However, through careful excavation of internal memoranda and
trade press reviews in combination with qualitative analysis of the shorts, it is
possible to uncover the techniques consciously employed by the Disney Studios
to convey ideology through their animated storylines. While it is true that these
conclusions can only be confidently articulated, it cannot be denied that many

of these techniques also apply to the Warner Brothers' animated shorts of the same period.

However, it would be a mistake to confine the application of this ideological framework to the wartime cartoons only. The techniques outlined in Carr's early war memoranda had their origins in the cartoons of the mid to late 1930s.

In the early 1930s, both Disney and Schlesinger's animation harnessed the popular mood through symbolism and caricature. Roosevelt's ascension to the presidency brought with it an intense feeling of community spirit. Using his war-like rhetoric of unity against a common enemy, the cartoons embraced the battle American society faced against the Depression and against the lethargy and despair associated with President Hoover. Optimism and a new embrace of family values found a home in early animation. Even FDR himself made the odd appearance in the cartoons as the signal that a new day had dawned and that things were changing for the American people, even in the animated world.

For the first time, an intrinsic connection was made between the world of Mickey Mouse, which had seemed nothing but a fairy tale creation, and the world that the American people were living in. This connection was recognized by the American people as early as 1933 due to the success of the Disney Silly Symphony *The Three Little Pigs*. The battle between the Pigs and the Big Bad Wolf resonated with the American people. They too, were doing battle with a dangerous foe. Regardless of Disney's intentions with this short, people identified with the animated world. And yet the Hays Office did not regard these productions as ideologically significant.

The productions of the Disney Studios and Schlesinger Studios moved swiftly from populist sentiment to the development of social and political commentary. Using its popular characters as psychological markers, the narratives of these shorts articulated the same moral dilemmas as the American people. How should one react in a situation where the choice between simple individualism and a tiresome communitarianism are the ideological paths laid out for action? These animated characters provided the answer for the American people, creating their own models for social action.

This intrinsic moral guidance was present in the Hollywood films of the time. However, these live action films were censored by the Hays Office, the animation was not. In this way, animation was able to develop as an unhindered ideological force within Hollywood. Hidden beneath the childlike characters and colourful fairy tales of the animated world lay a serious vehicle for serious social and political commentary. Mickey, Donald and Porky Pig were by no means immune from the economic pressures of Depression America. Shorts such as *Moving Day* and *Milk and Money* are explicit in their engagement with financial worries. Their narratives are an all too serious reminder of the difficulty faced by Roosevelt in rebuilding a broken America. These shorts also reflected the political frustrations inherent within society. *Self Control* and *Porky's Road Race* contain explicitly negative identifications with the FDR administration. They contain a political commentary that in the world of the live action feature film would have been discarded by the Hays Office.

This unchallenged ideological drive is perhaps more explicit in the world of international relations. Hollywood was taken to charge over the interventionist sentiment of its productions during the late 1930s and early 1940s. The furore over Warners' *Confessions* sparked an inquest. Animation, through subtle use of symbolism, provided a commentary on the way its characters felt about conflict. Through the caricature of the rise of the fascist leaders, it facilitated an explicit and radical analysis of the rising tensions within Europe. It is in these highly sophisticated politicized cartoons that scholars can identify the origins of the sophisticated wartime animated propaganda. The techniques used in these cartoons draw on the ideological associations of their characters in the early 1930s. The wolf was the overriding enemy, Mickey was a force for good, Donald was a reluctant hero and Porky was a hardworking pacifist. These characters are cast into their roles in the rapidly unravelling military drama of the 1930s, rehearsing for the main production. One cannot ignore the explicit ideological messages of cartoons such as *Three Little Wolves* and *What Price Porky*. Audience reviews from trade press reveal these cartoons were read in a political way and yet Hays still did not censor them. The explicit patriotic undertones of the cartoons of the late 1930s, in response to the threat from Europe and the strong isolationist and pacifist undertones within society cannot be mistaken for anything else.

These animated shorts were read ideologically by their audiences. The cartoons released just before the Second World War display pride in American national institutions, its geographical landmarks and its history. Through animating these ideas, a real connection is forged between the animated world and the real world. Audiences celebrated the greatness of their country through the cinema in this period in Hollywood's history. This celebration was also evident within the animated world.

The techniques used within these animated productions were again utilized in the wartime productions in order to raise morale on the American Home

Front and for the struggles of the United Nations. These were drawn into direct contrast with the ideology of the Axis powers in order to demean the enemy forces. Scholars can only guess at the reasons why animation was thought as ideologically unharmful by the Hays Office. It is likely that the categorical rejection of animation as a serious cinematic medium that plagued its treatment by scholars for many years was at the heart of this decision. How could the antics of mice, ducks and pigs be at the heart of any serious ideological rebellion? And yet, as proven by the reviews in the trade press, American audiences identified ideologically with these cartoons. Contemporary film analysts viewed Mickey Mouse as an important cultural symbol. Donald was interpreted as a personification of the violent spirit of the times, as a characterization of people's consistent frustration with their lot. Yet his eventual acceptance of the realities of war made it all the more significant when he was the first to sign up to pay his income taxes. These characters had a psychological significance for audiences.

It is also likely that the natural hyperbole and caricature of most animation made the Hays Office consider the medium generally, as opposed to looking at individual cartoons. It is true that not all of the animation produced by Warner Brothers and Disney was ideologically significant. Most were not. However, it is the collective effect of these cartoons over the period under study that is significant. The formation of Donald Duck's character throughout the 1930s until the outbreak of war made him all the more important as Disney's war hero. He was lazy at the beginning of the 1930s and a charter member of the Idle Hours Club. He struggled with his rent and he was reluctant to adopt the community spirit exemplified by the New Deal. He was frustrated by the administration's constant reminders for him to keep calm and hope for better times. His better self favoured intervention in Europe. But through this ideological journey, he emerged as Disney's poster child for war, employed by the Treasury to spur on the American people. Donald pays his taxes selflessly, joins up for armed service and fights the Nazis and the Japanese, emerging victorious.

Similarly, the transformation of the Big Bad Wolf from figurehead for the Depression, to a dangerous German passing on his appetite for destruction to a naïve youth, to his evolution as a Nazi was also an important ideological journey. This journey happened well before US involvement in the conflict in Europe. In a similar vein, the Pigs, through their interaction with the villainous Wolf came to symbolize patriotic, triumphant American citizens long before the attack on Pearl Harbor.

In combination with the ideological direction of its principal characters, this animation was also able to use music to its advantage when conveying its messages throughout the 1930s and 1940s. Through the innovative cartoon, *Steamboat Willie*, the Disney Studios was the first to use synchronized sound in its productions and quickly realized that music was as powerful as any other dimension within the animated production. *Who's Afraid of the Big Bad Wolf* became an anthem for the American people. They united behind these animated characters through music.

This became all the more powerful when such anthems were harnessed for a different cause. The Wolf turned into the Nazi enemy. Donald was given his own theme tune to rally people behind his efforts to pay his income taxes. Daffy sang that they were 'in it to win it'. These characters were living the war, along with their audiences and kept their spirits high. This transition from entertainment to political commentary found its origins in the animated shorts of the mid-1930s. Capitalizing on the techniques developed by these cartoons in this period to represent ideology, animation was then more than ready to take on the challenges of propaganda presented in wartime. As yet, no study has analysed this journey in the level of depth the cartoons warrant. Scholars speak of the cultural importance of the Disney cartoons without really giving mind to *why* they became culturally important. They speak of the popularity of Donald without explaining *how* his character became popular. Through charting the journey of animation in relation to the political, economic and social context into which these cartoons were released, it has been possible to explore, in depth, the historical importance of this animation.

Ultimately, these animated productions did not change the way they told stories during the Second World War. The techniques it used had been tried, tested and successful. In the Second World War, audiences had come to expect a certain type of animated production from the Disney Studios and the Warner Brothers Studios. They had come to expect animation to fulfil their ideological needs. Cartoon characters became emotional markers for their experiences of the Depression. Audiences expected them to fulfil the same ideological roles once the country was fighting another war. However, this time, the enemy was not domestic but international. What changed was the context into which these stories were received.

The government, now at war with an international enemy, called upon these studios to make their contribution, ignorant to the fact that animation had already been interpreting the decade's political, social and economic problems.

It was from the experiences of the Second World War that animation came to be seen and recognized by the government as a vehicle for education and interpretation; however, audiences and the studios themselves had recognized this from the mid-1930s. Indeed, Sybil DelGaudio has begun work on animation's interpretative potential as a link is forged between animation and the context in which it is produced (1997). However, as yet, there is little work done on the animated shorts produced after the war during the Cold War period. Disney's early feature films also remain relatively untouched in terms of their historical context. Byrne and McQuillan seem content to analyse Disney films only from the 1990s onwards (Bryne and McQuillan 1999). Herein lies a plethora of untouched animation, rich in history and contextual references which has not yet been full excavated by historians.

This research thus sets the bar for future work to be done on the medium of animation, particularly in how it conveys its historical ideology. How do the cartoons of Disney and Warner Brothers *do* history? How are the boundaries of animation transformed to make a traditionally uncomplicated medium translate inherently complex ideas? This research has merely scratched the surface of animation's interpretative potential. Disney saw animation, in the future, handling increasingly complex subjects. Through the lessons learnt throughout the war, it was recognized that in fact, there were few boundaries to what the medium was able to convey. Disney stated, 'Animation can explain whatever the mind of man can conceive. This facility makes it the most versatile and explicit means of communication yet devised for quick mass appreciation' (Krasniewicz 2010, 24). The potential for animation is limitless. Thus, the levels of interpretation for historians are also limitless.

Disney felt animation was capable of handling the intricacies of social, political and economic commentary as well as providing a simple way to educate and inform. He did not feel the content of his animation was for children. He fought for the recognition of animation to the level of the live action feature film. This book has sought to uncover untreated animated shorts and shed new light on the cultural significance of well-known productions. It has presented the interpretation of the Depression and the war of both the Disney Studios and by comparison, the Schlesinger Studios. These cartoons have left a deep impact on the landscape of history and will remain socially and politically significant for many years to come.

Works Cited

Adamson, J. (1968). *From This You Are Making A Living?*. Interview with Richard Huemer. American Film Institute, Los Angeles, CA.

Adamson, J. (1985). *Tex Avery: King of Cartoons*. New York: Da Capo Press.

Alexander, C. (1969). *Nationalism in American Thought 1920-1945*. Chicago: Rand-McNally.

Allen, F. (1940). *Since Yesterday: The Nineteen Thirties in America*. New York: Harper & Bros.

Alston, L. J. (1983). 'Farm Foreclosures in the United States During the Interwar Period'. *The Journal of Economic History*, 43 (4): 885–906.

Ambrose, S. E. (1998). *The Victors: Eisenhower and His Boys: The Men of World War Two*. New York: Simon & Schuster.

Ambrose, S. E., and D. Brinkley (1997). *Rise to Globalism: American Foreign Policy since 1938*. New York: Penguin Books.

Arieli, Y. (1964). *Individualism and Nationalism in American Ideology*. Cambridge, MA: Harvard University Press.

Badger, A. (1989). *The New Deal: The Depression Years, 1933-1940*. Basingstoke: Macmillan.

Balfour, M. (1979). *Propaganda in War 1939-1945: Organisations, Policies and Public in Britain and Germany*. London: Routledge & Kegan Paul.

Barrier, M. (1999). *Hollywood Cartoons: American Animation in its Golden Age*. New York: Oxford University Press.

Beckerman, H. (2001). *Animation: The Whole Story*. New York: Allworth Press.

Beckman, K. (2014). *Animating Film Theory*. Durham: Duke University Press.

Bell, E., L. Haas and L. Sells, eds. (1995). *From Mouse to Mermaid: The Politics of Film, Gender and Culture*. Bloomington: Indiana Press.

Bendazzi, G. (1994). *Cartoons: One Hundred Years of Cinema Animation*. London: John Libbey.

Bergman, A. (1971). *We're in the Money: Depression America and its Films*. New York: New York University Press.

Bernstein, M. A. (1987). *The Great Depression: Delayed Recovery and Economic Change in America, 1929-1939*. New York: Cambridge University Press.

Birdwell, M. (2005). 'Technically Fairy First Class: Is this any Way to Run an Army: Private Snafu and World War Two'. *Historical Journal of Film Radio and Television*, 25 (2): 202–12.

Blum, J. M. (1976). *V was for Victory: Politics and American Culture during World War Two*. New York: Harcourt.

Blumberg, B. (1979). *The New Deal and the Unemployed: The View from New York City*. Lewisburg: Bucknell University Press.

Bogdanovich, P. (1997). *Who the Devil Made It*. New York: Alfred A. Knopf.

Bonnifield, P. (1979). *The Dust Bowl: Men, Dirt and Depression*. Albuquerque: University of New Mexico Press.

Bordwell, D., and K. Thompson, eds. (2002). *Film History: An Introduction*: New York: McGraw-Hill.

Brighton, T. (2009). *Masters of Battle: Monty, Patton and Rommel at War*. London: Penguin.

Brinkley, A. (1995). *The End of Reform: New Deal Liberalism in Recession and War*. New York: Alfred A. Knopf.

Brode, D. (2004). *From Walt to Woodstock: How Disney Created the Counter-Culture*. Austin: University of Texas Press.

Brode, D. (2005). *Multi-Culturalism and the Mouse: Race and Sex in Disney Entertainment*. Austin: University of Texas Press.

Brogan, D. W. (1950). *The Era of Franklin D. Roosevelt*. New Haven: Yale University Press.

Brownstein, R. (1990). *The Power and the Glitter*. New York: Pantheon.

Bryne, E., and M. McQuillan (1999). *Deconstructing Disney*. London: Pluto Press.

Buel, T. B. (1984). *The Second World War, Europe & the Mediterranean*. Wayne: Avery Publishing Group.

Cavalier, S. (2011). *The World History of Animation*. London: Rotovision.

Carr, W. (1991). *A History of Germany 1815-1990*. London: Arnold.

Chapman, J. (1998). *The British at War: Cinema, State and Propaganda 1939-1945*. London: I. B. Tauris.

Cohen, K. F. (1997). *Forbidden Animation: Censored Cartoons and Blacklisted Animators*. New York: McFarland.

Cohen, M. (1975). 'Warners Revisited: Looney Tunes and Merrie Melodies'. *The Velvet Light Trap: A Critical Journal of Film and Television*, 15 (3): 33–7.

Crafton, D. (1993). 'The View From Termite Terrace: Caricature and Parody in Warner Brothers Animation'. *Film History*, 5 (2): 204–30.

Crafton, D. (2011). 'Infectious Laughter: Cartoons Cure the Depression'. In D. Goldmark and C. Kiel (eds), *Funny Pictures: Animation and Comedy in Studio-Era Hollywood*, 69–92 Berkeley: University of California Press.

Crafton, D. (2012). *Shadow of a Mouse. Shadow of a Mouse: Performance, Belief, and World-making in Animation*. Oakland: UC Press.

Crouse, J. M. (1986). *The Homeless Transient in the Great Depression*. Albany: State University of New York Press.

Culbert, D., ed. (1990). *Film and Propaganda in America: A Documentary History*. New York: Greenwood Press.

Cull, N. (1995). *Selling War: The British Propaganda Campaign against American 'neutrality' in World War One*. New York: Oxford University Press.

Daily Variety (1939–1944).

Dallek. R. (1979). *Franklin D. Roosevelt and American Foreign Policy 1932-1945*. New York: Oxford University Press.

Davis, A. M. (2005). *Good Girls and Wicked Witches: Women in Disney's Feature Animation*. London: John Libbey.

Davis, A. M. (2013). *Handsome Heroes and Vile Villains: Men in Disney's Feature Animation*. London: John Libbey.

DelGaudio, S. (1997). 'If Truth Be Told, Can Toons Tell It? Documentary and Animation'. *Film History*, 9 (2): 189–99.

Dick, B. F. (1985). *The Star Spangled Screen: The American World War Two Film*. Lexington: University of Kentucky Press.

Dorfman, A., and A. Mattelart (1975). *How to Read Donald Duck: Imperialist Ideology in the Disney comic*. New York: International General.

Edsforth, R. (2000). *The New Deal: America's Response to the Great Depression*. Oxford: Blackwell.

Ekirch, A. (1969). *Ideologies and Utopias: The Impact of the New Deal on American Thought*. Chicago: Quadrangle Books.

Eldridge, D. (2008). *American Culture in the 1930s*. Edinburgh: Edinburgh University Press.

Eliot, M. (1993). *Walt Disney: Hollywood's Dark Prince*. Secaucus: Carol Publishing Group.

Ellul, J. (1965). *Propaganda: The Formation of Men's Attitudes*. New York: Knopf.

Evans, G. (1984). *John Grierson and the National Film Board: The Politics of Wartime Propaganda*. Toronto: University of Toronto Press.

Fortune magazine (1939–42).

Fox, J. (2007). *Film and Propaganda in Britain and Nazi Germany*. Oxford: Berg.

Fjellman, S. (1992). *Walt Disney World and America*. Boulder: Westview Press.

Fowler, G. (1991). *Schnozzola: The Story of Jimmy Durante*. New York: Viking Press.

Friedel, F. (1973). *Franklin D. Roosevelt*. Boston: Little Brown.

Furniss, M. (2007). *Art in Motion: Animation Aesthetics*. London: John Libbey.

Gabler, N (2007). *Walt Disney: The Biography*. London: Aurum.

Giroux, H. (1999). *The Mouse That Roared: Disney and the End of Innocence*. Lanham: Rowman and Littlefield.

Goldmark, D., and C. Kiel (2011), *Funny Pictures: Animation and Comedy in Studio-Era Hollywood*. Oakland: UC Press,

Gordon, C. (1994), *New Deals: Business, Labour and Politics in America 1920-1935*. Cambridge: Cambridge University Press.

Grant, J. (2001). *Masters of Animation*. New York: Watson Guptill.

Heale, M. (1999). *Franklin D. Roosevelt: The New Deal & War*. London: Routledge.

Hearn, C. (1977). *The American Dream in the Great Depression.* Westport: Greenwood Press.

Hedda Hopper Papers. Collection 95. Margaret Herrick Library, Beverly Hills, Los Angeles, CA.

Higson, A. (1983). 'Critical Theory and British Cinema'. *Screen*, 24: 80–95.

Higson, A., and J. Ashby, eds (2000). *British Cinema: Past and Present.* London: Routledge.

Hollywood Reporter (1942).

Hollywood Spectator (1935–9).

Jackson, K. (1990). *Walt Disney: A Bio-Bibliography.* Westport: Greenwood Press.

Jacobs, L. (1939). *The Rise of the American Film: A Critical History.* New York: Harcourt.

Jamieson, G. H. (1985). *Communication and Persuasion.* London: Routledge.

Jones, D. B (1981). *Movies and Memoranda: An Interpretive History of the National Film Board of Canada.* Ottawa: Canadian Film Institute.

Jones, C. (1989). *Chuck Amuck: The Life and Times of an Animated Cartoonist.* New York: Farrar Straus.

Jowett, G., and V. O'Donnell (2006). *Propaganda and Persuasion.* London: Sage.

Katz, M. (1983). 'From Hoover to Roosevelt'. In K. Loucheim (ed.), *The Making of the New Deal*, 119–29. Cambridge, MA: Harvard University Press.

Kennedy, D. M. (1999). *Freedom from Fear: The American People in Depression and War.* New York: Oxford University Press.

Kirkendall, R. S. (1983). 'The New Deal and Agriculture'. In A. L. Hamby (ed.), *The New Deal: Analysis and Interpretation*, 61–90. New York: Weybright and Talley.

Koppes, C. R., and G. D. Black (1977). 'What to show the World: The Office of War Information and Hollywood 1942-1945'. *The Journal of American History*, 64 (1): 87–105.

Koppes, C. R., and G. D. Black (2000). *Hollywood Goes to War: Patriotism, Movies and the Second World War.* London: Tauris Parke.

Krasniewicz, L. (2010). *Walt Disney: A Biography.* Santa Barbara: Greenwood Press.

Laurie, C. (1996). *The Propaganda Warriors: America's Crusade Against Nazi Germany.* Lawrence: University Press of Kansas.

Leuchtenberg, W. E. (1963). *FDR Roosevelt and the New Deal 1932-1940.* New York: Harper & Row.

Louchheim, K. (1983). *The Making of the New Deal: The Insiders Speak.* Cambridge, MA: Harvard University Press.

Maltby, R. (1999). *Film Europe and Film America: Cinema, Commerce & Cultural Exchange 1920-1939.* Exeter: University of Exeter Press.

Maltin, L. (1980). *Of Mice and Magic: A History of American Animated Cartoons.* New York: McGraw-Hill.

Masnick, G. (2004). 'Home Ownership and Social Equality in the United States'. In K. Kurz and H. Blossfeld (eds), *Home Ownership and Social Inequality in Comparative Perspective*, 304–37. Stanford: Stanford University Press.

McCann, R. D. (1973). *The People's Films*. New York: Hastings House.

Merritt, R. (2005). 'Lost in Pleasure Island: Storytelling in Disney's Silly Symphonies'. *Film Quarterly*, 59 (1): 4–17.

Mock, J. R., and C. Larson (1939). *Words that Won the War: The Story of the Committee on Public Information 1917-1919*. Princeton: Princeton University Press.

Motion Picture Daily (1933–43).

Motion Picture Herald (1933–7).

Motion Picture Society for the America Records. Collection 233. Margaret Herrick Library, Beverly Hills, Los Angeles, CA.

Muscio, G. (1996). *Hollywood's New Deal*. Philadelphia: Temple University Press.

Neale, S., ed. (2002). *Genre & Contemporary Hollywood*. London: BFI.

New York Times, The (1933–46).

Offner, A. A. (1969). *American Appeasement: United States Foreign Policy and Germany 1933-1938*. Cambridge, MA: Harvard University Press.

Overy, R. (2004). *The Dictators: Hitler's Germany and Stalin's Russia*. London: Penguin.

Pallant, C. (2011). *Demystifying Disney: A History of Disney Feature Animation*. New York: Continuum International Publishing Group.

Parrish, M. (1992). *Anxious Decades: America in Prosperity & Depression 1920-1941*. New York: W. W. Norton.

Peterson, H. C. (1939). *Propaganda for War: The Campaign against American Neutrality*. Norman: University of Oklahoma Press.

Production Code Administration Certificates. Box 00179. Warner Brothers Archives, University of Southern California.

Pronay, N., and F. Thorpe, eds. (1980), *British Official Films in the Second World War: A Descriptive Catalogue*. Oxford: Clio,

Pronay, N., and D. W. Springs, eds. (1982), *Propaganda, Politics and Film 1918-1945*. London: Macmillan.

Read, A. (2004). *The Devil's Disciples: Hitler's Inner Circle*. London: Pimlico.

Rhodes, A. (1976). *Propaganda: The Art of Persuasion*. London: Angus and Robertson.

Riefenstahl, L. (1993). *A Memoir*. New York: St. Martin's Press.

Roddick, N. (1983). *A New Deal in Entertainment*. London: British Film Institute.

Roeder, G. H. (1993). *The Censored War: The American Visual Experience during World War Two*. New Haven: Yale University Press.

Rollin, L. (1996). 'Uncle Walt Un-masked'. *The Lion and The Unicorn*, 20 (2): 296–8.

Romasco, A. U. (1983). *The Politics of Recovery*. New York: Oxford University Press.

Rose, N. E. (1994). *Put to Work: Relief Programs in the Great Depression*. New York: Monthly Review Press.

Ross, S. H. (1996). *Propaganda for War: How the United States was Conditioned to Fight the Great War of 1914-1918*. London: McFarland.

Rosten, L. (1941). *Hollywood: The Movie Colony, the Movie Makers*. New York: Harcourt.

Sammond, N. (2005). *Babes in Tomorrowland: Walt Disney and the Making of the American Child*. Durham: Duke University Press.

Sandler, K. (1998). *Reading the Rabbit: Explorations in Warner Bros. animation*. New Brunswick, NJ: Rutgers University Press.

Schickel, R. (1968). *The Disney Version: The Life, Times, Art and Commerce of Walt Disney*. New York: Simon and Schuster.

Schindler, C. (1996). *Hollywood in Crisis: Cinema and American Society 1929-1939*. New York: Routledge.

Schneider, S. (1994). *That's All Folks: The Art of Warner Brothers Animation*. London: Aurum Press.

Service, R. (2004). *Stalin: A Biography*. London: Macmillan.

Shale, R. (1978). *Donald Duck Joins Up: The Disney Studio During World War Two*. Ann Arbor: UMI Research Press.

Sherry, M. S. (1990). *In the Shadow of War: The United States Since the 1930s*. New Haven: Yale University Press.

Short, K., ed. (1983). *Film and Radio Propaganda during World War Two*. London: Croom Helm.

Shortsleeve, K. (2004). 'The Wonderful World of Depression: Disney despotism and the 1930s. Or, why Disney scares us'. *The Lion and the Unicorn*, 28 (1): 1–30.

Shull, M., and D. Wilt (1987). *Doing Their Bit: Wartime Animated Short Films*. Jefferson: McFarland.

Sito, T. (2006). *Drawing the Line: The Untold History of the Animation Unions from Bosko to Bart Simpson*. Lexington, KY: University of Kentucky Press.

Sklar, R. (1978). *Movie Made America: A Cultural History of American Movies*. London: Chappell.

Sklar, R. (1980). 'The Making of Cultural Myths – Walt Disney'. In D. Peary and G. Peary (eds), *The American Animated Cartoon: An Anthology*, 47–105. New York: Dutton.

Smoodin, E. (1993). *Animating Culture: Hollywood Cartoons from the Sound Era*. London: Rutgers University Press.

Smoodin, E. (1994). 'Introduction: how to read Walt Disney'. In E. Smoodin (ed.), *Disney Discourse: Producing the Magic Kingdom*, 1–12. New York: Routledge.

Soloman, C. (1999). *Enchanted Drawings: The History of Animation*. New York: Alfred Knopf Doubleday.

Starr, K. (1996). *Endangered Dreams: The Great Depression in California*. New York: Oxford University Press.

Steele, R. W. (1985). *Propaganda in an Open Society: The Roosevelt Administration and the Media 1933-1941*. Westport: Greenwood Press.

Taylor, P. M., ed. (1988). *Britain and the Cinema in the Second World War*. London: Palgrave.

Taylor, P. M. (2003). *Munitions of the Mind: A History of Propaganda from the Ancient World to the Present Era*. Manchester: Palgrave Macmillan.

Thomas, B. (1976). *Walt Disney: An American Original.* New York: Simon and Schuster.

Tierney, D. (2007). *FDR and the Spanish Civil War: Neutrality and Commitment in a Struggle that Divided America.* Durham: Duke University Press.

Walt Disney Productions Release Information (1935–8). Hollywood Columnists' Clippings, Collection 1485, Margaret Herrick Library, Beverly Hills, Los Angeles, CA.

Wasko, J. (2001). *Understanding Disney.* Cambridge: Polity Press.

Watts, S. (1995). 'Walt Disney: Art and Politics in the American Century'. *Journal of American History*, 82 (1): 84–109.

Watts, S (1997). *The Magic Kingdom: Walt Disney and the American way of life.* Boston: Houghton Mifflin.

Welch, D. (2001). *Propaganda and the German Cinema.* London: I. B. Tauris.

Wells, M. K. (1995). *Courage and Air Warfare: The Allied Aircrew Experience in the Second World War.* Essex: Portland.

Wells, P. (1998). *Understanding Animation.* Abingdon: Routledge.

Wells, P. (2002). *Animation and America.* New Brunswick: Rutgers University Press.

Wheeler, M. (1998). *The Economics of the Great Depression.* Kalamazoo: W. E. Upjohn Institute for Employment Research.

Winkler, A. (1978). *The Politics of Propaganda: The OWI 1942-1945.* New Haven: Yale University Press.

Woll, A. L. (1983). *The Hollywood Musical Goes to War.* Chicago: Nelson-Hall.

Woodward, G. S. (1969). *Pocahontas.* Norman: University of Oklahoma Press.

Zipes, J. (1994). *Fairy Tale as Myth, Myth as Fairy Tale.* Lexington: University of Kentucky Press.

Filmography

For ease of reference, the filmography is divided into two sections. Listed first are the short subjects released by the Walt Disney Studios, in chronological order, followed by those released by the Schlesinger Studios. The second section includes feature length animation and live action pictures, again in chronological order.

Disney's short subjects

Mickey's Nightmare (1932) Dir. Burt Gillett. USA: Walt Disney Productions.
Mickey's Good Deed (1932) Dir. Burt Gillett. USA: Walt Disney Productions.
The Three Little Pigs (1933) Dir. David Hand. USA: Walt Disney Productions.
The Grasshopper and the Ants (1934) Dir. Wilfred Jackson. USA: Walt Disney Productions.
Mickey's Pal Pluto (1934) Dir. Burt Gillett. USA: Walt Disney Productions.
The Wise Little Hen (1934) Dir. Wilfred Jackson. USA: Walt Disney Productions.
The Dognapper (1934) Dir. David Hand. USA: Walt Disney Productions.
The Golden Touch (1935) Dir. Walt Disney. USA: Walt Disney Productions.
Mickey's Polo Team (1936) Dir. David Hand. USA: Walt Disney Productions.
Three Little Wolves (1936) Dir. David Hand. USA: Walt Disney Productions.
Moving Day (1936) Dir. Ben Sharpsteen. USA: Walt Disney Productions.
The Country Cousin (1936) Dir. Wilfred Jackson. USA: Walt Disney Productions.
Modern Inventions (1937) Dir. Jack King. USA: Walt Disney Productions.
Self Control (1938) Dir. Jack King. USA: Walt Disney Productions.
Donald's Better Self (1938) Dir. Jack King. USA: Walt Disney Productions.
Ferdinand the Bull (1938) Dir. Dick Rickard. USA: Walt Disney Productions.
The Practical Pig (1939) Dir. Dick Rickard. USA: Walt Disney Productions.
Donald's Penguin (1939) Dir. Jack King. USA: Walt Disney Productions.
The Riveter (1940) Dir. Dick Lundy. USA: Walt Disney Productions.
Window Cleaners (1941) Dir. Jack King. USA: Walt Disney Productions.
The Thrifty Pig (1941) Dir. Ford Beebe. USA: Walt Disney Productions. National Film Board of Canada.
The New Spirit (1942) Dir. Wilfred Jackson and Ben Sharpsteen. USA: Walt Disney Productions. U.S. Department of the Treasury.

Four Methods of Flush Riveting (1942) Dir. James Algar. USA: Walt Disney Productions.
Donald's Decision (1942) Dir. Ford Beebe. USA: Walt Disney Productions.
Stop That Tank (1942) Dir. Ub Iwerks. USA: Walt Disney Productions. National Film Board of Canada.
Donald Gets Drafted (1942) Dir. Jack King. USA: Walt Disney Productions.
Food Will Win the War (1942) Dir. Hamilton Luske. USA: Walt Disney Productions.
Out of the Frying Pan Into the Firing Line (1942) Dir. Ben Sharpsteen. USA: Walt Disney Productions.
Sky Trooper (1942) Dir. Jack King. USA: Walt Disney Productions.
Spirit of '43 (1943) Dir. Jack King. USA: Walt Disney Productions.
Education for Death (1943) Dir. Clyde Geronimi. USA: Walt Disney Productions.
Der Fuehrer's Face (1943) Dir. Jack Kinney. USA: Walt Disney Productions.
Fall Out, Fall In (1943) Dir. Jack King. USA. Walt Disney Productions.
Victory Vehicles (1943) Dir. Jack Kinney. USA. Walt Disney Productions.
Reason and Emotion (1943) Dir. Bill Roberts. USA: Walt Disney Productions.
Chicken Little (1943) Dir. Clyde Geronimi. USA: Walt Disney Productions.
Commando Duck (1944) Dir. Jack King. USA: Walt Disney Productions.

Warner Brothers' short subjects

Bosko in Person (1933) Dir. Hugh Harman and Isadore Freleng. Harman-Ising Productions.
I Like Mountain Music (1933) Dir. Rudolf Ising. USA: Harman-Ising Productions.
Bosko's Picture Show (1933) Dir. Hugh Harman. USA: Harman-Ising Productions.
Bosko the Musketeer (1933) Dir. Hugh Harman. USA: Harman-Ising Productions.
Porky's Poultry Plant (1936) Dir. Frank Tashlin. USA: Leon Schlesinger Productions.
Milk and Money (1936) Dir. Fred (Tex) Avery. USA: Leon Schlesinger Productions.
She Was An Acrobat's Daughter (1937) Dir. Isadore Freleng. USA: Leon Schlesinger Productions.
Porky's Road Race (1937) Dir. Frank Tashlin. USA. Leon Schlesinger Productions.
Porky's Building (1937) Dir. Frank Tashlin. USA: Leon Schlesinger Productions.
Porky's Poppa (1938) Dir. Robert Clampett. USA: Leon Schlesinger Productions.
What Price Porky (1938) Dir. Robert Clampett. USA: Leon Schlesinger Productions.
Johnny Smith and Poker-huntas (1938) Dir. Tex Avery. USA: Leon Schlesinger Productions.
Old Glory (1939) Dir. Charles (Chuck) Jones. USA: Leon Schlesinger Productions.
Detouring America (1939) Dir. Tex Avery. USA: Leon Schlesinger Productions.
Elmer's Candid Camera (1940) Dir. Chuck Jones. USA: Leon Schlesinger Productions.
Holiday Highlights (1940) Dir. Tex Avery. USA: Leon Schlesinger Productions.
Meet John Doughboy (1941) Dir. Robert Clampett. USA: Leon Schlesinger Productions.

The Fighting Sixty Ninth Half (1941) Dir. Isadore Freleng. USA: Leon Schlesinger Productions.
Meet John Doughboy (1941) Dir. Robert Clampett. USA: Leon Schlesinger Productions.
Aviation Vacation (1941) Dir. Tex Avery. USA: Leon Schlesinger Productions.
Rookie Revue (1941) Dir. Isadore Freleng. USA: Leon Schlesinger Productions.
Any Bonds Today? (1942) Dir. Robert Clampett. USA: Leon Schlesinger Productions.
The Ducktators (1942) Dir. Norman McCabe. USA: Leon Schlesinger Productions.
Fifth Column Mouse (1943) Dir. Isadore Freleng. USA: Leon Schlesinger Productions.
Tokio Jokio (1943) Dir. Norman McCabe. USA: Leon Schlesinger Productions.
Scrap Happy Daffy (1943) Dir. Frank Tashlin. USA: Leon Schlesinger Productions.
Bugs Bunny Nips the Nips (1944) Dir. Isadore Freleng. USA: Leon Schlesinger Productions.
Russian Rhapsody (1944) Dir. Robert Clampett. USA: Leon Schlesinger Productions.
Plane Daffy (1944) Dir. Frank Tashlin. USA. Warner Brothers Cartoons.
Herr Meets Hare (1945) Dir. Isadore Freleng. Warner Brother Cartoons.

Feature films

Steamboat Willie (1928) Dir. Walt Disney and Ub Iwerks. USA: Walt Disney Studios.
I Am A Fugitive From A Chain Gang (1932) Dir. Mervyn LeRoy. USA: Warner Brothers Pictures.
42nd Street (1933) Dir. Lloyd Bacon. USA: Warner Brothers Pictures.
Gabriel over the White House (1933) Dir. Gregory La Cava. Metro-Goldwyn Mayer.
Gold Diggers of '33 (1933) Dir. Mervyn LeRoy. USA: Warner Brothers Pictures.
This Day and Age (1933) Dir. Cecil B. Demille. USA: Paramount Pictures.
Footlight Parade (1933) Dir. Lloyd Bacon. USA: Warner Brothers Pictures.
Wild Boys of the Road (1933) Dir. William Wellman. USA: First National Pictures.
Our Daily Bread (1934) Dir. King Vidor. USA: United Artists.
The Spanish Earth (1937) Dir. Joris Ivens. USA: Contemporary Historians Inc.
Snow White and the Seven Dwarfs (1937) Dir. David Hand. USA: Walt Disney Productions.
Blockade (1938) Dir. William Dieterle. USA: United Artists.
Wings of the Navy (1939) Dir. Lloyd Bacon. USA: Warner Brothers Pictures.
Gone with the Wind (1939) Dir. Victor Fleming. USA: Selznick International Pictures. Metro-Goldwyn Mayer
Confessions of a Nazi Spy (1939) Dir. Anatole Litvak. USA: Warner Brothers Pictures.
Code of the Secret Service (1939) Dir. Noel M. Smith. USA: Warner Brothers Pictures.
Pinocchio (1940) Dir. Ben Sharpsteen and Hamilton Luske. USA: Walt Disney Productions.
The Mortal Storm (1940) Dir. Frank Borzage. USA: Metro-Goldwyn Mayer.
The Reluctant Dragon (1940) Dir. Alfred Werker and Hamilton Luske. USA. Walt Disney Productions.

Foreign Correspondent (1940) Dir. Alfred Hitchcock. United Artists.

The Great Dictator (1940) Dir. Charlie Chaplin. USA: United Artists.

Arise, My Love (1940) Dir. Mitchell Leisen. USA: Paramount Pictures.

Fantasia (1940) Dir. Samuel Armstrong, James Algar, Bill Roberts, Paul Satterfield, Ben Sharpsteen, David D. Hand, Hamilton Luske, Jim Handley, Ford Beebe, T. Hee, Norman Ferguson, Wilfred Jackson. Walt Disney Productions.

A Yank in the RAF (1941) Dir. Henry King. USA: Twentieth Century Fox Film Corporation.

Dumbo (1941) Dir. Ben Sharpsteen. USA: Walt Disney Studios.

Remember Pearl Harbor (1942) Dir. Joseph Santley. USA: Republic Pictures.

Yankee Doodle Dandy (1942) Dir. Michael Curtiz. USA: Warner Brothers Pictures.

Mrs Miniver (1942) Dir. William Wyler. USA: Metro-Goldwyn Mayer.

Danger in the Pacific (1942) Dir. Lewis D. Collins. USA: Universal Pictures.

A Prisoner of Japan (1942) Dir. Arthur Ripley and Edgar G. Ulmer. USA: Atlantis Pictures.

Casablanca (1942) Dir. Michael Curtiz. USA: Warner Brothers Pictures.

Journey for Margaret (1942) Dir. W.S. Van Dyke. USA: Metro-Goldwyn Mayer.

Hitler's Children (1943) Dir. Edward Dmytryk and Irving Reis. USA: RKO Radio Pictures.

This Land Is Mine (1943) Dir. Jean Renoir. USA: Jean Renoir-Dudly Nichols Productions.

Bataan (1943) Dir. Tay Garnett. USA: Metro-Goldwyn Mayer.

The Purple Heart (1944) Dir. Lewis Milestone. USA: Twentieth Century Fox Film Corporation.

Thirty Seconds Over Tokyo (1944) Dir. Mervyn LeRoy. USA: Loews Inc.

Song of the South (1946) Dir. Harve Foster and Wilfred Jackson. USA: Walt Disney Productions.

Pocahontas (1995) Dir. Mike Gabriel and Eric Goldberg. USA: Walt Disney Pictures. Walt Disney Feature Animation.

Frozen (2013) Dir. Chris Buck and Jennifer Lee. USA: Walt Disney Pictures. Walt Disney Animation Studios.

Inside Out (2015) Dir. Pete Docter. USA: Walt Disney Pictures. Pixar Animation Studios.

Index

9 781501 328770